THE BIG BOOK OF

WORDS

YOU SHOULD KNOW TO

SOUND SMART

A GUIDE *for* ASPIRING
INTELLECTUALS

———◆———

ROBERT W.

T0057191

Adams Media
New York London Toronto Sydney New Delhi

Adams Media
An Imprint of Simon & Schuster, Inc.
100 Technology Center Drive
Stoughton, MA 02072

For information about special discounts for bulk purchases, please contact Simon & Schuster Special Sales at 1-866-506-1949 or business@simonandschuster.com.

The Simon & Schuster Speakers Bureau can bring authors to your live event. For more information or to book an event contact the Simon & Schuster Speakers Bureau at 1-866-248-3049 or visit our website at www.simonspeakers.com.

Manufactured in the United States of America

6 2023

Library of Congress Cataloging-in-Publication Data has been applied for.

ISBN 978-1-4405-9106-8
ISBN 978-1-4405-9107-5 (ebook)

CONTENTS

Acknowledgments 4

Dedication 4

Introduction 5

About the Author 333

ACKNOWLEDGMENTS

Thanks to my editor, Peter Archer, and my agent, Bob Diforio, for having faith in me and this book. Thanks also to the many writers, authors, and other figures quoted throughout the book.

DEDICATION

To Dr. Jeffrey Segal

INTRODUCTION

A radio commercial for a mail-order course on building your vocabulary states, "People judge you by the words you use."

To help people judge you as wise and educated, we published our book *The Words You Should Know to Sound Smart*. It sold well and spawned an annual calendar. But our readers told us: "More big words to make us sound even smarter, please!"

The result is the book you now hold in your hands, *The Big Book of Words You Should Know to Sound Smart*. It was written so that people who hear you speak will see you as really smart—perhaps even smarter than you really are.

Some people who want to sound smart have cultivated a large vocabulary, which they unleash with great regularity. This book can serve as your "translator" when speaking with these pseudointellectuals.

Many other people possess a large vocabulary but use it sparingly, preferring to speak and write in plain English. As more than one writing instructor has put it, "Your goal is to express, not to impress."

It's possible that *The Big Book of Words You Should Know to Sound Smart* may even put some money in your pocket. People who have a good vocabulary come off as confident, intelligent, and motivated—qualities necessary for financial success.

The motivational speaker Earl Nightingale liked to tell students about a twenty-year study of college graduates. The study concluded, "Without a single exception, those who had scored highest on the vocabulary test given in college were in the top income group, while those who had scored the lowest were in the bottom income group."

Scientist John O'Connor gave vocabulary tests to executive and supervisory personnel in thirty-nine large manufacturing companies. On average: test scores for the company presidents were nearly three times higher than their shop foremen.

Vocabulary researchers Richard C. Anderson and William. E. Nagy write, "One of the most consistent findings of educational research is that having a small vocabulary portends poor school performance and, conversely, having a large vocabulary is associated with school success."

Whether this book helps you get higher grades or advance in your career, it's fun to improve your command of the English language—either to impress or express. Some of the words in *The Big Book of Words You Should Know to Sound Smart* can do just that: make you sound educated and intelligent.

With this book at your fingertips, you can command an expanded vocabulary enabling you to debate philosophical precepts with the intelligentsia, wax poetic with the literati, and lock academic horns with the clerisy. These bon mots can help you converse with the best of the portentous artistes and aesthetes—and impress the perfervid hoi polloi with your tarradiddle. With this compendious tome, you are only a daily erudite witticism away from true loquaciousness.

On the other hand, you may simply get pleasure out of knowing these words and adding them to your vocabulary quiver, even if you keep most of them in reserve.

It's your call.

A Note on the Pronunciation

Pronunciation keys given in this book are rendered phonetically, without using special symbols or systems.

Many of the words in this book have multiple meanings and pronunciations—in addition to those listed here—that are entirely correct.

Regional influences can affect pronunciation of certain words. In this book, we use the most commonly accepted pronunciation for each word, recognizing that it is by no means the only acceptable pronunciation.

A Note on the Sources

In his book *The Meaning of Everything: The Story of the Oxford English Dictionary*, Simon Winchester observes that there are essentially three sources for the words in any dictionary: (1) words found in existing dictionaries; (2) words overheard in conversation; and (3) words found "by a concerted trawl through the text of literature." *The Big Book of Words You Should Know to Sound Smart* is populated with words from all three sources. In particular, I owe a debt of gratitude to the *New York Review of Books*. I read every issue and find new words in each one.

More than a dozen of the words are from Jason Bateman's movie *Bad Words*. Many come from the books of Harlan Ellison, Pat Conroy, Nicholson Baker, and other authors who employ a sophisticated vocabulary.

As for dictionaries, my three primary references were *Webster's New World College Dictionary, Fifth Edition*, Merriam-Webster's online dictionary, and the *Shorter Oxford English Dictionary, Sixth Edition* which, contrary to its name, comes in two massive volumes.

"Of course the illusion of art is to make one believe that great literature is very close to life, but exactly the opposite is true. Life is AMORPHOUS, literature is formal."

———

Françoise Sagan, French novelist and playwright

abasement *(ah-BAYS-meant), noun*
A humiliation or dressing-down.
>*In his sermon, our pastor warned that pornography is a global ABASEMENT of all humankind, not just women.*

abate *(uh-BAIT), verb*
Reduce in intensity.
>*The police came round to cite me for failing to ABATE my smoky chimney.*

abatement *(ah-BAIT-ment), noun*
The reduction or elimination of a tax, claim, fine, or debt.
>*By having her daddy pull strings in the mayor's office, Sylvia received a quick ABATEMENT of her traffic ticket.*

abatjour *(ah-ba-ZHOO-er), noun*
An object that allows or diverts light into buildings.
>*As part of my remodeling project, I'm building a skylight as an ABATJOUR to lighten the front hallway.*

abecedarium *(ay-bee-see-DAIR-ee-um), noun*
An elementary school textbook used for teaching the alphabet.
>*In former years,* McGuffey's Eclectic Primer *was used in elementary schools as an ABECEDARIUM for young students.*

abessive *(uh-BESS-ev), adjective*
Indicating the absence of something.
>*The ABESSIVE character of game in the forest meant we had to rely on a vegetarian diet during our camping trip.*

abiogenesis *(ay-bye-oh-JEN-eh-sis), noun*
Spontaneous generation of life.
>*ABIOGENESIS is the mechanism in the Star Trek movies by which Spock is brought back from the dead.*

abiturient *(ah-bih-TUR-ee-ent), noun*
A German pupil about to leave high school and enter a university.
>*Rachel, having completed her high school years with flying colors, was an ABITURIENT on the verge of an Oxford education.*

abjure *(ab-JOOR), transitive verb*
To renounce or turn your back on a belief or position you once held near and dear.

Once Jodi tasted my mouth-watering, medium-rare filet mignon, she ABJURED the vegetarian lifestyle forever.

ablaut *(AHB-lout), noun*
An alteration in the internal structure of a word that affects its meaning.

In English, the words sing, sang, *and* sung *are an example of an ABLAUT, since the change of a letter changes their tense.*

ablution *(ah-BLEW-shin), noun*
A washing of the hands and face, or bathing of the entire body.

I begin each day with my morning ABLUTIONS.

abominate *(uh-BOM-in-ate), verb*
When you *abominate* something, you really, really hate and dislike it—and view it with considerable loathing.

"For my part, I ABOMINATE all honorable respectable toils, trials, and tribulations of every kind whatsoever." —Herman Melville, American author

aboral *(ab-AWR-ul), adjective*
Away from the mouth.

Johnny moved his fork in an ABORAL manner, showing his dislike of Brussels sprouts.

abraxas *(uh-BRAK-suhs), noun*
A mystical word sometimes found carved on gemstones.

Maryanne's New Age malachite pendulum was engraved with an ABRAXAS to enhance its power.

absconce *(ab-SKAWNS), noun*
An old-fashioned lantern formerly used in monasteries.

The monk illuminated his path with an ABSCONCE.

abscond *(ab-SKOND), verb*
To leave in a hurry but quietly, so as to escape notice, especially to avoid trouble.
> *Bored out of his wits, Jared ABSCONDED with the family Mercedes, but he wrapped it around a large oak tree.*

A

absquatulate *(ab-SKAW-chew-late), verb*
To exit without warning.
> *I routinely ABSQUATULATE from dull parties, social gatherings, and other events.*

abstemious *(ab-STEE-me-us), adjective*
To eat plain and simple food in moderation, avoiding overindulgence in drink and gluttony at the table.
> *Gandhi led an ABSTEMIOUS life.*

absterge *(ab-STIRJ), verb*
To wipe clean; to erase.
> *Because Roger had been a juvenile when he committed vandalism, the court agreed to ABSTERGE his record.*

abstruse *(ab-STROOS), adjective*
Arcane, complex, difficult to understand and learn.
> *Bob began to wish there was, in fact, a Santa Claus because he found the "simple instructions" to his son's bicycle far too ABSTRUSE.*

acanthous *(uh-KAN-thus), adjective*
Spiny; covered in spines.
> *Sea urchins are ACANTHOUS, which means beachgoers shouldn't step on them so as to avoid puncture wounds to the feet.*

acarine *(AK-uh-rayne), adjective*
Having to do with mites.
> *Dr. Moore's ACARINE studies resulted in his developing a new medicine to prevent ear mites in animals.*

acatour *(ak-uh-TOOR), noun*
Quartermaster or provisioner.
> *The expedition's ACATOUR made sure that everyone was well supplied with food, clothing, and adequate shelter.*

accidie *(AK-si-dee), noun*
Sloth; laziness; a feeling of torpor.
My cat, having chased a feather for ten minutes, was sunk in ACCIDIE, curled around her tail.

acclimate *(AK-luh-mate), verb*
Adjust oneself to a new set of climatic conditions.
As we ascended Mount Everest, we had to continually ACCLIMATE ourselves to the thinner air.

accoucheuse *(ak-oo-ZHOOZ), noun*
A midwife.
In many rural areas, babies were delivered by an ACCOUCHEUSE, since doctors were not immediately available.

accoy *(ah-KAWY), verb*
To pacify; to soothe.
The baby was so upset by his uncle's presence that it required his mother to ACCOY him and return him to calm.

accretion *(uh-KREE-shun), noun*
The gradual accumulation of something over time.
Mr. Scrooge's ACCRETION of money for many years had made him one of the richest men in London.

accubation *(ak-you-BAY-shun), noun*
The act of reclining on a couch.
Diners in ancient Rome engaged in ACCUBATION while eating, rising only to call for more food and wine.

acculturation *(ah-kul-cherr-AYE-shin), noun*
The process of adapting to a different culture.
Just because sushi makes me queasy doesn't mean I'm opposed to ACCULTURATION.

aceldama *(uh-SEL-duh-muh), noun*
A place of bloodshed and slaughter.
The old house was now a horrific ACELDAMA, with dead bodies scattered about the living room.

acerbate *(AA-sir-bayt), verb*
To irritate or make worse.
> *The Koch brothers' multimillion-dollar support of conservative candidates only ACERBATES the liberals' disdain of libertarianism.*

A

acersecomic *(uh-kare-suh-KAH-mik), noun*
Someone whose hair has never been cut.
> *The wild man, who had lived in the jungle his entire life with no contact with human society, was ACERSECOMIC, with his tangled hair reaching below his waist.*

achloropsia *(uh-klor-OP-see-uh), noun*
Color blindness in respect to the color green.
> *Margery's ACHLOROPSIA prevented her from seeing the coming of spring green grass to her lawn.*

achromatic *(ak-ruh-MAT-ik), adjective*
Completely without color.
> *The designers painted the entire room white and filled it with white furniture, leaving it starkly ACHROMATIC.*

acicular *(uh-SI-kyou-ler), adjective*
Needle-shaped.
> *The ACICULAR rock formations found in parts of the Rocky Mountains are spires that challenge the best climbers.*

acinaciform *(uh-SIN-uh-si-form), adjective*
Shaped like a scimitar.
> *Gaelen seized the ACINACIFORM piece of wood and used it to defend himself from his opponents' flashing swords.*

acouasm *(ah-COO-ahz-um), noun*
Thinking you are hearing strange sounds that are not really there.
> *Witnesses to the supernatural often suffer from ACOUASM.*

acquest *(uh-KWEST), noun*
Property acquired by some means other than inheritance.
> *I didn't inherit my house; it was an ACQUEST from a close friend, who gave it to me before he died.*

acrimonious *(ah-kri-MOAN-ee-us), adjective*
Angry; bitter; disputed.
> *"There is something about the literary life that repels me, all this desperate building of castles on cobwebs, the long-drawn ACRIMONIOUS struggle to make something important which we all know will be gone forever in a few years..."*
> —Raymond Chandler, American author

acropathy *(uh-KROP-uh-thee), noun*
Any disease affecting the body's extremities (hands, feet, etc.).
> *As a result of leprosy, many people in the Middle Ages suffered from ACROPATHY and lost fingers and toes.*

acroscopic *(ak-roh-SKOP-ik), adjective*
Moving toward the high point.
> *As we traversed the mountainside, we were aware of our ACROSCOPIC quest to get to the top.*

adelphogamy *(ah-del-FOE-gah-me), noun*
Marriage to your brother's wife.
> *All men practicing ADELPHOGAMY are polygamists.*

adjudicate *(ah-JOO-dih-kate), verb*
To preside over or listen to opposing arguments and help two parties settle their difference and come to an agreement.
> *As my daughters pummeled each other while screaming at top volume, I tried desperately to ADJUDICATE their quarrel.*

ad nauseam *(ad-NAW-zee-um), adverb*
Something that goes on and on, or is done over and over again, to a ridiculous, even sickening degree.
> *At first we were all impressed that Steve could recite the entire Gettysburg Address, but we all got kind of sickened when he repeated the feat AD NAUSEAM.*

adroit *(ah-DROYT), adjective*
Skilled or clever in a particular pursuit.
> *"It's kind of sad," Betty said to Barbara, "that Will thinks his ADROIT opera-singing abilities will impress women."*

adsorb *(add-SORB), verb*
To collect a dissolved liquid or gas on a surface.

He invented a dry chemical dehumidifier that ADSORBS excess moisture from a room.

A

aegis *(AYE-jis), noun*
The protection, support, and help rendered by a guardian, supporter, backer, or mentor.

Jill thinks she's above reproach because she's under the AEGIS of that marketing vice president with a penchant for younger women.

aesthetic *(es-THEH-tik), adjective*
Relating to beauty and the appreciation of beauty.

Covering your walls with pictures torn from the newspaper does not constitute a genuine AESTHETIC sense, Harold.

affectation *(ah-fek-TAY-shun), noun*
Behaviors or mannerisms that are exaggerated, extreme, eccentric, and deliberately showy, often an effort to attract attention.

"AFFECTATION is awkward and forces imitation of what should be genuine and easy." —John Locke, British philosopher

afflatus *(uh-FLAY-tuss), noun*
Inspiration that seems to come from divine origin.

The Nobel Prize–winning novelist attributed her abilities to AFFLATUS rather than to her own abilities.

aficionado *(uh-fish-ee-uh-NAH-doe), noun*
A devotee, someone who is enthralled with and supports a particular activity.

Dwight often refers to himself as an AFICIONADO of American-made microbrews.

aggrandize *(ah-GRAND-ize), verb*
To exaggerate, put on a false front, and make something look greater and grander than it really is.

Phil tries to AGGRANDIZE his reputation by stating that he is a charter member of the Bill O'Reilly fan club, but everybody just thinks this "feat" makes him pathetic.

agoraphobia *(ah-GORE-ah-foe-bee-ah), noun*
Fear of being outdoors or in public.
> *People believe Ms. Atkins to be antisocial, but it was her AGORAPHOBIA that made her a shut-in for decades.*

ailanthus *(a-LANN-thus), noun*
A type of tree with pointed leaves and green flowers.
> *"I was hoping to find a crack in the pavement where my AILANTHUS of a poem could take root." —Nicholson Baker, writer*

akimbo *(ah-KIM-bo), adverb*
With hands on hips and elbows turned outward.
> *When my father gets really mad, he stands stock-still, arms AKIMBO, and slowly turns red in the face.*

alacrity *(ah-LAK-rih-tee), noun*
Cheerful cooperation rendered with enthusiasm, promptness, and politeness.
> *The ALACRITY with which Steve responded to Helen's invitation is nothing short of astonishing.*

aleatory *(AIL-ee-ah-tore-ee), adjective*
An action that is unplanned, spontaneous, or spur of the moment rather than deliberately thought out and carefully considered; an outcome that is anything but certain and depends on luck, randomness, or chance.
> *"Of course you lost the election!" Miranda yelled. "An ALEATORY, fly-by-the-seat-of-your-pants campaign is never going to be a recipe for success!"*

allegory *(AL-eh-gor-ee), noun*
A story told to communicate a hidden meaning or deeper theme.
> *Many of the Grimm Brothers' fairy tales are clear ALLEGORIES of the consequences of children's rotten behavior.*

alliteration *(ah-lit-ter-AYE-shun), noun*
The repetition of similar sounds, especially at the beginnings of words, in written speech or the spoken word.
> *I'd forgotten how much Alicia likes to use ALLITERATION in her insults, but I was reminded quickly when she called me a cruel, callous cretin.*

amatory *(AM-uh-tore-ee), adjective*
Having to do with sexual love.
>Pete hasn't stopped sulking since Alice spurned his AMATORY advances at the office Christmas party.

A

ambiguity *(am-bih-GYOO-ih-tee), noun*
Uncertainty; lacking clear definition.
>Poets who revel in AMBIGUITY are one of the reasons many people hate poetry.

ambrosia *(am-BRO-zsha), noun*
Nectar, supposedly the food of the Greek gods on Mount Olympus.
>To my parents, sugary Passover wine was the AMBROSIA of the gods.

ameliorate *(ah-MEAL-your-ate), verb*
To correct a deficiency or defect; to make right a wrong; to take actions that make up, at least in part, for negative actions or failure to take action previously.
>After you insulted her mother, I don't think even the most expensive piece of jewelry will be enough to AMELIORATE your relationship with Marcia.

amenable *(ah-MEE-nah-bull), adjective*
One who readily and agreeably gives in to the wishes and desires of others.
>Mark considers himself AMENABLE, but the rest of us just think he's a pushover.

amorphous *(ah-MORE-fis), adjective*
Without definite shape, substance, or form; lacking definition and boundaries.
>"Of course the illusion of art is to make one believe that great literature is very close to life, but exactly the opposite is true. Life is AMORPHOUS, literature is formal." – Françoise Sagan, French novelist and playwright

amphibology *(am-fih-BAHL-ah-gee), noun*
Double meaning or ambiguity.
>Famous comic Norm Crosby based his routines of mangled words largely on mispronunciation and AMPHIBOLOGY.

anabasis *(a-nuh-BAY-sis), noun*
A military expedition from the coast of a country into its interior.
>The ancient Persian ruler Cyrus conducted an ANABASIS against his foe, Artaxerxes.

anabatic *(an-ah-BAT-ik), adjective*
Upward movement driven by air currents.
> *The glider pilot delighted the air show attendees with ANABATIC aerial acrobatics.*

anachronism *(ah-NAK-ruh-niz-em), noun*
A person, place, thing, or idea whose time has past, and who seems to belong to an earlier age.
> *His three record players—and the fact that he doesn't even know what an MP3 is—make Jim something of an ANACHRONISM.*

analemma *(an-al-EM-ah), noun*
A figure-eight pattern made by marking the position of the sun at the same time each day throughout the year.
> *ANALEMMAS are produced as the earth's tilt changes relative to the sun.*

analogous *(an-AL-a-gus), adjective*
Similar or comparable in some respects.
> *Nikki tried to argue that attending public school in Manhattan was ANALO-GOUS to attending the prestigious boarding school in the country, but her argument was weak and her grandmother wasn't buying it.*

anaphora *(an-AFF-for-ah), noun*
Repetition of a word or phrase at the beginning of successive sentences or stanzas.
> *ANAPHORA is a valuable arrow in the poet's quiver.*

anathema *(ah-NATH-eh-ma), noun*
Something so distasteful to you, so alien and foreign to your understanding, that you find it sickening and repellant—as if you were allergic to it.
> *Religious services were an ANATHEMA to Russ, what with him being a dedicated atheist and all.*

androcentrism *(an-druh-SEN-tri-zum), noun*
An outlook that emphasizes a masculine point of view.
> *"Larry," Joan warned, "that ANDROCENTRISM may be all the rage in the locker room, but you'd better leave it out of our bedroom if you know what's good for you."*

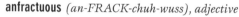

anfractuous *(an-FRACK-chuh-wuss), adjective*
Full of windings and intricacies, like a good mystery novel.
The novel's ANFRACTUOUS plot worked on paper, but it became stupefyingly confusing—actually, just plain stupid—onscreen.

animadversion *(an-uh-mad-VER-zhun), noun*
Very harsh criticism that suggests disapproval of what is being criticized.
My boss's frequent ANIMADVERSIONS have led to high staff turnover.

anomaly *(ah-NAHM-ah-lee), noun*
An exception to the norm; something different and unexpected that logically should not exist.
"After a thousand meters of this broken-field walking, Mitsuno came upon an ANOMALY: a patch of sand perhaps ten meters square." —Fred Pohl and Thomas Thomas, American science fiction authors

antebellum *(ant-eh-BELL-um), adjective*
Representative of or found in the Old South, meaning pre–Civil War.
"But John Allan was a successful immigrant merchant—by no means the type of gentleman planter who stood in the place of aristocrat in the self-conception of ANTEBELLUM Virginia." —Marilynne Robinson, novelist

antecedent *(an-tih-SEE-dent), noun*
The ancestor of an existing product, idea, etc.
IBM's electronic typewriter with storage was the ANTECEDENT of the modern PC.

antediluvian *(anne-tuh-dih-LOO-vee-uhn), adjective*
Old or primitive; pre-Biblical. Literally, before the Flood.
Archaeologists discovered an ANTEDILUVIAN voltaic pile—a battery—in an Egyptian pyramid a few years ago.

antidisestablishmentarianism *(anne-tie-diss-eh-stab-lish-meant-TAYR-ee-ah-nih-zim), noun*
The doctrine or political position that opposes the withdrawal of state recognition of an established church.
When people think of a really big word, ANTIDISESTABLISHMENTARIANISM is one of the ones that comes to mind.

antiquarian *(ann-tih-KWARE-ee-ann)*, *adjective*

Old, ancient, antique in nature.

Opening his ANTIQUARIAN bookstore was the realization of Howard's lifelong bibliophilic dream.

antithesis *(an-TIH-thuhs-siss)*, *noun*

The exact opposite; a thing that is completely different from another thing.

He tries so hard to be smooth, but Charles is the ANTITHESIS of cool.

apartheid *(Ah-PAR-thide)*, *noun*

South Africa's government-sanctioned policy of segregation and racial discrimination.

Since APARTHEID ended in 1994, South Africa has elected three native African presidents.

aphorism *(AH-for-iz-ihm)*, *noun*

A proverb, often-repeated statement, or cliché.

Danny, you say "I'm right. You're wrong." so much that it's become an APHORISM.

apocryphal *(ah-POCK-rih-full)*, *adjective*

An event, story, legend, or rumor that has been told so often, and so long after the fact, that one has good reason to doubt its authenticity, nor can it be verified through research.

John Henry may have been based on a real man, but in the story he has grown to APOCRYPHAL proportions.

apoplectic *(ap-uh-PLECK-tic)*, *adjective*

An extremely agitated state of rage.

Emily's careless event planning make me so APOPLECTIC that I just want to step in and plan the luncheon myself.

apostasy *(a-PA-stah-see)*, *noun*

The act of abandoning, ignoring, or openly flaunting an accepted principle or belief.

"It was his idea of grand APOSTASY to drive to the reform synagogue on the high holidays and park his pink-eye nag among the luxurious, whirl-wired touring cars of the rich." —Saul Bellow, American author

apotheosis *(ah-pa-thee-OH-sis), noun*
The culmination or highest point.
Winning the Silver Gutter Award at his local bowling alley was the APOTHEO-SIS of Wendell's less-than-stellar sports legacy.

appeasement *(ah-PEEZ-meant), noun*
The act of making others happy by agreeing to their demands.
Charlene realized too late that her policy of APPEASEMENT would not cause Warren to treat her with more respect.

appellation *(ah-pull-AYE-shun), noun*
A formal name, label, or title.
Even though he has only an honorary degree, he insists on being called by the APPELLATION of "doctor" everywhere he goes.

approbation *(ap-ruh-BAY-shun), noun*
Official approval or commendation.
"In a virtuous and free state, no rewards can be so pleasing to sensible minds, as those which include the APPROBATION of our fellow citizens. My great pain is, lest my poor endeavours should fall short of the kind expectations of my country." —Thomas Jefferson

apropos *(ah-pro-POE), adverb*
Appropriate, or at an opportune time.
Charlie began screaming the words "Too late! Too late!" APROPOS of nothing.

arcane *(are-CAYNE), adjective*
Strange and mysterious; understood by only a few.
Bill's ARCANE knowledge of all Lexus models and their accessories is just a waste.

archaeoloatry *(are-kay-oh-LOW-ah-tree), noun*
The worship or adoration of antiquity.
And it was Howard's ARCHAEOLOATRY that drove him to become an expert in antiquarian books, scrolls, and manuscripts.

archetype *(ARE-ke-type), noun*
A prototypical example; a recurrent theme or pattern; an original model that is widely imitated.
Boys never played with dolls until G.I. Joe became the ARCHETYPE of the "action figure."

archimandrite *(are-kih-MAN-dright), noun*
The head of a monastery.
The monk's dream was to one day be the ARCHIMANDRITE.

architrave *(ARE-kih-trayve), noun*
A beam resting on columns.
The ARCHITRAVE can be one of the less stable components of building construction.

argosy *(are-guh-SEE), noun*
A rich, seemingly endless, supply.
The deceased hermit's home turned out to be an ARGOSY of Cuban cigars, Swiss timepieces, and historical erotica.

artifice *(ARE-ti-fis), noun*
The use of clever strategies and cunning methods to fool or best others and tip an outcome in your favor.
"Every art and ARTIFICE has been practiced and perpetrated to destroy the rights of man." —Robert Ingersoll, American orator

ascetic *(ah-SEH-tick), noun*
A person who deliberately chooses to live a plain and simple life; characterized by lack of material possessions and strong self-discipline in all matters of behavior.
When Steve Jobs started Apple, a magazine profile portrayed him as an ASCETIC, noting that he had no furniture in his apartment.

assiduously *(ah-SID-you-us-lee), adverb*
Diligent and persistent, especially in an effort to help others, achieve a goal, or deliver on one's promises.
David worked ASSIDUOUSLY to complete his first novel, writing for three hours a night after work and dinner.

assuage *(ah-SWAYJ), verb*
To put someone at ease; to comfort or soothe; to erase doubts and fears.
"But history must not yet tell the tragedies enacted here; let time intervene in some measure to ASSUAGE and lend an azure tint to them." —Henry David Thoreau, American author and transcendentalist

assvogel *(ASS-voh-gul), noun*
South African vulture; slang term meaning ass or idiot.
   Man, that guy cut me off and didn't even slow down! He's such an ASSVOGEL!

asunder *(ah-SUN-derr), adjective*
A whole that has been split into parts; a union that has been eliminated, leaving the people or things once joined now separate.
   His marriage torn ASUNDER, Mike decided to quit his job, move to Tangiers, and become a year-round beach bum.

asynchronous *(aye-SINK-crow-nuss), adjective*
Acting or functioning with no regularity or discernible time schedule.
   Maggie's ASYNCHRONOUS habits drive her friends crazy because they can never make advance plans with her.

athwart *(ah-THWORT), preposition*
Against; in opposition to.
   His politics set him ATHWART the current administration.

attainder *(ah-TAYNE-der), noun*
To give up one's rights and properties after being convicted of a crime.
   ATTAINDER magnifies the dishonor and makes worse the material consequences of committing a felony, which inspired Walter Gibson to write, "Crime does not pay."

augur *(AW-ger), verb*
To predict or foretell the future.
   The three witches of Shakespeare's Macbeth *AUGUR the cataclysmic fate of the play's titular character.*

auspicious *(awe-SPIH-shus), adjective*
A good beginning giving rise to the belief that the venture, journey, or activity will end in success.
   The blind date did not have an AUSPICIOUS start because Max kept calling his friend's cousin "Mary" instead of "Mallory."

austere *(aw-STEER), adjective*
Stern; grim and lacking humor or warmth; clean and unornamented; severe or strict in manner.
   In the movie Dead Poets Society, *Robin Williams clashes with an AUSTERE headmaster at a private boys' school.*

autodidact *(aw-toe-diE-dakt), noun*
A self-educated person.
> *In the twentieth century, the library was the university of the AUTODIDACT; in the twenty-first century, it is the Internet.*

autonomy *(aw-TAHN-ah-mee), noun*
Maintaining independent thought and action; free; self-governing; without dependence on, or under control of, a higher authority.
> *Herb claims he wants AUTONOMY, but he goes absolutely nuts whenever his boss gives him unstructured assignments.*

avant-garde *(ah-vant-GARD), noun, adjective*
New and experimental; especially referring to art, writing, architecture, and music.
> *"He seemed to toss them all into the mixed salads of his poetry with the same indifference to form and logic, the same domesticated surrealism, that character-ized much of the American AVANT-GARDE of the period." —Frank O'Hara, American poet*

avarice *(AH-ver-iss), noun*
The insatiable desire to have a lot of money; greed.
> *"What you call AVARICE," Mary said, "I just call getting my share."*

aver *(uh-VER), verb*
To assert the truthfulness of a statement.
> *"'Has she no faults, then (Envy says), sir?' / Yes, she has one, I must AVER: / When all the world conspires to praise her, / The woman's deaf, and does not hear." —Alexander Pope, British poet*

avuncular *(a-VUN-cue-lar), adjective*
Kind; genial; benevolent; like an uncle.
> *Myron's AVUNCULAR personality makes women think of him as a friend, not as a lover.*

axiom *(AKS-e-um), noun*
A truth or fact that is seen as self-evident, leaving no room for question or debate.
> *Much to the chagrin of his creditors, Max adopted the AXIOM of those who have amassed great wealth: "Pay yourself first."*

"A woman moved is like a fountain troubled. / Muddy, ill-seeming, thick, BEREFT of beauty, / And while it is so, none so dry or thirsty / Will deign to sip or touch one drop of it."

———

William Shakespeare, English playwright

babeldom *(BAY-bell-dum), noun*
A confused mixture of voices.
> *From the crowd, there arose a BABELDOM that was cut short by the speaker clearing his throat, preparatory to beginning.*

B

bacchanal *(bah-kan-AL), noun*
A wild celebration; a party at which the partygoers are loud and out of control, often fueled by excessive alcohol consumption.
> *The initiation ceremony at the fraternity turned into a full-blown BACCHA-NAL requiring the intervention of the campus police to restore order.*

baculine *(BAA-kew-lyne), adjective*
Relating to the practice of corporeal punishment in the classroom.
> *The BACULINE philosophy is: "Spare the rod, spoil the child."*

badinage *(BAH-dih-nadge), noun*
Light, good-natured, even playful banter.
> *"If you don't care for me, you can move out now. I'm frankly not up to BADI-NAGE." —Harlan Ellison, American author*

baft *(BAFT), noun*
A cheap cotton fabric.
> *His new shirt was chiefly made of BAFT, which did not survive the rainstorm very well.*

bailiwick *(BALE-ee-wick), noun*
A person's specific area of expertise, experience, skill, knowledge, education, or authority.
> *Foreign language is not my BAILIWICK, I soon realized after failing out of Hebrew school.*

bailment *(BAYLE-ment), noun*
The act of transferring possession of property, for purposes of safekeeping, from one person to another.
> *I came into possession of my father's coin collection through a BAILMENT with my mother.*

baisemain *(BAYZ-mayn), noun*
A kiss on the hand, often as a sign of respect.
> *When you greet the movie star, you should plant a BAISEMAIN on her to show your respect for her status.*

balanism *(BA-lan-iz-um), noun*
The use of suppositories to administer medicine.
> *Rather than taking the drugs orally, the patient was required to use BALANISM.*

baptistery *(BAHP-tiss-tree), noun*
The pool or basin in a church where people are baptized.
> *Ironically, Stephen was taken to a BAPTISTERY as a child but only a few short years later would proclaim himself to be an atheist.*

barbican *(BAR-bih-can), noun*
A tower, usually of stone, built as a defensive measure against invaders or trespassers.
> *Duke Gardens in New Jersey is guarded by two small BARBICANS at the main gate.*

barometric *(bah-rah-MET-trick), adjective*
Relating to atmospheric pressure as measured by a barometer.
> *Meteorologists can often predict changes in weather by monitoring BAROMETRIC pressure.*

basial *(BAY-zuhl), adjective*
Relating to a kiss.
> *A make-out session centers around BASIAL pleasures.*

basilisk *(BAH-sill-isk), noun*
A mythical reptile with a lethal stare or breath.
> *With poisonous saliva that can kill a man with one bite, the Komodo dragon is truly a modern-day BASILISK.*

bastion *(BAS-tee-uhn), noun*
An institution, individual, or something else protecting or preserving a particular way of life, society, set of beliefs, or moral code.
> *Cliff, a Yale BASTION, continuously quibbles with Irene, who graduated summa cum laude from Harvard.*

bathos *(BAY-thoss), noun*
A sudden change in mood from the solemn and serious to a more light-hearted, relaxed, and humorous outlook.

> *When the clock ticked at midnight on December 31, 1999, and we moved into the new century without the computers shutting down, the grim look and worried faces disappeared, and the IT department was suddenly enveloped in a feeling of BATHOS.*

beatific *(bee-uh-TIH-fick), adjective*
Displaying sheer delight or joy.

> *She was radiant with a BEATIFIC smile on her face.*

beatitude *(bee-AT-ih-tood), noun*
Being in the highest possible state of happiness, good humor, and contentment.

> *"Kindness is a virtue neither modern nor urban. One almost unlearns it in a city. Towns have their own BEATITUDE; they are not unfriendly; they offer a vast and solacing anonymity or an equally vast and solacing gregariousness."*
> *—Phyllis McGinley, American author and poet*

beguiling *(bee-GUY-ling), adjective*
Charming; bewitching; enchanting.

> *The BEGUILING charm Monica learned at finishing school more than makes up for her vapid personality.*

behemoth *(bee-HEE-meth), noun*
A thing or creature of gigantic proportions.

> *In the anime cartoons of the sixties, there were two robots: man-sized Tobor and the BEHEMOTH Gigantor.*

beleaguer *(beh-LEE-gir), verb*
To persistently surround, harass, or pester until you get what you want.

> *To the embarrassment of her friends, Kristen BELEAGUERED the sommelier until he brought her a satisfactory Bordeaux.*

belie *(bee-LYE), verb*
To contradict or misrepresent.

> *Luther's mild-mannered, almost sickly appearance BELIED his physical conditioning and surprising strength.*

belles-lettres *(bell-LET-ruh), noun*
Novels, short stories, poems, and other writings read for their grace and literary style and not necessarily their content.

> *"Learning has been as great a Loser by being...secluded from the World and good Company. By that Means, every Thing of what we call BELLES LETTRES became totally barbarous, being cultivated by Men without any Taste of Life or Manners." —David Hume, Scottish philosopher*

B

bellicose *(BELL-ih-kose), adjective*
Belligerent; surly; ready to argue or fight at the slightest provocation.

> *Doug is so touchy about his new Jaguar that he'll instantly grow BELLICOSE if you so much as brush against it.*

bellwether *(BELL-weather), noun*
A leading indicator or important factor in determining a course of action or outcome.

> *The fact that Robert got thrown out of Groton and Exeter was a BELLWETHER for his lackadaisical years at Dartmouth.*

beneficent *(be-NEF-ih-sent), adjective*
Kindly in action, purpose, or speech.

> *In a BENEFICENT gesture, the neighborhood raised $10,000 to help pay for the young boy's leukemia treatments.*

benighted *(bee-NYE-ted), adjective*
To be lost, ignorant, or unenlightened.

> *The Medieval period was a BENIGHTED era of superstition.*

benign *(beh-NINE), adjective*
Kindly; gentle; generous of spirit; not harmful.

> *We thought Amanda BENIGN until she began to inflate her family pedigree.*

bereaved *(beh-REEVD), adjective*
To be in a state of grief as the result of the death of someone you love or care deeply about.

> *"Laughter would be BEREAVED if snobbery died." —Peter Ustinov, British writer and dramatist*

bereft *(beh-REFT), adjective*
Lacking a certain characteristic, possession, or trait; isolated and lonely.
> *"A woman moved is like a fountain troubled. / Muddy, ill-seeming, thick, BEREFT of beauty, / And while it is so, none so dry or thirsty / Will deign to sip or touch one drop of it." —William Shakespeare, English playwright*

besotted *(bih-SOTT-ed), adjective*
Made foolish, stupid, or dull due to an infatuation with love, money, the pursuit of power, etc.
> *Aline thinks Jake is BESOTTED with her, but he's really BESOTTED with her father's stock portfolio.*

bespoke *(bih-SPOHK), adjective*
Clothes, shoes, and other goods custom-made for a particular client.
> *Taylor's big secret is that though he wears BESPOKE clothing, he's only leasing his new Lexus.*

bête noire *(bett-NWAR), noun*
A thing for which one has an intense dislike or great fear; a dreaded enemy or foe.
> *Sunlight was Dracula's greatest BÊTE NOIRE.*

betoken *(bee-TOE-ken), verb*
To serve as a warning.
> *For Mary and Paul, the breakdown of their new Porsche while they were still two hours away from their summer home BETOKENED a disastrous vacation.*

bezoar *(beh-ZOAR), noun*
A solidified mass found in the stomach or intestines of some animals.
> *Dissection uncovered a disgusting BEZOAR inside the cow.*

bibelot *(BIB-low), noun*
A small object of beauty or rarity.
> *The Rossington's collection of BIBELOTS contains numerous Fabergé eggs.*

bibliomania *(bib-lee-oh-MAY-nee-uh), noun*
A preoccupation with the acquisition and ownership of books.
> *Lauren's BIBLIOMANIA extends only to her stockpile of catalogues for exclusive shops.*

bibulous *(BIB-yuh-luss), adjective*
Related to drinking or to drunkenness.
> *Arthur thinks he's "fine," but his BIBULOUS activities are causing the club to consider permanent expulsion.*

bicameral *(by-KAM-er-el), adjective*
A government or parliament with two chambers or houses.
> *With a Senate and a House of Representatives, the United States has a BICAMERAL legislature.*

bifurcate *(BYE-fur-kate), verb*
To divide something into two branches or forks.
> *"François Truffaut defined a great movie as a perfect blend of truth and spectacle. Now it's become BIFURCATED. Studio films are all spectacle and no truth, and independent films are all truth and no spectacle." —Howard Franklin, American screenwriter and director*

bilateral *(By-LAT-ur-ul), adjective*
Touching, existing on, or having or being agreed to by two sides.
> *The president signed a BILATERAL disarmament agreement with the nation bordering to the north.*

bildungsroman *(BILL-dungs-roh-man), noun*
A coming-of-age novel, such as *The Catcher in the Rye* or *A Portrait of the Artist as a Young Man.*
> *Alex has started writing a BILDUNGSROMAN about his experiences in prep school.*

bilious *(BILL-yuss), adjective*
Having a nasty temperament or disagreeable disposition; to be "full of bile" and hatred.
> *The polo team's BILIOUS captain made his players miserable as he proceeded to criticize their every move.*

billet *(BILL-uht), noun*
A job, position, or appointment.
> *With his wealthy father's influence, Miles was able to secure a lucrative BILLET in a major brokerage house.*

biloquist *(BILL-oh-kwist), noun*
A person able to speak in two voices.
> *In exorcisms, priests who think they hear a demon speaking may actually be treating a BILOQUIST.*

B

biomechanics *(by-oh-meh-CAN-iks), noun*
The science of motion in living organisms and their limbs, joints, and digits.
> *To work in prosthetics required an understanding of BIOMECHANICS.*

blandishments *(BLAN-dish-ments), noun*
Compliments rendered primarily to influence and gain favor with the person you are praising.
> *The BLANDISHMENTS heaped upon the consultant by his client were not sufficient to persuade him to take a staff position with them.*

blazon *(BLAY-zuhn), noun or verb*
A coat of arms; or, to proclaim something widely.
> *You'll find the Rutherford's family BLAZON on every one of Prescott's ties.*

bloviate *(BLOH-vee-ayt), verb*
To speak pompously and at length.
> *Maxwell BLOVIATES about his "excellent" golf game, but everyone knows he deflates his handicap.*

boethetic *(bo-eh-THET-ik), adjective*
Able to help with a problem or cure an ailment.
> *He did not know whether the bottle contained a BOETHETIC elixir or snake oil.*

bona fide *(BO-nah-fyed), adjective*
Legitimate; the real thing; the genuine article.
> *He may not come across as particularly intelligent, but Brian's Phi Beta Kappa key is, in fact, BONA FIDE.*

bonhomie *(bon-uh-MEE), noun*
A good-natured, genial manner.
> *Even though he has no family pedigree, Walker is accepted into our group because of his contagious BONHOMIE.*

bourgeois *(boor-ZHWAH), adjective*
Pertaining or relating to the middle class, as opposed to the upper class or royalty on one end and the peasants or common laborers on the other.

"The representation of the garrison thus turned out to be incomparably more moderate and BOURGEOIS than the soldier masses." —Leon Trotsky, Bolshevik revolutionary and Marxist theorist

bovine *(BO-vyne), adjective*
Anything related to or reminiscent of cows or other dull, docile, slow-moving, grazing mammals.

"The cow is of the BOVINE ilk; One end is moo, the other, milk." —Ogden Nash, American poet

bowdlerize *(BOWED-ler-eyes), verb*
To remove obscenity, violence, and other inappropriate content from a novel, play, or story so as to make it appropriate for a younger reader.

Hollywood BOWDLERIZED his script, so instead of being R-rated, the film was rated PG-13.

brachet *(brah-KET), noun*
A female hound that hunts by scent.

That short-haired BRACHET is a beautiful bitch.

bradawl *(BRAD-all), noun*
A straight awl with a chisel edge.

He had no idea how to use the BRADAWL that came with the toolset he bought.

braggadocio *(brag-uh-DOH-see-oh), noun*
Empty boasting or bragging.

Eric claims he is a consummate wine connoisseur, but it is just BRAGGADOCIO.

breviary *(BREE-vee-air-ee), noun*
A brief summary or abridgement.

She called it a BREVIARY, but Lana's recounting of her family's month on the Riviera was anything but short.

Brobdingnagian *(brahb-ding-NAG-ian), adjective*
Describes a thing or person of enormous size; huge.
Andre the Giant was a man of BROBDINGNAGIAN proportions, standing seven foot five inches and weighing over 500 pounds.

bromide *(BRO-mide), noun*
A cliché or tired saying used to express an idea without any thought or originality.
Helen's Harvard education does not stop her from peppering her speech with insipid BROMIDES.

brouhaha *(BREW-ha-ha), noun*
A confusing, exciting, and turmoil-rife event.
Madeline caused a BROUHAHA when she told her parents she was eschewing Harvard for a state school in order to be closer to her boyfriend.

brummagem *(BRUHM-uh-juhm), noun, adjective*
Describes something that looks great but performs poorly.
"Our press is certainly bankrupt in . . . reverence for nickel plate and BRUMMA-GEM." —Mark Twain, American author

bucolic *(byoo-KOL-ick), adjective*
A peaceful, serene, rural object, place, or environment.
We bought a weekend place in a BUCOLIC little village in the country.

bugaboo *(BUHG-uh-boo), noun*
Something that causes fear and worry, often needlessly.
Angela caused a BUGABOO when she informed her family that she was leaving the Episcopal Church.

bulbous *(BUHL-bus), adjective*
Shaped like a bulb.
A BULBOUS nose crisscrossed with veins is sometimes called a drinker's nose.

bulwark *(bull-werk)*, *noun*
A defensive, protective barrier, wall, or force.
> *"Since he aims at great souls, he cannot miss. But if someone should slander me in this way, no one would believe him. For envy goes against the powerful. Yet slight men, apart from the great, are but a weak BULWARK."* —*Sophocles, Greek tragedian*

B

bumptious *(BUMP-shuss)*, *adjective*
Loud and assertive in a crude way.
> *The club's golf pro was fired due to his BUMPTIOUS behavior on the links.*

burgeon *(BURR-jin)*, *verb*
To sprout, to grow; to blossom and flourish.
> *Natalia does her part for the BURGEONING "green" movement by having her gardener turn manure from her stables into fertilizer.*

bursary *(BURR-sir-ee)*, *noun*
The treasury of a university or college.
> *The dean was caught dipping into the BURSARY to fund his vacation to Bermuda.*

byzantine *(biz-ann-teen)*, *adjective*
A convoluted plan; a scheme that is overly complicated; a puzzle or task that's difficult to figure out because of its complexity.
> *We found it impossible to follow the BYZANTINE plot of how Eileen made Mariah a laughingstock by replacing her Prada shoes with nearly identical knockoffs.*

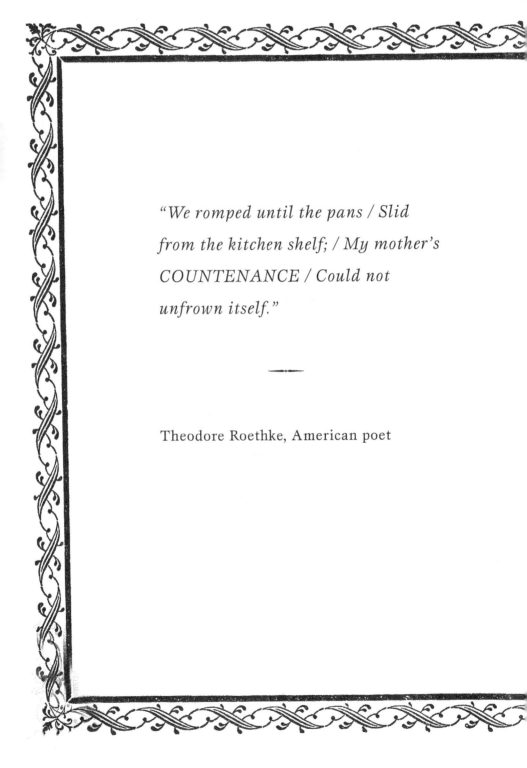

"We romped until the pans / Slid from the kitchen shelf; / My mother's COUNTENANCE / Could not unfrown itself."

Theodore Roethke, American poet

cabal *(kah-BAHL), noun*
An underground society, secret religious sect, or other private group assembled for purposes hidden from those around them.

> *I was shocked when our neighbor asked us to join a CABAL of devil worshippers; after all, he is a deacon at the local church!*

cabotage *(KAB-uh-tij), noun*
The right of a country to control all air traffic flying in its skies.

> *After 9/11, CABOTAGE became a major concern of New York City and its mayor.*

cache *(KASH), noun*
Something hidden or stored.

> *Everyone was jealous when they learned of Moira's CACHE of acceptances to the finest schools.*

cachexia *(kah-CHECK-see-ah), noun*
Wasting away of bones and muscles in patients who do not eat, such as some AIDS and cancer sufferers.

> *CACHEXIA is the main cause of death in 50 percent of cancer patients.*

cacodoxy *(kah-kuh-docs-see), noun*
Incorrect opinions or doctrine.

> *To the atheist, religion is a CACODOXY for which there is not a shred of proof.*

cadaverous *(kah-DAV-er-us), adjective*
Corpse-like.

> *Lurch in the old* The Addams Family *series had a CADAVEROUS appearance.*

caducous *(kuh-DOO-kuss), adjective*
Transitory; short-lived; perishable.

> *"Some thing, which I fancied was a part of me, falls off from me and leaves no scar. It was CADUCOUS." —Ralph Waldo Emerson, American poet, essayist, and transcendentalist*

caitiff *(KAY-tiff), noun*
A mean, evil, dastardly person.

> *Underdog's nemesis was the CAITIFF Simon Bar Sinister.*

callithump *(KAL-ih-thump), noun*
A loud and lively band or parade.
Every year my high school band marched in the annual town CALLITHUMP.

calumny *(KAL-um-nee), noun*
The act of libel or slander; to besmirch a person's reputation by spreading false statements and rumors.
"CALUMNY will sear virtue itself." —William Shakespeare, English playwright

cambist *(KAM-bist), noun*
One who trades currencies, exchanging the currency of one nation for that of another.
The streets of London, catering as they do to international tourists in need of changing currency, are full of CAMBISTS.

canard *(kah-NARD), noun*
A groundless rumor or belief.
"This sampling should once and for all put an end to the base CANARDS leveled against this column and this columnist." —Harlan Ellison, writer

cannonade *(can-non-ayd), noun*
A continuous, relentless bombardment or effort.
A CANNONADE of questioning greeted Eva's statement that she was quitting the club's tennis team.

capacious *(kuh-PAY-shus), adjective*
A huge open space; roomy; a large interior or room.
All of our meetings take place in the high school's CAPACIOUS private auditorium.

capillaceous *(kap-ih-LAY-shus), adjective*
Possessing thin filaments.
The atyid shrimp is a CAPILLACEOUS bottom feeder.

capitulation *(kah-pih-chew-LAY-shun), noun*
The act of surrendering or giving up.
Ross offered James no CAPITULATION during the confrontational lacrosse game.

capricious *(kah-PREE-shus), adjective*
Prone to quickly change one's mind, decision, or course of action at the drop of a hat or on impulse.

> *"I do not understand the CAPRICIOUS lewdness of the sleeping mind." —John Cheever, American novelist*

captious *(KAP-shuss), adjective*
A person who enjoys giving unsolicited advice; a nitpicker; a petty individual who takes pleasure in pointing out the flaws in and mistakes made by others, no matter how small.

> *Audrey is a CAPTIOUS individual eager to show others how smart she is, often by belittling them.*

carouse *(kuh-ROWZ), verb*
To engage in boisterous social activity.

> *We CAROUSED until dawn at the annual New Year's Eve party that the Weatherton's hold on their yacht.*

cassock *(KAH-sok), noun*
A long, tight-fitting outer garment often worn by priests and ministers.

> *The Father's ample girth made wearing a CASSOCK nearly impossible.*

castigate *(KAS-tuh-gate), verb*
To scold or criticize harshly, with the objective of assigning blame and motivating the other person to correct their error.

> *The bartender was CASTIGATED by his boss for serving alcohol to two teenage girls without checking their ID first.*

catharsis *(kah-THAR-sis), noun*
The purging of the senses through tragic drama or through music; or, in general, a discharge of negative emotions.

> *After losing matches at the club's courts, Puccini's "Madame Butterfly" always leads Celeste to CATHARSIS.*

caveat *(KAV-ee-ott), noun*
A precaution or warning.

> *Before Arthur applied to college, his sister offered him a CAVEAT: "Many of us do not consider Columbia to be a true Ivy League school."*

chafe *(shayf), verb*
To cause irritation by rubbing.
The tight boots caused his ankles to CHAFE.

chambray *(SHAM-bray), noun*
A smooth fabric made of cotton.
Nothing is quite as comfortable and soft as a CHAMBRAY shirt.

chimera *(kih-MER-ah), noun*
An object, place, event, or combination of things so strange, odd, and improbable that it logically should not exist in the real world—and yet, it does.
"What a CHIMERA then is humankind. What a novelty! What a monster, what a chaos!" —Blaise Pascal, French philosopher

chivalry *(SHIV-ul-ree), noun*
Brave, kind, courteous, or gentlemanly behavior.
"We hear much of CHIVALRY of men towards women; but . . . it vanishes like dew before the summer sun when one of us comes into competition with the manly sex." —Martha Coston, American author

cholers *(KOH-lers), noun*
The mood of anger, irritability, grumpiness, or being short-tempered and impatient.
When Franklin is in the grip of CHOLERS, even his closest friends avoid his table at the club.

cineaste *(SIN-ee-ast), noun*
A person who is either a professional in the movie business or just a big fan.
My cousin Gary is a CINEASTE specializing in indie films.

circadian *(sir-KAY-dee-en), adjective*
Biorhythms regulated by the twenty-four-hour cycle of the earth's rotation.
A disruption in CIRCADIAN rhythm can cause nocturnal animals to wander about in the daytime.

circuitous *(sir-CUE-uh-tuss), adjective*
Extremely twisty and winding; indirect.
Blanche called it a shortcut, but her CIRCUITOUS directions caused us to arrive very late at the debutante ball.

circumlocution *(sir-kum-low-CUE-shun), noun*
Language that is pompous, overly formal, wordy, and redundant.
> *Grant used CIRCUMLOCUTION to suggest that he attended a prep school, but all of us know he is a product of public education.*

circumspect *(SIR-kum-spekt), adjective*
Prudent, cautious, and well considered.
> *"I smiled, / I waited, / I was CIRCUMSPECT; / O never, never, never write that I / missed life or loving."* —Hilda Doolittle, American poet and memoirist

cirrate *(SIR-rate), adjective*
Having tendrils.
> *In H.P. Lovecraft's story "Pickman's Model," the fantasy artist Pickman often painted CIRRATE monstrosities.*

clandestine *(klan-DES-tyne), adjective*
Refers to activities that are secret, covert, and perhaps not fully authorized or sanctioned.
> *"CLANDESTINE steps upon imagined stairs / Climb through the night, because his cuckoos call."* —Wallace Stevens, American poet

claque *(klak), noun*
A group of admiring followers or fans.
> *In modern parlance, members of your CLAQUE would be called peeps.*

clarion *(KLAR-ee-uhn), adjective*
Clear and shrill sound.
> *On the day classes began at his prep school, Paul groaned at the CLARION call of his morning alarm.*

claviform *(KLAH-vih-form), adjective*
A club-shaped object that is thin on one end and thick on the other.
> *His CLAVIFORM walking stick doubled as a formidable weapon.*

clough *(KLOW), noun*
A narrow gorge.
> *In Ithaca we traversed a rickety bridge over a deep CLOUGH through which a stream flowed.*

cloying *(KLOYE-ing), adjective*
Sickeningly sweet, sappy, or sentimental.
"Minerva save us from the CLOYING syrup of coercive compassion!" —Camille Paglia, American author, feminist, and social critic

coadunate *(ko-ADD-you-nate), adjective*
Joined; grown together.
The COADUNATE brothers are Siamese twins.

coagulate *(koh-AG-you-late), verb*
To congeal or clump together.
The leftover gravy COAGULATED into a disgusting mess.

coaxial *(koh-AX-ee-ul), adjective*
A cable with a solid conductor at its center that is used to transmit cable television and broadband signals.
With COAXIAL cable installed, his TV picture was much clearer and sharper.

codify *(KAHD-uh-fye), verb*
To organize into a system of rules, codes, or principles; to make clear and coherent.
Fiona set out to CODIFY the rules associated with her exclusive clique.

coeval *(ko-EVE-ul), adjective*
Of the same time period.
The invention of the automobile and the first powered airplane flight are COEVAL events.

cogent *(KOH-gent), adjective*
A case or argument presented in a reasoned, well-thought-out, logical, compelling, and persuasive argument.
Corey offered a very COGENT argument in favor of insider trading.

cognizant *(KOG-nih-sint), adjective*
Aware of the realities of a situation.
Amanda is always COGNIZANT of her acquaintances' pedigrees.

cognoscente *(kon-yuh-SHEN-tee), noun*
Person with superior knowledge or understanding of a particular field.
> *As a result of my many years living in the Bordeaux region of France, I am a COGNOSCENTE of wine and winemaking.*

colloquial *(kah-LOW-kwee-ul), adjective*
Informal, conversational, everyday language.
> *"COLLOQUIAL poetry is to the real art as the barber's wax dummy is to sculpture." —Ezra Pound, American expatriate poet*

colluctation *(kahl-yook-TAY-shin), noun*
A conflict.
> *In marketing there has always been a COLLUCTATION between direct marketers and general advertising.*

commodious *(kah-MOW-dee-us), adjective*
Very spacious.
> *Though COMMODIOUS, the Barrows' Cape Cod home is austere and lacks charm.*

compendious *(kuhm-PEN-dee-us), adjective*
Concise, succinct; to the point.
> *Sheila is unable to tell COMPENDIOUS stories about her trips to the Riviera.*

compere *(KAM-per), noun*
The master of ceremonies.
> *As a COMPERE, he is incomparable.*

complaisant *(kuhm-PLAY-zuhnt), adjective*
Agreeable and eager to please.
> *Eleanor is far too COMPLAISANT with common strangers.*

comport *(kum-PORT), verb*
To conduct oneself; to behave in a particular way.
> *Roger always embarrasses us because he seems to think his family name frees him to COMPORT himself foolishly.*

compunction *(kuhm-PUHNGK-shun), noun*
Anxiety caused by regret for doing another harm.
> *Thomas never feels COMPUNCTION for the bruises he leaves on the lacrosse field.*

compurgation *(kom-purr-GAY-shun)*, *noun*
A practice by which an accused person can be found not guilty if twelve or more people take an oath testifying to the validity of his claim of innocence.
The Anglo-Saxon process of COMPURGATION is the basis of the modern American jury system.

conciliatory *(kon-SILL-ee-ah-tore-ee)*, *adjective*
Actions or words meant to settle a dispute or resolve a conflict in a manner that leaves no hard feelings on either side.
"If you are not very clever, you should be CONCILIATORY." —Benjamin Disraeli, British statesmen and literary figure

concomitant *(kon-kohm-ih-tant)*, *noun*
Something that exists or occurs with something else.
"Each action of the actor on the stage should be the visible CONCOMITANT of his thoughts." —Sarah Bernhardt, nineteenth-century French actress and author

concupiscence *(kon-KYOO-pih-suhns)*, *noun*
Unbridled lust in the extreme—horniness.
"You're talking to a young vampire, a fountain of CONCUPISCENCE." —Mario Acevedo, American fantasy author

confabulate *(kuhn-FAB-yuh-late)*, *verb*
To chat or converse informally.
Jarod proceeded to CONFABULATE about the wines most recently added to the family cellar.

connubial *(kuh-NEW-bee-ul)*, *adjective*
Relating to being married.
The groom was eager to exercise his CONNUBIAL rights.

consecrate *(KON-seh-krayt)*, *verb*
To declare something sacred, true, sacrosanct, or involuble.
"It is regarded as normal to CONSECRATE virginity in general and to lust for its destruction in particular." —Karl Kraus, Austrian writer

consuetude *(kahn-SWI-tood)*, *noun*
Established custom or behavior.
Holding the door for women was once a CONSUETUDE in polite society.

consummate *(KON-suh-mitt), adjective*
Complete or perfect; showing supreme skill.
> *"[John F. Kennedy is] a new star with a tremendous national appeal, the skill of a CONSUMMATE showman." —Russell Baker, American author*

contiguous *(kon-TIG-yew-us), adjective*
Adjacent; sharing a common border; sitting next to one another in a row or sequence.
> *The network extends to the forty-eight CONTIGUOUS states.*

contretemps *(KON-truh-tahn) noun*
An inopportune occurrence with embarrassing results.
> *"Pan had been amongst them . . . the little god Pan, who presides over social CONTRETEMPS and unsuccessful picnics." —E.M. Forster, English novelist*

conundrum *(kuh-NUN-drum), noun*
A difficult problem or situation that is not easily resolved.
> *Knowing whether to attend MIT, Yale, or Harvard was quite a CONUNDRUM: MIT had the courses he wanted, but Harvard and Yale offered him full sports scholarships.*

convalescence *(con-vah-LESS-sense), noun*
The time you spend recovering from—and getting back to full health—after an illness, during which the patient usually rests while being taken care of by others.
> *"CONVALESCENCE is the part that makes the illness worthwhile." —George Bernard Shaw, Irish playwright*

convivial *(kuhn-VIV-ee-ull), adjective*
Fond of feasting, drinking, and companionship.
> *"One does not leave a CONVIVIAL party before closing time." —Winston Churchill, British statesman and orator*

coquette *(ko-KET), noun*
A woman who dresses promiscuously or flirts excessively to make men think she is sexually available when in fact she has no intention of sleeping with them.
> *Marla doesn't intend to play the COQUETTE at society balls, but her alluring looks attract other debutantes' dates constantly.*

countenance *(KOUN-tn-unts), noun*
A facial expression, either deliberate or unconscious, conveying the person's mood, thoughts, or emotions.
> *"We romped until the pans / Slid from the kitchen shelf; / My mother's COUNTENANCE / Could not unfrown itself." —Theodore Roethke, American poet*

coup *(koo), noun*
When a person already in a position of power forcibly seizes control.
> *Sophia took control of her father's company while he was in the hospital, an act the investors considered a bit of a COUP.*

couture *(kuh-TOUR), noun*
Clothing in the latest and most popular styles created by in-vogue fashion designers.
> *If Alyssia does not have the latest COUTURE prior to its debut on Paris runways, she will not deign to consider wearing it.*

crepuscular *(kri-PUS-kyoo-ler), adjective*
Relating to twilight.
> *"CREPUSCULAR rays stream down through a tree in Olympic Park in Washington." —Michael Carlowicz, science writer*

cull *(KULL), verb*
To gather, amass, or collect.
> *Consumer behavior data was CULLED from online surveys and focus groups.*

cynosure *(SIN-uh-sure), noun*
A center of attention or attraction.
> *"This lighthouse was the CYNOSURE of all eyes." —Henry David Thoreau, American author and transcendentalist*

"Everything we shut our eyes to, everything we run away from, everything we deny, DENIGRATE or despise, serves to defeat us in the end."

Henry Miller, American author and painter

D

dabchick *(DAB-chik), noun*
A small diving bird.
> *The DABCHICK is the smallest of the European grebes.*

dactylogram *(dak-TILL-oh-gram), noun*
An image of a fingerprint.
> *The biometric security system scans the retina or uses a DACTYLOGRAM.*

dalliance *(DAL-ee-anss), noun*
A brief, casual flirtation with or interest in someone or something; the act of tarrying rather than proceeding swiftly and deliberately.
> *Her DALLIANCE with the pool boy made her husband angry and jealous.*

Darwinian *(dar-WIN-ee-in), adjective*
Relating to Charles Darwin.
> On the Origin of Species *lays out the DARWINIAN view of evolution.*

dauntless *(DAWNT-liss), adjective*
Fearless, intrepid, and bold.
> *"For Thought has a pair of DAUNTLESS wings." —Robert Frost, American poet*

dearth *(dearth), noun*
A dire shortage.
> *Besieged by the enemy, the city suffered a DEARTH of water, food, medicine, fuel, and much else besides.*

debauchery *(deh-BAW-chair-ee), noun*
Frequent indulgence in sensual pleasures.
> *"The geniuses, the mad dreamers, those who speak of DEBAUCHERY in the spirit, they are the condemned of our times." —Harlan Ellison, American author*

debilitate *(dih-BILL-uh-tayt), verb*
To make weak or feeble.
> *Several hours on the polo fields are enough to DEBILITATE even the most robust player.*

decimate *(DESS-ih-mate), verb*
To reduce something greatly, to the point of wiping it out.

"Every doctor will allow a colleague to DECIMATE a whole countryside sooner than violate the bond of professional etiquette by giving him away." —George Bernard Shaw, Irish playwright

decimestrial *(dess-ih-MEH-stree-il), adjective*
Having ten months.

With two months for summer break, the Academy had a DECIMESTRIAL school year.

déclassé *(day-klass-AY), adjective*
Of a fallen social position or inferior status.

Jean thought her imitation designer bag looked exactly like the real thing, but the other girls in her exclusive private school quickly ridiculed Jean—and her bag— for being DÉCLASSÉ.

decorous *(DEH-kore-us), adjective*
Behaving in a manner acceptable to polite society; having good taste and good manners.

"Another week with these DECOROUS drones and I'll jump out the window," the young girl complained to her mother of her fellow debutantes.

decoupage *(day-koo-PAJH), noun*
A craft project made by cutting out designs in paper and foil.

The senior citizens at the elder-care facility spent the afternoon making DECOUPAGE Christmas ornaments for the tree.

de facto *(dee-FAK-toe), adjective*
Existing in fact.

Although we eschew titles, Sasha clearly is the DE FACTO head of our arts patronage club.

deflation *(dee-FLAY-shun), noun*
A weakened economy in which prices fall because of a decline in consumer spending.

We were pleased to learn that DEFLATION has not harmed sales at Wempe's on Fifth Avenue, our favorite purveyor of watches.

defunct *(dih-FUNKT), adjective*
An institution, object, etc., that has ceased to exist.

> *"Practical men, who believe themselves to be quite exempt from any intellectual influence, are usually the slaves of some DEFUNCT economist." —John Maynard Keynes, British economist*

deification *(dee-if-ih-kay-shin), noun*
The process of making someone or something into—and worshipping them as—a god.

> *"Poetry is the DEIFICATION of reality." —Edith Sitwell, British poet*

deleterious *(dell-ih-TEAR-ee-us), adjective*
Harmful; damaging.

> *Smoking has been proven to have a DELETERIOUS effect on one's health.*

delineate *(dih-LINN-ee-ate), verb*
To use words to outline or describe with precision an object or person.

> *With efficiency, Prescott DELINEATED plans for the new wing of his family's Connecticut beach house.*

delope *(dee-LOPE), verb*
To fire a gun into the air in the hopes of ending a duel.

> *Failing to DELOPE, Alexander Hamilton was killed in a duel.*

demagogue *(DEM-ah-gog), noun*
A politician who owes his popularity largely to pandering to popular opinion and catering to the wishes of his constituency.

> *"A DEMAGOGUE is a person with whom we disagree as to which gang should mismanage the country." —Don Marquis, American journalist and humorist*

demiurge *(DEM-ee-urj), noun*
A powerful creative force or a creative personality.

> *After trying a few different professions, Jackson realized that his ability with artifice, combined with his family connections, would make him a marketing DEMIURGE.*

demotic *(dih-MAH-tik), adjective*
Language used by ordinary people.
> *Eileen always avoids the DEMOTIC because she does not want to be mistaken for someone from the middle class.*

demur *(di-MURR), verb*
To make an objection on the grounds of scruples.
> *"Assent, and you are sane; / DEMUR,—you're straightway dangerous, / And handled with a chain." —Emily Dickinson, American poet*

denigrate *(DEN-ih-grayt), verb*
Insulting; put down; demean; belittle.
> *"Everything we shut our eyes to, everything we run away from, everything we deny, DENIGRATE or despise, serves to defeat us in the end." —Henry Miller, American author and painter*

dénouement *(day-new-MAHN), noun*
The conclusion of a complex series of events.
> *Marjorie was disappointed with the opera because she felt its DÉNOUEMENT left too many loose ends.*

deonerate *(dee-ON-err-rate), verb*
To unload or relieve yourself of a burden.
> *In the movie Sin City, Marv DEONERATES to a corrupt priest, played by Frank Miller, and then kills him.*

deprecate *(DEPP-rih-kate), verb*
To express severe disapproval of another's actions.
> *"Those who profess to favor freedom and yet DEPRECATE agitation, are men who want crops without plowing up the ground." —Frederick Douglass, American abolitionist and orator*

de rigueur *(duh-rih-GUR), adjective*
Conforming to current standards of behavior, fashion, style, and etiquette.
> *A two-carat diamond engagement ring that cost a young man a year's salary was DE RIGUEUR for proposing to a girl in the 1950s.*

derivative *(deh-RIV-uh-tiv), adjective*
Copied or adapted from others.
> *"Only at his maximum does an individual surpass all his DERIVATIVE elements, and become purely himself." —D.H. Lawrence, British author*

D

descant *(des-KANT), verb*
To talk freely and without inhibition.
> *Eloise is always more than willing to DESCANT concerning her past liaisons.*

descry *(dih-SCRY), verb*
To make a discovery through careful examination.
> *With barely more than a casual glance, Amanda was able to DESCRY that the handbag was a knockoff.*

desideratum *(deh-sih-deh-RAH-tum), noun*
Something that one covets or desires.
> *Ever since she was an adolescent, Evangeline's DESIDERATUM has been a first edition of Virginia Woolf's first novel,* The Voyage Out.

desultory *(dee-SULL-ter-ee), adjective*
Acting without plan or purpose; activity that seems random or haphazard.
> *"Find time still to be learning somewhat good, and give up being DESULTORY."*
> *—Marcus Aurelius, Roman Emperor*

deus ex machina *(DAY-oos eks mah-kih-nuh), noun*
An unexpected and fortunate event solving a problem or saving someone from disaster; a stroke of good luck.
> *The author used a DEUS EX MACHINA to work his way out of the mess he got the characters in toward the end of the novel.*

dexterity *(decks-TER-ih-tee), noun*
The ability to use one's hands to perform delicate tasks.
> *Building model ships requires great DEXTERITY.*

dextrorotatory *(decks-tro-row-TAY-tore-ee), adjective*
Turning in a clockwise direction.
> *A DEXTROROTATORY turn of the wheel when in the right lane in London could get you killed.*

diaphanous *(die-APH-uh-nuss), adjective*
Fine and sheer; insubstantial and vague.

"To behold the day-break! / The little light fades the immense and DIAPHA-NOUS shadows, / The air tastes good to my palate." —Walt Whitman, American poet and humanist

diatribe *(DIE-uh-tribe), noun*
A speech railing against injustice; a vehement denunciation.

The editorial was a mean-spirited DIATRIBE against school vouchers written to prevent children from other towns from being sent by bus to Centerville High School.

dibble *(DIH-bull), noun*
A gardener's tool for making holes in the soil.

For a successful planting, use a DIBBLE and then drop your seeds in the holes.

dichotomy *(die-KOT-uh-me), noun*
Division into two parts, especially into two seemingly contradictory parts.

A DICHOTOMY between good and evil is present in every human heart.

didactic *(dye-DAK-tik), adjective*
Designed, made, or tailored for purposes of education, self-improvement, or ethical betterment.

"The essential function of art is moral ... But a passionate, implicit morality, not DIDACTIC." —D.H. Lawrence, British author

diffident *(DIFF-ih-dent), adjective*
To be uncertain or unsure about making a decision or taking an action; to lack confidence and boldness.

If you feel DIFFIDENT about driving a Rolls Royce, you can always buy a Bentley.

dilettante *(DILL-ih-tont), noun*
A person who studies a subject in a casual fashion, learning the topic for the fun of it rather than to apply it to solve real problems.

Joseph Priestly could be considered a DILETTANTE, and yet his work led to the discovery of oxygen.

diorama *(die-a-RAH-ma), noun*

A miniature scene.

For his fifth-grade project, my son made a DIORAMA of dinosaurs in prehistoric times in a shoe box.

D

disabuse *(diss-uh-BYOOZ), verb*

To free oneself or someone else from an incorrect assumption or belief.

We had to DISABUSE Lorraine from her belief that her family connections would immediately make her a member of our group.

discomfit *(diss-KUM-fit), verb*

To embarrass someone to the point where they become uncomfortable.

Maggie's public mispronunciation of the designer's name at the charity benefit DISCOMFITED her mother.

discursive *(dis-KER-siv), adjective*

A manner or style of lecturing in which the speaker jumps back and forth between many topics.

Paul's DISCURSIVE lectures on American history jumped from century to century, yet it all came together in an understandable and fresh fashion.

disenfranchise *(dis-en-FRAN-chyz), verb*

To deny someone a right or privilege; to make someone feel rejected and apart.

"Some states specify felonies that condemn the citizen to DISENFRANCHISEMENT for life." —Andrew Hacker, American political scientist

dishabille *(dis-uh-BEEL), noun*

Casual dress, or a casual manner.

Jensen is such a stickler for proper attire he feels he is in a state of DISHABILLE if he leaves the house without an ascot.

disparage *(dih-SPAIR-ihj), verb*

To bring reproach or discredit upon through one's words or actions.

"Man's constant need to DISPARAGE woman, to humble her, to deny her equal rights, and to belittle her achievements—all are expressions of his innate envy and fear." —Elizabeth Gould Davis, American feminist and author

disparate *(dis-PAHR-at), adjective*
Two or more things that differ greatly from one another and cannot be logically reconciled.

"As if, as if, as if the DISPARATE halves / Of things were waiting in a betrothal known / To none." —*Wallace Stevens, American modernist poet*

disport *(dih-SPOHRT), noun*
A diversion or amusement; can also be used as a verb, meaning to amuse oneself.

Felicia has turned the act of arguing with the proprietors of her favorite boutiques into a DISPORT.

disseminate *(diss-SEM-in-ate), verb*
To distribute something so as to make it available to a large population or area.

The Internet is rapidly replacing newspapers as the primary medium for the DISSEMINATION of news.

dissimulate *(diss-IHM-you-late), verb*
To hide one's feelings from another by using untruths.

"To know how to DISSIMULATE is the knowledge of kings." —*Cardinal Richelieu, French clergyman, noble, and statesman*

diurnal *(die-UR-nal), adjective*
Taking place or being active during daylight hours.

The house staff knows not even to approach Nora's bedroom door before twilight because she totally rejects a DIURNAL lifestyle.

dogmatic *(dawg-matt-ick), adjective*
A person who adheres rigidly to principles, rules, and beliefs, even when there is ample evidence that doing so may not be the best course of action.

Leroy is DOGMATIC in his assertion that the Maserati Gran Turismo is superior to the Mercedes-Benz SLR McLaren.

doromania *(door-oh-MAIN-ee-ah), noun*
A compulsion to shower people with excessive and unnecessary gifts.

Many people with DOROMANIA are obsessive-compulsive.

douceur *(doo-SIR), noun*
A bribe or a conciliatory gift.
> *After Francine's father refused to buy her another polo pony, he offered her the DOUCEUR of a weekend at an exclusive spa.*

doyen/doyenne *(doy-EN), noun*
A man or woman who is the senior member of a group, based on rank, age, experience, etc.
> *Though she is the youngest member of our group, Brittany is our DOYENNE, based on her extensive family connections.*

Draconian *(drah-KONE-ee-an), adjective*
Strict; mean-spirited; excessively harsh; cruel; punishment or restriction meant to cause misery to those receiving it.
> *Ophelia was distraught over the DRACONIAN way that her father forced her to stay with her chaperone throughout their vacation on the Greek Isles.*

dreadnought *(DRED-naut), noun*
A large, heavily armored battleship or tank with many big guns.
> *In the movie* Star Trek Into Darkness, *the* Enterprise *is attacked by a DREAD-NOUGHT—a giant starship twice the size of the* Enterprise.

duffer *(DUFF-uhr), noun*
An incompetent or ineffectual person.
> *Maxwell can't help being a DUFFER. After all, his family has only been wealthy for two generations.*

dun *(done), verb*
To pursue a deadbeat customer in collection of a debt.
> *The first step when you DUN a no-pay customer is to send a collection letter.*

duodenum *(doo-WAH-den-um), noun*
The first section of the small intestine.
> *Your DUODENUM contains bacteria, but they do not harm you in any way.*

dyslogistic *(diz-luh-JISS-tick), adjective*
Showing disapproval or censure.
> *We gave Elizabeth DYSLOGISTIC glances when she told us she had decided to stop shopping at Cartier.*

dysphoria *(diss-FOR-ee-ah), noun*
A feeling that overall one is not well.
DYSPHORIA is sometimes a by-product of depression.

dystopia *(diss-TOE-pee-uh), noun*
An imagined future society where conditions are terrible.
There have been countless science fiction films set in a DYSTOPIA, Soylent
Green *and* Demolition Man *among them.*

"There is no man, however wise, who has not at some period of his youth said things, or lived in a way the consciousness of which is so unpleasant to him in later life that he would gladly, if he could, EXPUNGE it from his memory."

———

Marcel Proust, French novelist, essayist, and critic

ebberman *(EBB-er-mun), noun*
A person who fishes under bridges.
> *Beneath the arched bridge I spied two EBBERMEN casting their lines over the river.*

ebriection *(ebb-ree-EK-shun), noun*
A mental collapse suffered after too much alcoholic intake.
> *As a result of binge drinking at his fraternity, Biff suffered an EBRIECTION and had to be taken to the psychiatric ward of the local hospital.*

ebullient *(ih-BOOL-yent), adjective*
Feeling joy and positive emotions at an extreme level; the state of being wildly enthusiastic about something.
> *Lorne was EBULLIENT when he found that his mother had given the college enough money to overturn his rejection.*

ecbole *(ek-buh-LEE), noun*
Ancient Greek rhetorical figure in which a speaker introduces a digression into his speech.
> *The politician, concerned with the looming sex scandal, launched his speech with an ECBOLE about recent terrorist threats.*

ecclesiolatry *(ih-klee-zee-OL-ah-tree), noun*
Excessive reverence for churches and church practices.
> *During the nineteenth century's Great Awakening, many historians feel that Americans suffered from ECCLESIOLATRY.*

ecdemic *(ek-DEM-ik), adjective*
Referring to a disease whose place of origin is distant from where it is first observed.
> *The ECDEMIC plague of the fourteenth century was first noted by historians in Italy, although it probably originated in Asia.*

ecdysiast *(ek-DEEZ-ee-ast), noun*
A stripper.
> *Although she never took off all her clothes on stage, Gypsy Rose Lee was among the most famous ECDYSIASTS during the heyday of vaudeville.*

echelon *(ESH-uh-lonn), noun*

A level of command or authority.

Family connections helped Michael ascend quickly to the upper ECHELON of his brokerage firm.

eclaircise *(eh-KLARE-size), verb*

To make clear; to clarify.

Since many of you didn't understand the remarks I made yesterday, in today's lecture I will attempt to ECLAIRCISE them.

éclat *(ay-KLAH), noun*

Great public acclaim; great public notoriety.

Although they are the height of Paris fashion, Martina's five-inch heels earned her much ÉCLAT in the society pages.

eclosion *(ih-KLOH-zhun), noun*

The emergence of an insect from its pupa.

The ECLOSION of the monarch butterfly is an amazing sight, when the bright wings of the insect unfold from the case of its pupa.

ecru *(EK-roo), adjective*

A light gray-yellow brown.

The model was wearing an ECRU skirt with a ruffled cream-colored blouse and shoes.

ectype *(EK-typ), noun*

Reproduction or copy of something.

The clones of Star Wars: Attack of the Clones are ECTYPES of Jango Fett.

edacious *(ih-DAY-shuss), adjective*

Greedy, eager, and consumed with consumption.

It's not fair to label Rosella EDACIOUS because she only wants the same luxury items the rest of us desire.

educe *(ee-DOOS), verb*

To come to a conclusion or solve a problem through reasoning based on thoughtful consideration of the facts.

After Roger's family purchased a Mercedes C class, rather than its usual Mercedes E class, we EDUCED the Wallertons were enduring financial difficulties.

effable *(EF-uh-buhl), adjective*
Capable of being expressed (as opposed to *ineffable*).
> *Many feel that the financial plan is too complicated to explain easily, but I find it very EFFABLE and have expounded it in my speeches.*

efface *(ih-FAYSS), verb*
To erase, obliterate, make inconspicuous.
> *"It is also true that one can write nothing readable unless one constantly struggles to EFFACE one's own personality. Good prose is like a windowpane." —George Orwell, British author*

effervescent *(ef-fur-VES-sent), adjective*
Bubbly; upbeat; cheerful; possessing a positive attitude and joyful personality.
> *After getting the acceptance letter from Cornell, Sabrina was positively EFFER-VESCENT and celebrated with a trip to Neiman Marcus.*

effete *(eh-FEET), adjective*
Decadent and lacking in vigor due to decadence or self-indulgence.
> *The Eddingtons donated one of their serving sets to charity, so only the truly EFFETE would deign to label the family as snobs.*

efficacious *(eff-ih-KAY-shuss), adjective*
Capable of having a desired effect.
> *"Example is always more EFFICACIOUS than precept." —Samuel Johnson, British moralist and poet*

effleurage *(ef-luhr-AHZH), noun*
A delicate stroking given during a massage session.
> *The masseuse performed an EFFLEURAGE on Mark's legs and feet that made him feel completely relaxed.*

efflorescent *(ef-fluh-RES-suhnt), adjective*
Something that has reached the final stage of its development or is at the peak of perfection.
> *Thomas is convinced that the Bugati Veyron Fbg represents the EFFLORES-CENT automobile.*

effluvium *(ih-FLOO-vee-uhm), noun*
An unpleasant exhalation, vapor, or mist.
The break in the sewage line caused a noxious EFFLUVIUM to waft through the neighborhood, driving people indoors.

effrontery *(eh-FRON-ter-ee), noun*
To have offended someone through inappropriate or aggressive behavior or audacious requests; audacity.
After doing a terrible job on the project, he had the EFFRONTERY to ask me, "Can I do extra credit?"

effulgent *(ih-FULL-junt), adjective*
Shining brightly; glowing; radiant.
The lightning storm made the evening sky positively EFFULGENT.

effusive *(eh-FEW-siv), adjective*
Profuse and overflowing; without reservation.
In an effort to butter up the senator, the lobbyist was transparently EFFUSIVE in his praise of the new bill.

egalitarian *(ih-gal-uh-TARE-ee-uhn), adjective*
To be fair and balanced in the extreme; to act in the belief that all men are created equal and should be treated so.
"Chinks in America's EGALITARIAN armor are not hard to find. Democracy is the fig leaf of elitism." —Florence King, American author

egregious *(ih-GREE-jus), adjective*
A serious mistake or offense, often with dire consequences.
Pauline made the EGREGIOUS mistake of asking the price of a piece of jewelry that caught her eye, rather than simply asking to purchase the necklace.

eidetic *(aye-DETT-ick), adjective*
Of visual imagery that is nearly photographic in detail.
We were displeased with the Howlands' recent art purchase because the so-called artist harkens back to the tired old school of EIDETIC representation.

eidolon *(eye-DOH-luhn), noun*
A phantom or apparition; the image of an ideal.

> *"By a route obscure and lonely, / Haunted by ill angels only, / Where an EIDO-LON, named Night, / On a black throne reigns upright." —Edgar Allan Poe, American author and poet*

ejectamenta *(ee-jek-tah-MEN-tah), noun*
Material ejected from some source.

> *If Mount Rainier were to erupt, its EJECTAMENTA might well destroy large parts of Seattle.*

élan, *(ey-LAHN), noun*
Enthusiasm; energy; flair; zest.

> *Bryanna reacted with ÉLAN when she was tapped to be part of a feature for Elite Travel Magazine.*

elapid *(EL-uh-pid), noun*
One of the snakes belonging to the family that have permanently erect fangs, including cobras and coral snakes.

> *To ensure our freedom from the ELAPIDS that were found in that part of India, we had with us a mongoose, an intrepid cobra chaser.*

eleemosynary *(el-ih-MAHS-in-err-ee), adjective*
Funded by voluntary contributions or supported by charity.

> *"Don contributes to favored political causes, think tanks, theater groups, educational organizations, and other worthy ELEEMOSYNARY efforts."*

elegy *(EL-eh-gee), noun*
A lament for the dead.

> *"Modern ELEGIES tend to be unconvincing because the poet so clearly believes in the immortality that an ELEGY traditionally claims for its subject."*
> *—Edward Mendelson, professor of English and comparative literature at Colombia University*

elephantine *(EH-luh-fan-tyne), adjective*
Large and clumsy; similar to an elephant.

> *The Incredible Hulk is possessed of an ELEPHANTINE tread that shakes the ground and terrifies evildoers.*

elide *(ee-LIDE), verb*
To leave out a sound or syllable when speaking; to eliminate the distinctive barrier separating levels.

When Catherine ELIDES the g's at the end of certain words, she betrays her Southern origins.

elocution *(el-oh-CUE-shun), noun*
The ability to deliver a public speech in a clear and persuasive manner.

He's a brilliant man, but he needs to work on his ELOCUTION.

eloign *(ih-LOYN), verb*
To remove to a distant place.

When I was identified as the person who had testified against the mob, the government ELOIGNED me to a secret location.

elucidate *(ee-LOO-sih-date), verb*
To lecture, explain, or pontificate about a subject in great detail so as to make it exceeding clear.

"It[was] the mission of the twentieth century to ELUCIDATE the irrational."
—Maurice Merleau-Ponty, French philosopher

elucubrate *(ih-LOO-kyoo-brait), verb*
To produce a written work through lengthy, intensive effort.

Thanks to a few hundred bucks passed along to a classmate, Miles did not have to ELUCUBRATE his term paper and could, instead, attend parties with us.

elution *(ee-LOO-shun), noun*
The act of removing material from something by dissolving it.

Many companies along the coast extract salt from sea water by a process of ELUTION, leaving a rich mineral crust behind.

em *(EM), noun*
In typesetting, a space between words or letters equivalent to the width of a capital *M*.

In designing the page, the compositor inset quotations two EMS to the right of the rest of the text's margin.

emblements *(EM-bluh-muhnts), noun*
Crops grown on a piece of land.
> *Despite the drought, my father succeeded for a time in harvesting EMBLE-MENTS from our acreage and selling them above market price.*

E

embrangle *(em-BRAN-guhl), verb, adjective*
To embroil or entangle; the state of being entangled.
> *"'He has got himself EMBRANGLED—fine old English word that!'" —Dorothy Sayers, English author,* The Nine Tailors

emend *(ih-MEND), verb*
To correct or remove faults, as from a text.
> *Blanche EMENDED her holiday wish list, removing the Ferrari watch and replacing it with a Versace dinner plate.*

emmew *(ee-MYOO), verb*
To imprison or confine.
> *To take the cat to the vet for her operation, it was necessary to EMMEW her in an animal carrier.*

emollient *(ih-MOHL-yunt), adjective*
Able to soften something, especially skin.
> *The EMOLLIENT lotion I put on after our trip to the beach made my arms and legs feel less scaly and itchy.*

empennage *(EM-pen-azh), noun*
The rear part of a plane, including the rudder and stabilizer.
> *Due to problems with the EMPENNAGE, the pilot had to make an emergency landing, as he was no longer able to steer the plane properly.*

empressement *(ahn-press-MAHN), noun*
A display of effusive cordiality.
> *Those at the party who belonged to the nouveau riche set were easy to recognize, due to their constant and distasteful EMPRESSEMENT.*

empyreal *(em-PEER-ee-uhl), adjective*
Elevated and sublime; or, of the sky.
> *The beautiful three-carat sapphire her fiancé gave her shone with an EMPY-REAL, almost celestial, light.*

encipher *(en-SY-fur), verb*
To scramble or convert data into a secret code, prior to transmission, thereby making it impossible for unauthorized users to understand or decipher.
Mathematicians were employed by the Army to crack ENCIPHERED messages during the war.

encomium *(en-KO-me-um), noun*
Effusive praise given in a public forum.
The CEO's ENCOMIUM at Phil's retirement dinner caused his eyes to mist over.

endemic *(en-DEM-ik), adjective*
A widespread condition or characteristic found in a certain region, area, or group.
Affluence and influence seem to be just ENDEMIC to our group.

enervate *(EN-er-vayt), transitive verb*
To rob a person, organization, place, or thing of its energy, strength, and vitality.
Greenhouse gases ENERVATE the protective ozone layer surrounding the earth.

enigmatic *(en-ig-MATT-ik), adjective*
Mysterious, puzzling, and difficult to figure out.
"The interest in life does not lie in what people do, nor even in their relations to each other, but largely in the power to communicate with a third party, antagonistic, ENIGMATIC, yet perhaps persuadable, which one may call life in general." —Virginia Woolf, British essayist and novelist

enjambment *(en-JAMB-meant), noun*
A run-on sentence or line in a poem.
"Because of this one ENJAMBMENT, I can almost not bear to read the poem."
—Nicholson Baker, American author

enjoin *(ehn-JOYN), verb*
To direct or order someone to do something.
After purchasing one too many Bentleys, Alex's father ENJOINED him to be more frugal.

E

enmity *(EN-mih-tee), noun*
Mutual dislike; animosity; hatred; antagonism; or disagreement between two groups or parties.
  Was the ENMITY between Muhammad Ali and Joe Frasier an act, genuine, or a combination of both?

ennui *(on-WEE), noun*
Apathy and lack of energy caused by boredom and disinterest.
  "And he spoke of ENNUI, of jaded appetites, of nights and days aboard a moonstone vessel as large as a city." —Harlan Ellison, American author

ensconce *(en-SKONTS), verb*
To settle oneself warmly or snugly; to hide something in a secure place.
  Julia ENSCONCED herself in a leather chair in the family's library and perused recent catalogs.

entablature *(en-TAB-luh-cher), noun*
In classical Greek architecture, the space on top of and between the columns.
  The marble carvings that were part of the ENTABLATURE of the Parthenon in Athens were removed to England by Lord Elgin.

entropy *(EN-troh-pee), noun*
The tendency of any system to run down and revert to total chaos.
  "Just as the constant increase of ENTROPY is the basic law of the universe, so it is the basic law of life to be ever more highly structured and to struggle against ENTROPY." —Václav Havel, Czech playwright, writer, and politician

enumerate *(eh-NOO-muh-rate), verb*
To list or to count off individually, one by one.
  "One might ENUMERATE the items of high civilization, as it exists in other countries, which are absent from the texture of American life, until it should become a wonder to know what was left." —Henry James, American-born British author

enunciate *(ee-NUN-see-ate), verb*
To pronounce words carefully and clearly; to speak in a manner that makes you easily understood.
  No one will listen to him until he stops mumbling and learns to ENUNCIATE.

envisage *(en-VIZ-ij), verb*
To envision, imagine, or create a mental picture.
"I don't ENVISAGE collectivism. There is no such animal, it is always individualism." —Gertrude Stein, American author

epexegesis *(ep-ex-ih-JEE-sis), noun*
The addition of a word or words to explain a preceding term.
The annotated text is filled with EPEXIGESIS, that is to say, explanations of various obscure or archaic words.

ephemeral *(eh-FEM-er-uhl), adjective*
A short-lived condition temporary event, or fleeting moment.
"There remain some truths too EPHEMERAL to be captured in the cold pages of a court transcript." —Irving Kaufman, Chief Judge, United States Court of Appeals

epicurean *(eh-pih-CURE-ee-an), noun*
Devoted to the enjoyment of good food and comfort.
Mother's Thanksgiving meal at the Cape Cod compound was an annual EPICUREAN delight.

epideictic *(ep-ih-day-IK-tik), adjective*
Designed to show off a speaker's skills.
The Sunday sermon was deemed by the congregation a perfect EPIDEICTIC opportunity for the new minister to impress them.

epigraph *(EH-pih-graf), noun*
A short quotation or saying at the beginning of a book or book chapter, or a brief inscription on a coin, statue, or building.
"Benfey begins his book with a curious EPIGRAPH from John Ruskin." —Joyce Carol Oates, American author

epiphany *(eh-PIH-fan-ee), noun*
A sudden, unexpected insight that seems to come from nowhere and throws great illumination on a subject previously not well understood.
One day Marcus had an EPIPHANY and realized that, to find true happiness, he should become a philanthropist.

epistaxis *(ep-uh-STAK-sis), noun*
A nosebleed.
> *Our seats for the concert were so far and high in the back of the arena that we were in danger of EPISTAXIS, hence the term "nosebleed section."*

E

epistolary *(eh-PISS-toe-lar-ee), adjective*
Having to do with the writing or letters or other literary works.
> *Madeline continues the EPISTOLARY tradition by eschewing e-mail, opting for fine parchment and her great-grandfather's diamond-encrusted quill pen for her correspondence.*

eponymous *(eh-PON-eh-muss), adjective*
To be named after something, such as a child being named after his grandfather or the mythical Romulus giving his name to Rome.
> *Josephine spends as much time as possible sailing in her EPONYMOUS yacht.*

equable *(ECK-wuh-bull), adjective*
Unvarying, steady, and free from extremes.
> *"He spake of love, such love as spirits feel / In worlds whose course is EQUABLE and pure." —William Wordsworth, British Romantic poet*

equanimity *(ee-kwa-NIM-ih-tee), noun*
The ability to keep one's cool during times of stress, conflict, or trouble.
> *When his mother locked her keys in the car, her young son responded with surprising EQUANIMITY.*

equatorium *(eh-kwa-TOR-ee-um), noun*
An antique device used to find the positions of the sun, moon, planets, and other heavenly bodies.
> *The court astrologer brought out his EQUATORIUM and other instruments in order to cast the king's horoscope.*

equivocate *(ee-KWIV-uh-kate), verb*
To change one's mind or be unable to stick with a decision or resolution; to vacillate in one's opinion or position.
> *The candidate seemed to EQUIVOCATE on the energy crisis with each speech he made.*

erotesis *(er-oh-TEE-sis), noun*
A rhetorical form in which the speaker asks a question to which the apparently right answer is really the wrong one.

An example of EROTESIS is the question, "Shall I be frightened by such ravings of the opposition in answer to my reasonable proposals?"

E

ersatz *(er-ZATS), adjective*
A phony; a fake; a counterfeit; an inferior copy; a pale imitation of an original.

Before his sentencing and jail term, the artist made an impressive living selling ERSATZ Rembrandt paintings.

erudite *(AIR-yoo-dyte), adjective*
Sophisticated; well educated; deeply learned; knowledgeable; scholarly.

Beneath his ERUDITE image, Dr. John Brinkley was a money-grubbing con man.

esbat *(EZ-bat), noun*
A meeting of witches, especially a witches' coven.

The three Weird Sisters are engaged in an ESBAT when Macbeth confronts them about his future as king of Scotland.

escritoire *(ess-krih-TWAR), noun*
A writing desk.

In the upper hallway of my house I have an ESCRITOIRE at which I do most of my serious writing.

escutcheon *(ess-KUHCH-uhn), noun*
A shield depicting a coat of arms.

"My late Uncle Henry, you see, was by way of being the blot on the Wooster ESCUTCHEON." —P.G. Wodehouse, English author and humorist, Jeeves Takes Charge

esoteric *(es-oh-TER-ik), adjective*
Something known or appreciated by an elite few who have the taste, sophistication, and education to understand its merits.

"My ESOTERIC doctrine, is that if you entertain any doubt, it is safest to take the unpopular side in the first instance." —William Lamb Melbourne, British prime minister

estival *(ES-tuh-vuhl), adjective*
Pertaining to summer.
> *In this ESTIVAL season, the beaches are full, coolers are overflowing with beer bottles, and the smell of grilling meat is everywhere.*

E

ethereal *(eh-THEER-ee-uhl), adjective*
Light and airy; possessing a heavenly or celestial quality.
> *"ETHEREAL, their mauve / almost a transparent gray, / their dark veins bruise-blue." —Denise Levertov, British-born American poet*

ethos *(EE-thos), noun*
The core principles or beliefs of a religion, culture, or community.
> *Even the eating of cheese violates the ETHOS of the vegan culture.*

etiolate *(EE-tee-uh-late), verb*
To cause to become weak and appear sickly.
> *Over time, Brad's excesses—and his refusal to see a plastic surgeon—increasingly ETIOLATED his once-handsome appearance.*

euphemism *(YOU-feh-miz-im), noun*
A synonym that is less offensive than the word it is used to replace.
> *"The doctor told me I'm big boned," said Chuck defensively. "That's just a EUPHEMISM for fat," his brother said meanly.*

euphony *(YOU-fone-ee), noun*
The habit of changing the pronunciation of words or the wording of phrases so they are pleasing to the ear and roll off the tongue with greater ease.
> *In finishing school, Alsace learned the art of EUPHONY, and she has parlayed that into a hobby of earning roles in television commercials.*

euphuism *(YOU-few-iz-im), noun*
A phrase, sentence, or thought expressed in an ornate, flowery, overly elaborate style of writing, often making the exact meaning difficult to discern.
> *Felicia's words are full of EUPHUISM, particularly when describing the architecture of her family's various houses.*

eupraxia *(you-PRAK-see-ah), noun*
In medicine, the normal ability to perform coordinated movements.
The police, suspecting the man was drunk, engaged him in exercises designed to demonstrate his EUPRAXIA, which he failed miserably.

eustasy *(YEW-stah-see), noun*
A change in sea level caused by melting of ice, movement of ocean floors, or major deposits of sediment.
Global warming is already triggering EUSTASY with the melting of the polar ice caps.

eutony *(YOU-tun-ee), noun*
The pleasant sound of a word.
To the starving man, words such as "hot tomato soup" and "grilled cheese sandwich" are heavy with EUTONY.

evanescent *(ev-eh-NESS-ent), adjective*
Having the qualities of a mist or vapor, capable of vanishing seemingly into thin air.
"Nobody thinks it's silly to invest two hours' work in two minutes' enjoyment; but if cooking is EVANESCENT, well, so is the ballet." —Julia Child, American cook, author, and television personality

evince *(ee-VINCE), verb*
To reveal or indicate the presence of a particular feeling or condition.
The blocky lines of Van Gogh's paintings EVINCE a feeling of depression and madness.

exacerbate *(egg-ZASS-err-bayt), verb*
To take action that makes a situation worse or aggravates it further.
The problem with the mission was further EXACERBATED when the outer tiles ripped away from the Space Shuttle.

excoriate *(eggs-KORE-ee-ate), verb*
To criticize; to attempt to censure or punish.
We EXCORIATED Melanie for inviting people with no family connections to her birthday party.

E

exculpate *(EKS-kull-payte), verb*
To prove the innocence of someone suspected of being guilty, or free someone from an obligation or burden.
> *Gerald Ford's pardon EXCULPATED Richard Nixon legally, but history consigned him to the role of a disgraced president forever.*

execrate *(EGGS-eh-krayt), verb*
To loath; to subject to scorn and derision.
> *We EXECRATED William for weeks due to his casual rejection of an invitation to join Yale's Skull and Bones.*

exemplar *(eggs-EM-plar), noun*
A role model; a shining example of a desired state, status, or behavior.
> *"The system—the American one, at least—is a vast and noble experiment. It has been polestar and EXEMPLAR for other nations." —Phyllis McGinley, American poet*

exhort *(ig-ZORT), verb*
To urge or advise earnestly.
> *"The function of the moralist is not to EXHORT men to be good but to elucidate what the good is." —Walter Lippman, American journalist*

exigency *(EKS-ih-jen-see), noun*
A condition or problem of some urgency such that when it arises requires an immediate effort to alleviate or solve it.
> *"We should never despair, our Situation before has been unpromising and has changed for the better, so I trust, it will again. If new difficulties arise, we must only put forth New Exertions and proportion our Efforts to the EXIGENCY of the times." — George Washington, American president*

existential *(eggs-ih-STEN-shul), adjective*
Refers to ideas, beliefs, and philosophies that support the belief in free will and the freedom of the individual.
> *"No phallic hero, no matter what he does to himself or to another to prove his courage, ever matches the solitary, EXISTENTIAL courage of the woman who gives birth." —Andrea Dworkin, American radical feminist and author*

expiate *(EKS-pee-ate), verb*
To make amends for doing something wrong.
> *"Killing himself and the woman must certainly have occurred to him as a way of EXPIATING guilt." —John D. MacDonald, American author*

expropriate *(eks-PRO-pree-ate), verb*
To seize property or wealth from its owner for the public's use or benefit, as when the state takes someone's home under eminent domain to build a road through it.
> *The Bradfords are still reeling from the fact that the state EXPROPRIATED a portion of their formal gardens for a new highway.*

expunge *(eks-PUNJ), verb*
To rid oneself of an annoyance; to cast out; to get rid of; to forcibly eject.
> *"There is no man, however wise, who has not at some period of his youth said things, or lived in a way the consciousness of which is so unpleasant to him in later life that he would gladly, if he could, EXPUNGE it from his memory."*
> *—Marcel Proust, French novelist, essayist, and critic*

expurgate *(EKS-per-gate), transitive verb*
To purge sexually inappropriate, disgusting, or otherwise undesirable material prior to presentation.
> *For her parents' benefit, Marina EXPURGATED stories related to the weekend she spent slumming in Greenwich Village.*

extemporaneous *(eks-tem-por-ayne-ee-us), adjective*
Off the cuff; done without preparation.
> *My ability to speak EXTEMPORANEOUSLY makes me very comfortable speaking in front of a group that asks a lot of questions.*

extol *(eks-TOLE), verb*
To praise with great enthusiasm.
> *Iris has not ceased to EXTOL the virtues of her new Romain Jerome Day & Night watch.*

extrapolate *(eks-TRAP-oh-late), verb*
To infer, by taking known information into account.
> *The tasteful four-carat diamond on her finger allowed us to EXTRAPOLATE that Portia had accepted James's proposal.*

"Never lose sight of the fact that all human FELICITY lies in man's imagination, and that he cannot think to attain it unless he heeds all his caprices."

—

Marquis de Sade, French aristocrat and revolutionary

fabricant *(FA-brih-kant), noun*
A manufacturer or maker of goods.
> *In his quest to become a FABRICANT, the first step was to find a building suitable for a factory.*

façade *(fah-SAHD), noun*
The front of a building; a deceptive appearance masking a thing's true nature.
> *"A good man often appears gauche simply because he does not take advantage of the myriad mean little chances of making himself look stylish. Preferring truth to form, he is not constantly at work upon the FAÇADE of his appearance." —Iris Murdoch, Irish author and philosopher*

facetious *(fuh-SEE-shus), adjective*
Comments made specifically to get a laugh out of those around you; something said in jest; sarcastic.
> *"Boarding school manners and attitudes—stoic denial, FACETIOUS irony— are still deeply entrenched in the character of the country." —Jonathan Raban, British travel writer and novelist*

facile *(FASS-ill), adjective*
Accomplished easily and with little effort.
> *"The hunger for FACILE wisdom is the root of all false philosophy." —George Santayana, author and philosopher*

faction *(FAK-shin), noun*
A small dissenting group within a larger one.
> *"I will keep where there is wit stirring, and leave the FACTION of fools." —William Shakespeare, English playwright*

factitious *(fack-TISH-uss), adjective*
Contrived; fabricated.
> *At first, we thought the rumor FACTITIOUS, but then we learned that couture-producer Hermès does, in fact, plan to design and market a helicopter.*

factoid *(FAK-toyed), noun*
An interesting short fact.
> *His editor asked him to use a lot of FACTOIDS in his book.*

factotum *(fak-TOE-tum), noun*
A person who does many different types of work or activities.
He is a real *FACTOTUM*—a jack of all trades and master of none.

fadoodle *(fah-DOO-duhl), noun*
Nonsense; ridiculousness.
"You must be drunk! You're talking mere FADOODLE! No one's taking you seriously."

fain *(FAYN), adverb*
Happily or willingly.
I would FAIN assist you in your endeavor to send your children to college and see that they get ahead in the world.

fallacious *(fuh-LAY-shus), adjective*
An idea or conclusion based on one or more false assumptions.
Since my online subscriber list is double opt-in, accusing me of being a spammer is a wholly FALLACIOUS assumption.

fallible *(FAL-ih-bull), adjective*
Capable of screwing up, making errors, or being wrong.
At a fairly young age children realize their parents are eminently FALLIBLE.

familistery *(fam-ihl-ISS-ter-ee), noun*
A society in which the community functions as an extended family.
During the 1960s, some communes in the American Southwest tried to set themselves up as FAMILISTERIES in which children were raised by the entire community.

famulus *(FAM-you-luhs), noun*
Assistant or aide.
I usually leave the preparing of such papers to my FAMULUS, who is paid to do these things.

fanfaronade *(fan-far-oh-NAYED), noun*
Boasting; bragging; showing off.
Muhammad Ali's FANFARONADE was part of his charm.

fanion *(FAN-yun), noun*
A small flag used to indicate the location of surveying stations.
The surveyors had set up a FANION about every twenty yards to indicate the direction of the roadbed.

fantod *(FAN-todd), noun*
Being nervous or anxious.
His FANTOD concerning crowds made him swoon when a large group of people entered the room.

farandole *(FAR-uhn-dole), noun*
A dance originating in Provence, France.
At the party, dancers performed a lively FARANDOLE, reminding many of them of their Provençal origins.

farcical *(FAR-sih-kuhl), adjective*
Ludicrous, absurd, or laughably inept.
"To conjure up such ridiculous questions, the answers to which we all know or should know are in the negative, is to build up a whimsical and FARCICAL straw man which is not only grim but Grimm." —Tom C. Clark, Supreme Court Justice

farctate *(FARK-tate), adjective*
Stuffed full of something.
The walls of the cabin were made FARCTATE with dried leaves and branches to provide a measure of insulation.

fardel *(FAR-dill), noun*
A burden.
His penniless, ever-mooching relatives were a FARDEL on Wayne.

farouche1 *(fah-ROOSH), adjective*
To become sullen, shy, or withdrawn in the presence of company.
His FAROUCHE demeanor gave people the impression that he didn't like them, when in fact, he was merely an introvert.

farouche2 *(fah-ROOSH), adjective*
Wild; ferocious.
Wolverine is the most FAROUCHE superhero in comic-book literature.

farrier *(FAR-ee-err), noun*
A person who shoes horses.
> *"Putting shoes on horses is a dangerous business," said the FARRIER, who noted that one swift kick could end him.*

fascicle *(FAS-ih-kuhl), noun*
A section of a book that is bound in separate parts.
> *The binder gathered together the FASCICLES and sewed them into a single book, onto which he then bound a leather cover.*

fascinorous *(fah-sih-NOR-uhs), adjective*
Wicked; infamous for evil deeds or thoughts.
> *History has declared that Adolf Hitler and Joseph Stalin were among the most FASCINOROUS men who ever lived, inasmuch as they were responsible for millions of deaths.*

fastidious *(fah-STID-ee-us), adjective*
To be particular about things, particularly good housekeeping and personal hygiene; to place great importance on even the smallest of details.
> *"A FASTIDIOUS person in the throes of love is a rich source of mirth." —Martha Duffy, Arts editor,* Time *magazine*

fatidic *(fah-TIHD-ik), adjective*
Prophetic.
> *Nostradamus was a particularly prolific and FATIDIC figure whose words were widely studied.*

fatuous *(FACH-oo-us), adjective*
Trivial; silly; absurd; unimportant; pointless.
> *"I'm sick of pretending that some FATUOUS male's self-important pronouncements are the objects of my undivided attention." —Germaine Greer, Australian writer and scholar*

Faustian *(FOW-stee-in), adjective*
Evil; malicious; dark and brooding with malevolent intent; demonic; satanic; having sold one's soul to the devil—metaphorically or literally—in exchange for wealth and power.
> *In the movie* The End of Days *a group of police officers make a FAUSTIAN bargain with Satan himself.*

F

fauteuil *(FOH-til), noun*
A French-made upholstered armchair without sides.
> *My front parlor is filled with furniture I brought back from Paris, including a FAUTEUIL from the nineteenth century.*

faux *(FOH), adjective*
Fake; phony; artificial.
> *She wore a cheap secondhand dress and a FAUX pearl necklace made out of white beads.*

faux pas *(foh pah), noun*
A serious breach of social protocol or etiquette.
> *Looking a Japanese business customer directly in the eye during conversation is considered an egregious FAUX PAS not easily forgiven.*

faviform *(FAHV-ih-form), adjective*
Shaped like a honeycomb.
> *Design elements on some Roman baroque buildings were FAVIFORM, reflecting the important role of the Barberini family, whose symbol was bees.*

fealty *(FEE-ul-tea), noun*
A sense of obligation or loyalty, usually existing because one person feels beholden to another.
> *The only reason that Bryson pledged FEALTY to David is because David's social connections helped Bryson get a job on Wall Street.*

febricity *(feh-BRIS-ih-tee), noun*
The state of being feverish.
> *Ron's FEBRICITY and our inability to lower his temperature finally convinced us to send for a doctor.*

feckless *(FEK-less), adjective*
Possessing an air of casual indifference; lacking definitiveness of purpose.
> *Some accuse us of being FECKLESS, but they have no idea how difficult it is to live a wealth-infused lifestyle.*

fecundity *(fe-KUN-di-tee), noun*
A person, organization, resource, or activity that is exceptionally productive, creative, fertile, or fruitful.
> *"Blistering heat suddenly took the place of Carboniferous moisture and FECUN-DITY." —Simon Winchester, British author and journalist*

felicitous *(fih-LISS-ih-tuss), adjective*
Appropriate and well suited for a particular occasion.
> *"O to be a dragon / a symbol of the power of Heaven—of silkworm / size or immense; at times invisible. FELICITOUS phenomenon!" —Marianne Moore, modernist American poet and writer*

felicity *(fih-LISS-ih-tee), noun*
A state of blissful happiness.
> *"Never lose sight of the fact that all human FELICITY lies in man's imagination, and that he cannot think to attain it unless he heeds all his caprices." —Marquis de Sade, French aristocrat and revolutionary*

femerall *(FEM-urh-ahl), noun*
An opening in a roof to allow smoke to escape.
> *Structures in ancient cities often had FEMERALLS so that the interiors would not become choked with smoke from open fires.*

feral *(FERR-ill), adjective*
Wild; undomesticated.
> *The field was overrun with FERAL cats.*

feretory *(FER-eh-taw-ree), noun*
A reliquary for the remains of a saint.
> *The bones of St. Cuthbert were kept in the cathedral in a magnificent jeweled FERETORY made of intricately carved ivory.*

ferrous *(FERR-iss), adjective*
A metal containing iron.
> *Contrary to popular belief, magnets cannot attract all metals—only FERROUS metals.*

ferruginous *(fuh-ROO-juh-nus), adjective*
Containing iron; rust colored; the color of rusty iron.
> *As a result of years exposed to the rains and wind, the iron girders had become FERRUGINOUS, standing out against the bleached white sand.*

ferrule *(FEH-rool), noun*
A metal cap or ring placed around the end of a cane, club, or tool to give it added strength.
> *In the TV movie* The Strange Case of Dr. Jekyll and Mr. Hyde, *Jack Palance beat his victims to death with the FERRULE on his walking stick.*

ferule *(FER-uhl), noun*
A cane or flat piece of wood made for punishing schoolchildren.
> *For our misbehavior, the teacher caned us on the hands with his FERULE.*

fervent *(FUR-vuhnt), adjective*
Showing great enthusiasm and intensity of spirit.
> *Packing up the family's castoffs for myriad charities each December places Contessa in a FERVENT state.*

fescue *(FESS-kew), noun*
A type of grass used in many of the golf courses of the British Isles.
> *Shinnecock Hills is one of the few U.S. courses planted with FESCUE grass.*

fetlock *(FEHT-lahk), noun*
The tuft of hair at the base of a horse's hind legs just above the start of the hoof.
> *The FETLOCKS on the legs of the horses that pull the Budweiser wagon almost cover their hooves.*

fiat *(FEE-aht), noun*
An authoritative decree or order.
> *Everyone interested in receiving a sizeable portion of his inheritance simply allows grandfather to rule the household by FIAT.*

fiddle-faddle *(FID-ill-fad-uhl), adjective*
Something that is trivial, nonsensical, or a waste of time and attention.
> *"FIDDLE-FADDLE!" declared the octogenarian when his grandson showed off his new iPhone.*

fiduciary *(fih-DO-she-err-ee), adjective*
Pertaining to money or finances.
An accountant has a FIDUCIARY responsibility to his clients to prepare tax returns in accordance with current tax laws.

filibeg *(FIL-uh-beg), noun*
A kilt, as worn in the Scottish Highlands.
After the uprising of 1745, Scots were forbidden by the English government for many years to wear the FILIBEG, since it was an expression of Scottish nationalism.

filibuster *(FILL-ih-bus-ter), noun*
Making a prolonged speech or using other tactics to delay legislative actions or other important decisions.
The room breathed a collective sigh when the senator finally ended his eight-hour FILIBUSTER.

fillip *(FILL-uhp), noun*
Something that revives or arouses excitement.
"Faithful horoscope-watching, practiced daily, provides just the sort of small, but warm and infinitely reassuring FILLIP that gets matters off to a spirited start."
—Shana Alexander, American author

firkin *(FUR-kin), noun*
A small wooden tub or container.
Run next door and borrow some butter from the neighbors; here's a FIRKIN you can bring it back in.

flabellate *(fluh-BEL-uht), adjective*
Fan-shaped.
FLABELLATE vaulting in medieval English cathedrals extends outward in great fans of decorative ribbing.

flagitious *(fluh-JISH-uss), adjective*
Shamefully wicked or particularly heinous.
Now that the paparazzi hangs on her every move, Natasha goes out of her way to engage in FLAGITIOUS behavior.

F

flagrante delicto *(fluh-grahn-tay di-LIK-toh) noun*
In the act of committing an offense; most widely used today to describe a couple caught in the act of sexual intercourse.

> *"No cheating spouse, no teen with a wrecked family car, no mayor of Washington, DC, videotaped in FLAGRANTE DELICTO has ever come up with anything as farfetched as U.S. farm policy." —P.J. O'Rourke, American satirist*

flambeau *(FLAHM-boh), noun*
Torch or candlestick.

> *To find our way through the dark wood, we each bore a FLAMBEAU that burned brightly.*

flautino *(flaw-TEE-noh), noun*
A small flute; one of several types of small flutes.

> *To create the high-pitched sounds necessary for the musical theme, the composer employed a melodic line played by a FLAUTINO.*

fleuret *(floor-ET), noun*
A small flower.

> *The edges of the tablecloth were embroidered with FLEURETS, which gave it a bucolic, spring-like appearance.*

flibbertigibbet *(FLIB-err-tee-jih-bet), noun*
A flighty or whacky person.

> *Friends and family saw Mark as a FLIBBERTIGIBBET until he became a millionaire by opening a chain of clown schools.*

floccinaucinihilipilification *(flock-in-awe-sin-ih-lip-ih-fih-KAY-shin), noun*
To value a thing as worthless.

> *The appraiser's FLOCCINAUCINIHILIPILIFICATION dashed his hopes of making a killing selling the oil painting he found in an attic.*

floccose *(FLOHK-ohs), adjective*
Of plants, bearing small tufts of fur or long hairs.

> *The pods of the milkweed plant are FLOCCOSE, the seeds carried on the wind supported by tufts of white hair.*

florid *(FLOOR-id), adjective*
Excessively ornate and showy, as prose.

> *"All men are really most attracted by the beauty of plain speech, and they even write in a FLORID style in imitation of this."* —Henry David Thoreau, American author and transcendentalist

fluke *(flook), noun*
One of the tines of a ship's anchor.

> *The FLUKE of our anchor caught on the sandy bottom of the lagoon and held us fast.*

flux *(fluks), noun*
The rate of flow of some substance or thing per unit area.

> *The FLUX of water through the tapering pipe gave the shower greater force.*

foible *(FOY-bull), noun*
A small flaw, weakness, or defect.

> *For all his flaws and FOIBLES, Richard Nixon was perhaps the most effective president on foreign policy in the twentieth century.*

foin *(FOYN), noun*
A thrust with a bladed weapon.

> *Gaelen made a FOYN with his sword, which Harlech parried with his own blade in a shower of sparks.*

foment *(foe-MEHNT), verb*
To rouse or incite.

> *"If perticuliar care and attention is not paid to the Laidies we are determined to FOMENT a Rebelion, and will not hold ourselves bound by any Laws in which we have no voice, or Representation."* —Abigail Adams, second First Lady of the United States

foraminated *(fohr-AM-ihn-a-tud), adjective*
Having small openings; pierced by small holes.

> *The container was FORAMINATED, which meant that when it was filled with water it sprinkled the garden through its holes.*

forbear *(for-BEAR), verb*
To not do something; to do without.
> *The landlord decided to FORBEAR raising the rent until the repairs to the building had been completed.*

forby *(fawr-BAY), preposition*
Near.
> *Aye, the loch is FORBY, not more than a quarter mile distant.*

forestall *(for-STAWL), verb*
To thwart an action in advance; or, to buy up goods in order to increase their resale price.
> *Arthur's family thrives during financially insecure times because it always seems to FORESTALL exactly the right commodities.*

forinsecal *(fohr-IN-say-kahl), adjective*
Foreign; alien.
> *To paraphrase Horace, nothing human is FORINSECAL to me.*

fortuitous *(for-TOO-ih-tuss), adjective*
A happy event taking place by accident or chance.
> *"The most FORTUITOUS event of my entire life was meeting my wife Eleanor."*
> *—Franklin Delano Roosevelt*

foulard *(foe-LARD), noun*
A scarf, tie, or ascot made of silk or another lightweight material.
> *FOULARDS are colorful and stylish yet won't make you too warm.*

founder *(FOUN-der), verb*
To fail utterly; to become a complete wreck.
> *"Who would not rather FOUNDER in the fight / Than not have known the glory of the fray?" —Richard Hovey, American poet*

frabjous *(FRAB-jus), adjective*
Magnificent; wonderful; extraordinary; delightful.
> *Her wedding dress was absolutely FRABJOUS.*

fractious *(FRACK-shuss), adjective*
Easily angered or irritable; quarrelsome; unruly.

> *"Sex is metaphysical for men, as it is not for women. Women have no problem to solve through sex. Physically and psychologically, they are serenely self-contained. They may choose to achieve, but they do not need it. They are not thrust into the beyond by their own FRACTIOUS bodies." —Camille Paglia, American author, feminist, and social critic*

frangible *(FRAN-juh-bull), adjective*
Easily breakable.

> *The Worthington's staff knows to be excessively careful around the family's collection of FRANGIBLE Ming vases.*

fratricide *(FRA-trih-side), noun*
The act of killing a relative, friend, or neighbor.

> *"Similar FRATRICIDE occurs with submitted manuscripts, with reviewers denigrating competing research so it is not published." —Jerome Groopman, Harvard Medical School*

frenetic *(fruh-NET-ick), adjective*
Frantic and frenzied.

> *"I love my work with a FRENETIC and perverse love, as an ascetic loves the hair shirt which scratches his belly." —Gustave Flaubert, French writer*

freon *(FREE-on), noun*
A chemical used in air conditioners to produce cold temperatures.

> *Every spring, before you will need the AC to cool the house in summer, have the FREON levels checked.*

frippery *(FRIHP-uh-ree), noun*
Ostentatious or affected elegance.

> *The FRIPPERY of Lara's couture belied her nouveau riche origins.*

frisson *(FREE-son), noun*
A sudden strong feeling of excitement, conflict, or danger.

> *"Pregnant women! They had that weird FRISSON, an aura of magic that combined awkwardly with an earthy sense of duty." —Ruth Morgan, American novelist*

frowst *(frowst), noun*
Stale, musty, stifling air.
> *The FROWST in the concert hall caused my sister to feel ill at my son's college graduation.*

F

fruition *(froo-ISH-un), noun*
The completion of a task; the achievement of a goal as the result of significant and persistent effort.
> *John Nash, a mathematician whose life was featured in* A Beautiful Mind, *received the Nobel Prize for the FRUITION of his work in game theory decades after he completed it.*

fulgent *(FULL-gent), adjective*
To shine or glitter.
> *Her new diamond ring was FULGENT under the ballroom's bright lights.*

fuliginous *(fyoo-LIH-jih-nus), adjective*
Sooty or smoky.
> *The FULIGINOUS appearance of our house's walls was caused by the smoke from the nearby forest fire.*

fulminate *(FULL-mihn-ayt), verb*
To have a sudden, angry outburst.
> *When his son turned down a college offering a $100,000 scholarship, Bob FULMINATED long and loud.*

fulsome *(FULL-sum), adjective*
Describes words or actions that praise or flatter someone to an excessive degree.
> *Katie's introduction of the keynote speaker was so FULSOME that he led his speech with a few self-effacing remarks.*

fumarole *(FYOO-muh-rohl), noun*
An opening near a volcano that expels vapors and fumes.
> *The fact that the eruptions from the FUMAROLES were getting bigger and closer together indicated to the geologist that the probability of an explosion was increasing.*

fungible *(FUHN-jih-bull), adjective*
Freely exchangeable for another of like nature; interchangeable.
Stella was incensed to find that not all Cartier watches are FUNGIBLE.

furtive *(FUR-tiv), adjective*
Acting guilty of some misstep or possessing knowledge one would just as soon keep secret.
"For a while the two stared at each other—Denison embarrassed, Selene almost FURTIVE." —Isaac Asimov, Russian-born American author and biochemist

fustian *(FUHS-chun), adjective*
Pompous or bombastic.
As his speech to the Rotary continued, the congressman's language grew ever more FUSTIAN, and his audience was more and more bored.

fustigate *(FUHS-tih-gate), verb*
To beat or chastise.
When his critics caught him outside the office, they threatened to FUSTIGATE him severely for what he'd written about them.

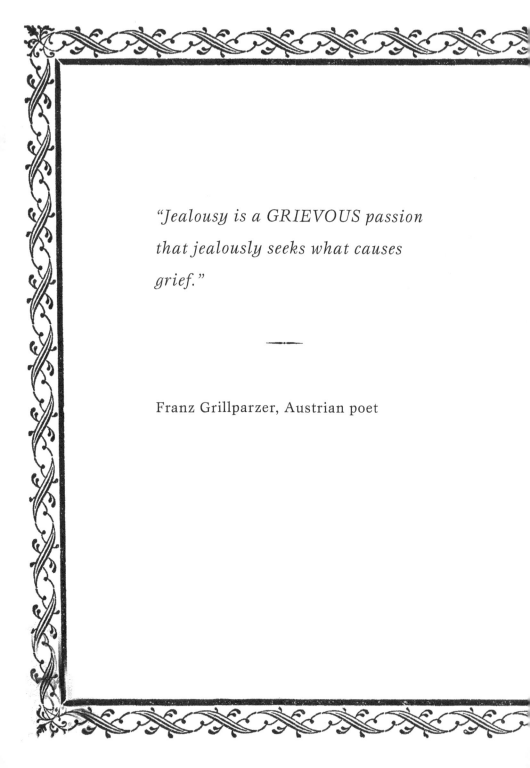

"Jealousy is a GRIEVOUS passion that jealously seeks what causes grief."

—

Franz Grillparzer, Austrian poet

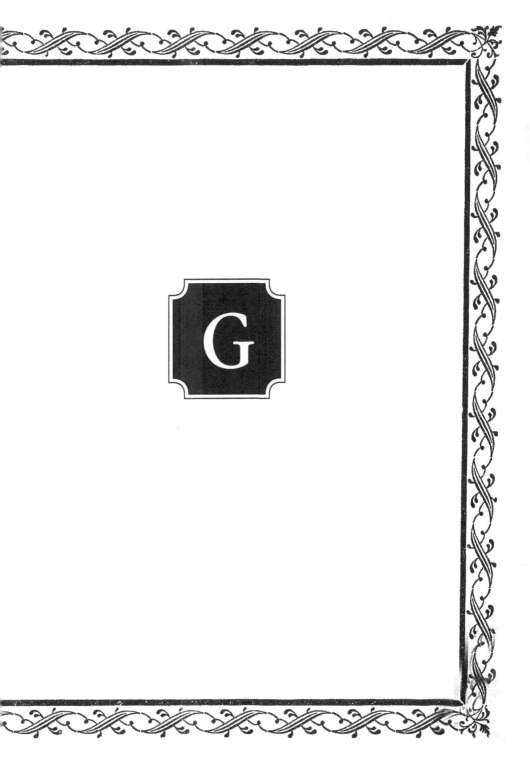

gable *(GAY-bull), noun*
The triangular upper part of a wall at the end of a rigid roof.
> *The Sandersons could not resist purchasing a second Cape Cod home because they fell in love with the home's colorful GABLES.*

gadabout *(GAD-uh-bowt), noun*
Someone only interested in having fun.
> *Jay Gatsby was quite the GADABOUT.*

gadarene *(GAD-uh-reen), adjective*
Moving quickly and without control.
> *The GADARENE pilot flew into the side of a mountain.*

gainsay *(GANE-say), verb*
To deny, dispute, or contradict.
> *Michael has made no attempt to GAINSAY the persistent rumors that his family's fortune rests solely on insider trading.*

galeiform *(gah-lee-ih-form), adjective*
Helmet-shaped.
> *His GALEIFORM head drew stares and laughter wherever he went.*

galivant *(GAL-ih-vant), verb*
To wander widely; to constantly travel to many different places, without an itinerary or plan; to freely go wherever and whenever the mood strikes you, and doing so frequently.
> *Some accuse us of GALIVANTING around the world, but cultural knowledge is de rigueur for cocktail conversation.*

galleon *(GAL-ee-un), noun*
A Mediterranean sailing vessel used by explorers for ocean voyages.
> *The GALLEONS of the Spanish fleet sailed annually from Seville to Panama and Cartagena.*

galliard *(GAL-yerd), adjective*
In a good mood; happy; lively.
> *Depression has destroyed his once GALLIARD disposition.*

gallipot *(GAL-ih-paht), noun*
A small jar used by pharmacists containing medications.
My godfather used a mortar and pestle to blend compounds from his GALLIPOTS.

galvanize *(GAL-vuh-nyze), verb*
To propel someone or something into sudden activity.
The unveiling of new yachts quickly GALVANIZED the regatta.

gambit *(GAM-bit), noun*
A remark used to redirect a conversation; or, a maneuver used to seek advantage.
"The catchphrase positively rejoices in being a formula, an accepted GAMBIT, a ready-made reaction." —John Gross, British literary critic

gambol *(GAM-bowl), verb*
To run, skip, or jump about in a playful or joyous fashion.
"We all have these places where shy humiliations GAMBOL on sunny afternoons." —W.H. Auden, Anglo-American poet

gambrel *(GAM-brill), noun*
The joint bending backward in the hind leg of a horse.
Butchers hang meat on GAMBREL-shaped frames.

gamesome *(GAYM-suhm), adjective*
Playful and frolicsome.
"[Nature] is GAMESOME and good, / But of mutable mood,— / No dreary repeater now and again, / She will be all things to all men." —Ralph Waldo Emerson, American poet, essayist, and transcendentalist

gamine *(gah-MEEN), noun*
A girl with a boyish demeanor and mischievous nature who is somehow still appealing.
Her GAMINE behavior and looks only made her that much more attractive to teenage boys her age.

gamut *(GAM-utt), noun*
The full spectrum of possibilities or choices.
> *The choice of places to eat near the mall ran the GAMUT from chain restaurants to five-star dining.*

gardyloo *(gar-dee-LOU), interjection*
A warning that slop or waste was about to be thrown from a second-story window to the street below.
> *"GARDYLOO!" the young mother cried before dumping the contents of the potty out the window.*

garnish *(GAR-nihsh), verb*
A legal procedure for taking a portion of a person's wages, property, and assets to pay his debts.
> *If you do not pay your taxes within thirty days, the county reserves the right to GARNISH a portion of your wages until the back taxes are paid in full.*

garrulity *(gah-ROO-lih-tee), noun*
The habit of talking way too much.
> *"The interview is an intimate conversation between journalist and politician wherein the journalist seeks to take advantage of the GARRULITY of the politician and the politician of the credulity of the journalist" —Emory Klein, American journalist*

gastropod *(GAS-troh-pod), noun*
A mollusk having a straight shell, small shell, one-piece shell, or no shell.
> *Escargot are cooked GASTROPODS.*

gauche *(GOHSH), adjective*
Sorely lacking in the social graces and good manners; crude behavior.
> *Rhett was under the impression that one needed only money to join the country club. However, his GAUCHE demeanor caused him to be denied membership.*

gazetteer *(gaz-ih-TEERr), noun*
A geographical index or dictionary of places organized by name.
> *The Rothschilds prefer their pilot simply head for the sun, rather than consult a GAZETTEER prior to short flights.*

gazumping *(gah-ZUM-ping), verb*
Reneging on an oral commitment to buy or sell a property.
The seller was GAZUMPING because he had received a better offer.

gelastic *(jel-AA-stick), adjective*
Relating to laughter.
Bobo had a GELASTIC nature, appropriate because he was a professional clown.

gelid *(JELL-uhd), adjective*
Extremely cold; icy.
The Vangelder's yacht sluiced easily through the GELID waters of the bay.

geniculate *(jen-IK-you-late), adjective*
Severely bent.
He had the GENICULATE posture of a much older man.

genome *(JEE-nome), noun*
The collection of chromosomes that makes an individual organism unique from all others except its clone or identical twin.
Blake has become convinced that the GENOMES of those among his most important social contacts have more commonalities than differences.

genteel *(jehn-TEEL), adjective*
Well-bred and possessing a refined temperament.
"[I am] a journalist in the field of etiquette. I try to find out what the most GENTEEL people regularly do, what traditions they have discarded, what compromises they have made." —Amy Vanderbilt, American etiquette expert

geopolitical *(gee-oh-poh-LIH-tih-kull), adjective*
Anything having to do with the politics affecting the relationships of two or more countries, especially when influenced by geographical factors.
GEOPOLITICAL instability in the Middle East is fueling rising crude oil prices.

geostationary *(jee-oh-STAY-shin-air-ee), adjective*
A satellite in orbit 22,236 miles above the earth's surface so that the satellite is always directly over the same spot of ground.
Arthur C. Clarke was the first to propose that three GEOSTATIONARY satellites orbiting earth could provide a global communications network effectively covering every location on the planet.

geosynchronous *(jee-oh-SIN-krin-us), adjective*
In orbit 22,236 miles above the earth so that the orbiting object is always over the same spot on the planet below.

Arthur C. Clarke first suggested using GEOSYNCHRONOUS satellites to create a global communications network in a technical paper he wrote for a magazine.

G

germane *(jehr-MANE), adjective*
Relevant, pertinent, and fitting.

"Quotes from Mao, Castro, and Che Guevara . . . are as GERMANE to our highly technological, computerized society as a stagecoach on a jet runway at Kennedy airport." —Saul Alinksy, American social activist

germinal *(JUHR-muh-nuhl), adjective*
Related to the earliest stage of development.

Roland's foray into art-buying is in its GERMINAL phase.

gerontology *(jer-on-TAH-lah-jee), noun*
The study of biological aging.

Some biologists specializing in GERONTOLOGY believe the maximum human life span will never be much more than 120 years.

gestalt *(geh-STALT), noun*
A unified whole.

"Feminism is an entire world view or GESTALT, not just a laundry list of women's issues." —Charlotte Bunch, American feminist

gesticulate *(jes-TIH-cue-late), verb*
To use gestures when talking, especially when the speaker is eager or excited to get his ideas across.

"Okay, the man in the yellow shirt," the seminar leader said, pointing to an audience member who was GESTICULATING wildly.

gibbet *(JIH-bit), noun*
A gallows.

In Hang 'Em High, Clint Eastwood was hung on a GIBBET but survived.

gimcrack *(JIHM-krack), noun*
A showy object of little or no value.
> *"Haul them off! Hide them! / The heart winces / For junk and GIMCRACK, / for jerrybuilt things." —Richard Wilbur, American poet*

glabrous *(GLAH-bross), adjective*
Bald.
> *Sy Sperling founded the Hair Club for GLABROUS men.*

glean *(GLEEN), verb*
To discover or learn slowly and deliberately.
> *Bentley GLEANED from the drop in Ferrari sales that a looming recession even had some of his social contacts feeling nervous.*

glibber *(GLIH-bur), adjective*
Able to speak in a smooth, slick manner.
> *No one is GLIBBER than a professional orator.*

globalization *(glow-bull-ih-ZAY-shin), noun*
The movement toward a true world economy with open and free trading across national borders.
> *"Proponents of GLOBALIZATION insist that, as trade and investment move across borders, economic efficiencies raise the standards of living on both sides of the exchange." —Arthur Goldwag, American author*

globule *(GLAHB-yewl), noun*
A small globe or ball.
> *"In yourself is the law of all nature, and you know not yet how a GLOBULE of sap ascends." —Ralph Waldo Emerson, American poet, essayist, and transcendentalist*

Gnosticism *(NAH-stih-sih-zim), noun*
The religious belief that salvation is attained through secret knowledge rather than through prayer, ritual, faith, divine grace, or good works.
> *Many of the key principles of Christianity were formed as a direct response to GNOSTICISM.*

gogliak *(GO-glee-ak), noun*
In golf, a shot with a wood that first glances off the ground before hitting the ball.
> *GOGLIAK is a synonym for dropkick.*

gonfalon *(GONE-fal-in), noun*
A banner.
> *The majorettes carried the school GONFALON during the Fourth of July parade.*

gorgonize *(GORE-guh-nize), verb*
To paralyze or mesmerize with one's looks or personality.
> *Even without her family's wealth and connections, Marla would likely GOR-GONIZE all the men who enter her orbit.*

gormandize *(GORE-mun-dize), verb*
To eat like a glutton, as if one was starving.
> *We find GORMANDIZING on even the finest French cuisine to be quite tasteless and, therefore, to be avoided.*

gossamer *(GAHSS-uh-muhr), adjective*
Something delicate, light, and flimsy that will flutter in the slightest breeze.
> *Fairies flitted among the flowers on GOSSAMER wings.*

grabble *(GRAH-bull), verb*
To feel for something with your hands.
> *The kids had a great time as they GRABBLED for Easter eggs.*

grandiloquent *(grand-EL-oh-kwent), adjective*
Having a pompous, overly inflated, hyperbolic, or pretentious way of presenting oneself in speech and mannerism.
> *The architect waxed GRANDILOQUENT about the visionary design of his new skyscraper.*

granular *(GRAN-you-ler), adjective*
The ability to divide, organize, and search through something at a fine level of detail.
> *Julian's GRANULAR abilities allow him to extract the absolute best from among even the largest pile of uncut diamonds.*

gratuitous *(grah-TOO-ih-tuss), adjective*
Unnecessary; inappropriately excessive; uncalled for.

> *"Being accused of making money by selling sex in Hollywood, home of the casting couch and the GRATUITOUS nude scene, is so rich with irony that it's a better subject for a comic novel than a column." —Anna Quindlen, American author and opinion columnist*

gravid *(GRAH-vid), adjective*
Pregnant.

> *An ultrasound showed she was GRAVID with child.*

gravimetric *(grav-ih-MEH-trick), adjective*
Acted upon by gravity.

> *The material dumped from the silo was GRAVIMETRICALLY conveyed to the dump truck underneath it.*

gravitas *(grav-ih-tas), adjective*
Behavior or manner that is dignified and serious, perhaps even a bit stiff, formal, and pompous.

> *The GRAVITAS with which Lionel viewed the Harvard-Yale football game was quite amusing to many of us.*

gravure *(grev-YOOR), noun*
A printing process where the matter to be duplicated is etched into the printing surface.

> *GRAVURE printing has a soft, velvety property.*

greave *(GREEV), noun*
Armor covering the leg from the knee to the ankle.

> *His GREAVE prevented a serious leg wound.*

gregarious *(greh-GARE-ee-us), adjective*
An extrovert; an outgoing person; one who is friendly and cheerful in nature.

> *"We are easy to manage, a GREGARIOUS people, / Full of sentiment, clever at mechanics, and we love our luxuries." —Robinson Jeffers, American poet*

grievous *(GREE-vuhss), adjective*
Flagrant and outrageous; or, causing grief and great sorrow.

"Jealousy is a GRIEVOUS passion that jealously seeks what causes grief." —
Franz Grillparzer, Austrian poet

G

grognard *(GROG-nard), noun*
A veteran soldier.

As a GROGNARD with a Purple Heart, he collected a monthly check from the
Veterans Benefits Administration.

grouse *(GRAUSS), verb*
To complain or grumble about one's situation.

We decided not to return to the restaurant after the maitre d' continuously
GROUSED about the slovenliness of his wait staff.

grumous *(GRUM-us), adjective*
Thick; clotted.

The body was covered with a sticky, GRUMOUS substance.

gryphon *(GRIFF-uhn), noun*
A mythical beast with the legs and body of a lion and the claws, head, and
wings of an eagle.

"The GRYPHON'S claws were greatly prized, as they were reputed to change
color in the presence of poison." —Richard Barber, British historian

guaranty *(gar-an-TEE), noun*
The taking of responsibility by one person for another person's debts or other
financial obligations. Also, the act of giving security.

"The Constitution is the sole source and GUARANTY of national freedom."
—Calvin Coolidge

guerrilla *(guh-RILL-uh), noun*
One who engages in warfare through small acts of harassment and sabotage.

With her keen eye for detail and authenticity, Lorissa has begun to wage a
GUERRILLA war against stores that proffer knockoffs as legitimate couture.

guile *(GILE), noun*
Deceitful cunning; trickery.
> *"Gaze no more in the bitter glass / The demons, with their subtle GUILE, / Lift up before us when they pass, / Or only gaze a little while."* —William Butler Yeats, *Irish poet and dramatist*

gurgitation *(gur-jih-TAY-shin), noun*
A whirlpool.
> *The river formed a GURGITATION where it went underground.*

gustatory *(GUSS-tuh-tore-ee), adjective*
Of the sense of taste.
> *"Food has it over sex for variety. Hedonistically, GUSTATORY possibilities are much broader than copulatory ones."* —Joseph Epstein, *American author and critic*

gyrating *(jye-RAY-ting), adjective*
Of a circular or spiral pattern.
> *When he first appeared on* The Ed Sullivan Show, *Elvis Presley's GYRATING hips during his act caused quite a stir.*

"The HAUGHTY sommelier, with his talismanic tasting cup and sometimes irritating self-assurance, is perceived more as the high priest of some arcane rite than as a dining room functionary paid to help you enjoy the evening."

———

Frank J. Prial, former *New York Times* wine columnist

habeas corpus *(HAY-bee-us-CORE-puss), noun*
A written order requiring a prisoner or person under arrest or confinement to be brought before a judge to assess whether the restraint of said person is lawful and proper.

H

> *Following the nightclub brawl, Chad and Wendell managed to receive a writ of HABEAS CORPUS only after their father called the authorities and reminded them of his social contacts.*

habile *(HAB-ill), adjective*
Skillful and able; handy.

> *Our HABILE gardener has helped render our topiary into the shapes of dollar and pound signs.*

habiliment *(haa-BILL-ih-meant), noun*
Clothing.

> *The emperor has new HABILIMENTS.*

habitude *(HAB-uh-tyood), noun*
Customary behavior or customary procedure.

> *Alistair's HABITUDE is for the servants to awake him just prior to noon.*

hackney *(HAK-nee), noun*
A cab, particularly of the horse-drawn variety used in Victorian and Edwardian England.

> *My friend hailed the HACKNEY, and we stepped inside, little knowing what adventures the evening would bring us.*

haemal *(HI-mahl), adjective*
Of or relating to blood.

> *We've performed a number of HAEMAL tests on the patient to determine if his white count is low.*

hagiography *(hag-ee-OG-ruh-fee), noun*
A biography that idealizes its subject.

> *The Van Gelders were disappointed with the volume written about their illustrious ancestors because the book fell far short of being a HAGIOGRAPHY.*

hagioscope *(HAG-ee-oh-SKOHP), noun*
An opening in the interior walls of a cruciform church.
Looking through the HAGIOSCOPE, we had a clear view of the altar.

haggis *(HAH-gis), noun*
A traditional Scottish dish made from the liver and heart of a sheep that is minced, mixed with oatmeal and suet, and boiled in the sheep's stomach.
For our Burns Night supper in Edinburgh, we dined on HAGGIS, bashed neeps, and greens, with Atholl brose to drink.

halation *(hal-AYE-shun), noun*
A blurred image or ring of light caused by the reflection or dispersal of light.
The mysterious white ring he claims is a ghost is merely HALATION caused by the photographer's lighting.

halcyon *(HAL-see-on), adjective*
Calm; peaceful; carefree; prosperous.
"It was the most HALCYON summer I ever spent." —Rick Bass, American author and environmental activist

halfpace *(HAF-pase), noun*
A platform on which the stair turns back in exactly the reverse direction of the lower flight of the staircase.
Climbing the long flight of stairs, we sat down on the HALFPACE and rested for a few moments.

haligraphy *(ha-LEE-gruh-fee), noun*
A book about salt.
Since I wanted to understand the importance of salt to early Romans, I studied a HALIGRAPHY that explained the question to my satisfaction.

halitosis *(hal-ih-TOE-sis), noun*
Bad breath.
Listerine gets rid of HALITOSIS.

halogen *(HAL-oh-jen), noun*
A classification on the Periodic Table of five highly reactive chemical elements.
The HALOGEN fluorine combines with hydrogen to form hydrofluoric acid.

H

halyard *(HAL-yerd), noun*
A rope used to secure a spar or sail aboard a ship.
Pull on that HALYARD to help me raise the mainsail so we can get underway.

hamartia *(ha-mar-tee-ah), noun*
A tragic flaw.
Don's HAMARTIA was his inability to understand people's feelings.

hamshackle *(HAM-sha-kul), verb*
To hobble a cow by placing a rope around its head and one of its legs.
Before giving that cow the injection, help me HAMSHACKLE her so she doesn't kick us.

handfast *(HAND-fast), noun*
A contract, especially a betrothal or wedding, formally sealed by the clasping of hands.
I would like to thank all of you for coming here today to our HANDFAST ceremony at which we declare our love and commitment to one another.

hansom *(HAN-sum), noun*
A two-wheeled, horse-drawn covered carriage.
In a hansom, the driver sits above and behind the passengers.

hapless *(HAP-liss), adjective*
Unlucky and unfortunate.
"Exile is the noble and dignified term, while a refugee is more HAPLESS."
—Mary McCarthy, American author

harangue *(ha-RANG), verb, noun*
Verbally accost; yell at; berate.
"But on that hot July day she breaks—HARANGUING strangers in the street."
—Oliver Sacks, British neurologist

harbinger *(HAR-bin-jer), noun*
A forerunner or warning sign of a future event or trend.
The asteroid's shadow blotted out the sun as it speeded on a collision course with earth, a HARBINGER of impending doom.

hariolate *(HAR-ee-oh-layt)*, *verb*

To predict or foretell.

> *If I were to HARIOLATE your fortune, I do not think you would be pleased with the result.*

harpagon *(HAR-puh-gahn)*, *noun*

A grappling iron or harpoon.

> *During the battle, the soldiers aboard Nelson's* Victory *hurled HARPAGONS at the French ship, allowing them to board the enemy vessel.*

harpy *(HAR-pee)*, *noun*

A greedy and predatory person; a scolding and shrewish woman.

> *"That HARPY Charlotte can't wait to get her claws into Bruce," Nancy observed.*

harridan *(HAR-ih-den)*, *noun*

An old, mean, crabby woman.

> *A difficult and hard life had turned her into an angry HARRIDAN.*

harry *(HAR-ee)*, *verb*

To torment with constant attacks.

> *"At middle night great cats with silver claws, / Bodies of shadow and blind eyes like pearls, / Came up out of the hole, and red-eared hounds / With long white bodies came out of the air / Suddenly, and ran at them and HARRIED them."*
> —*William Butler Yeats, Irish poet and dramatist*

hauberk *(HAW-burk)*, *noun*

Chainmail shirt that extends from the neck to the knees.

> *Rather than weighty plate armor, the knight was clad in a HAUBERK and light steel helm.*

haughty *(HAW-tee)*, *adjective*

Snobbish and arrogant.

> *"The HAUGHTY sommelier, with his talismanic tasting cup and sometimes irritating self-assurance, is perceived more as the high priest of some arcane rite than as a dining room functionary paid to help you enjoy the evening." —Frank J. Prial, former* New York Times *wine columnist*

haurient *(HAW-ree-ent), adjective*
Refers to a fish or other marine creature swimming vertically and rising, as if to breathe.
> *The HAURIENT bodies of the whales could be seen amid the waves, breaking the foamy surface of the ocean.*

haute couture *(OAT-koo-TOOR), noun*
Highly fashionable clothing on the cutting edge of the latest design fads and trends.
> *"HAUTE COUTURE should be fun, foolish, and almost unwearable."*
> —Christian Lacroix, French fashion designer

haut monde *(oh-MAHND), noun*
High society.
> *"The literary wiseacres prognosticate in many languages, as they have throughout so many centuries, setting the stage for new HAUT MONDE in letters and making up the public's mind." —Fannie Hurst, American novelist*

haver *(HEY-ver), verb*
Vacillate; waver.
> *There's no need to HAVER and hem over a simple offer like this.*

hawser *(HAW-zer), noun*
A heavy rope used for mooring ships in dock or at anchor.
> *"The HAWSER was as taut as a bowstring, and the current so strong she pulled upon her anchor." —Robert Louis Stevenson,* Treasure Island

headland *(HED-luhnd), noun*
A point of land extending into a body of water.
> *"Far-called, our navies melt away; / On dune and HEADLAND sinks the fire: / Lo, all our pomp of yesterday / Is one with Nineveh and Tyre!"*
> —Rudyard Kipling, English poet, "Recessional"

hearsay *(HEER-say), noun*
Information gathered from another that is not part of one's direct knowledge.
> *"My talk to thee must be how Benedick / Is sick in love with Beatrice. Of this matter / Is little Cupid's crafty arrow made, / That only wounds by HEARSAY."*
> —William Shakespeare, English playwright

hebdomad *(HEB-dough-mad), noun*
A group of seven.
> *A week is a HEBDOMAD of days.*

hectare *(HEK-tair), noun*
A unit of land measurement, equal to 2.471 acres.
> *The farm amounted to some 2,500 HECTARES, enough to produce a substantial crop of wheat.*

hedonism *(HEE-duh-niz-im), noun*
The nonstop pursuit of personal pleasure as one's primary goal.
> *"[Bad] taste supervenes upon good taste as a daring and witty HEDONISM. It makes the man of good taste cheerful, where before he ran the risk of being chronically frustrated." —Susan Sontag, American literary theorist, philosopher, and political activist*

hegemon *(HEDJ-ey-mahn), noun*
One who exercises control.
> *With the triumph of the Chinese revolution in 1949, Mao became the chief HEGEMON of the Chinese people for the next thirty years.*

hegemony *(hih-JEHM-uh-nee), noun*
Domination of a region or the entire world by a single nation, or the authority of one individual over an entire group.
> *Alison should not achieve HEGEMONY over the rest of us merely because her list of social contacts is slightly longer than ours.*

hegumene *(heh-gyoo-meh-nee), noun*
Leader of a convent.
> *Sister Maria had been HEGUMENE of the Convent of the Sacred Order of St. Theresa for five years.*

hekistotherm *(heh-KISS-toe-therm), noun*
A plant that can grow at low temperatures.
> *Among the HEKISTOTHERMS are lichens and mosses.*

heliacal *(hi-LY-ah-kuhl)*, *adjective*
Concerning phenomena near the sun.
> *The HELIACAL appearance of Venus in the morning sky while the sun is rising is highly unusual.*

heliotrope *(HEEL-ee-oh-trope)*, *noun*
A plant whose flowers turn toward the sun.
> *The sunflower is so named because it is a HELIOTROPE.*

hellacious *(hel-AYE-shus)*, *adjective*
Extremely brutal, violent, and severe.
> *Madison's foray into the corporate world was so HELLACIOUS that she quickly went back to being supported solely by her trust fund.*

hemialgia *(hem-ee-AL-jee-ah)*, *noun*
Pain that occurs only on one side of the body.
> *Since falling from a ladder a few years ago, I've been subject to HEMIALGIA on my left side.*

heptamerous *(hep-TAM-err-us)*, *adjective*
Having seven parts in each whorl.
> *She daintily picked HEPTAMEROUS flowers.*

Heptarchy *(HEP-tar-kee)*, *noun*
The confederation of seven English kingdoms from the fifth through the ninth century.
> *Academics specializing in early Anglo-Saxon kingdoms study the HEPTARCHY.*

herculean *(her-kyuh-LEE-uhn)*, *adjective*
Of extraordinary power or difficulty. Often capitalized because the word alludes to Hercules.
> *"We found it a HERCULEAN effort not to chortle at the outlandish clothing of the nouveau riche attendees of our party," said Lillian. "How inappropriate to wear evening attire to an afternoon garden party!"*

heretic *(HER-eh-tik), noun*
A person who boldly, loudly, and publicly defies the conventions of a religion, society, culture, or set of beliefs.

> *"The HERETIC is always better dead. And mortal eyes cannot distinguish the saint from the HERETIC." —George Bernard Shaw, Irish playwright*

hermeneutics *(her-men-NEW-tiks), noun*
The interpretation of obscure texts.

> *He specialized in hermeneutics of Greek manuscripts.*

hermetic1 *(her-MEH-tik), adjective*
Isolated; unaffected by outside influences.

> *"Reality, whether approached imaginatively or empirically, remains a surface, HERMETIC." —Samuel Beckett, Irish writer, dramatist, and poet*

hermetic2 *(her-MEH-tik), adjective*
Of or relating to the occult sciences.

> *The cult left all sorts of HERMETIC documents relating to their worship of the god Mithras.*

herpetic *(her-PEH-tik), adjective*
Creeping; spreading.

> *After the Fall, the snake in Eden was HERPETIC; before then, possibly, it went on two legs.*

herpetology *(her-peh-TAH-la-gee), noun*
The study of reptiles.

> *The HERPETOLOGIST was fined for keeping a three-foot alligator in his apartment's bathtub.*

heuristic *(her-IS-tick), adjective*
Solving problems using trial and error or rules of thumb.

> *Engineers eschew pure theory in favor of HEURISTIC problem solving.*

heuristics *(her-IS-ticks), noun*
The study of heuristic methods and processes.

> *Engineers study HEURISTICS to hone their problem-solving skills.*

H

heyday *(HEY-dey), noun*
The period of something's greatest strength or prominence.
> *The HEYDAY of colonialism was in the nineteenth century, particularly in Britain and France.*

hiatus *(high-AY-tuss), noun*
An interruption or break.
> *Lorelei's coming-out party was a welcome HIATUS in our otherwise uneventful social calendar.*

hibernaculum *(high-bur-NAK-you-lum), noun*
A den or other place where an animal hibernates.
> *It is extremely dangerous to disturb a slumbering bear in its HIBERNACULUM.*

hidebound *(HIDE-bound), adjective*
Inflexible and holding narrow opinions.
> *Wallace can be rather HIDEBOUND when pontificating on the virtues of classic Mercedes-Benz models versus the condition of the automobile company at present.*

hierarchy *(HIGH-uhr-ahr-key), noun*
A pecking order or ranking according to status or level of authority.
> *In the HIERARCHY of the military, a medical doctor, who is assigned the rank of captain but is not a military man, automatically outranks a lieutenant who may have years of battle experience.*

hierophant *(HEAR-oh-fant), noun*
A person who understands and explains obscure or mysterious knowledge.
> *Our parapsychology professor was a dedicated HIEROPHANT.*

hirsute *(HER-soot), adjective*
Hairy or shaggy.
> *Bigfoot is a HIRSUTE primate.*

histrionics *(hiss-tree-AHN-iks), noun*
Over-the-top, unnecessarily dramatic behavior.
> *"Enough with the HISTRIONICS!" his mother scolded, immediately shutting off the flow of tears and silencing his bawling.*

hoary *(HOAR-ee), adjective*
Impressively old; ancient.
> *"Feminism has tried to dismiss the femme fatale as a misogynist libel, a HOARY cliché. But the femme fatale expresses women's ancient and eternal control of the sexual realm."* —Camille Paglia, American author, feminist, and social critic

H

hobbish *(HAHB-ish), adjective*
Like a clown; foolish.
> *The only explanation for Stanley's HOBBISH behavior at the party is that he was intoxicated.*

Hogmanay *(hawg-muh-NAY), noun*
New Year's Eve, especially in Scotland.
> *For HOGMANAY this year, we're going to do a pub crawl in Glasgow and then ring in the New Year with a haggis feast.*

hoi polloi *(HOY-puh-LOY), noun*
A pejorative term used to describe the masses or the common people.
> *"My practice is to ignore the pathetic wishes and desires of the HOI POLLOI,"* the governor said haughtily.

holarctic *(hole-ARK-tik), adjective*
Anything relating to the geographical distribution of animals in the Arctic region.
> *Our so-called Arctic safari was a bust. No one told us that, due to HOLARCTIC conditions, we would find no polar bears near our encampment.*

holistic *(ho-LISS-tik), adjective*
Refers to medical practices that treat the whole person and not just a specific organ, condition, or disease.
> *Marsha's HOLISTIC approach to healing involves channeling energy through crystals.*

holosteric *(ho-low-stehr-ik), adjective*
A barometer that does not use liquid.
> *You can only get HOLOSTERIC barometers in antique shops and online.*

homage *(HOM-ij), noun*
Respect paid and deference shown to a superior or other person one admires, fears, or wishes to emulate or praise.

Gary took black and white photos with a nondigital camera in HOMAGE to Ansel Adams, whose works he greatly admired.

homeopathy *(HOME-ee-oh-path-ee), noun*
The medical practice of giving patients minerals, metals, herbs, and other bioactive compounds in extremely diluted form.

Most modern scientists believe the effectiveness of HOMEOPATHY in some cases is due mainly to the placebo effect.

homeostatis *(ho-me-oh-STAY-sis), noun*
A dynamic system in which balance between input and output has been achieved, so no net changes take place.

When HOMEOSTATIS is achieved in a sealed biosphere, the animals and plants can live without outside air, food, or water.

homiletics *(home-ih-LET-iks), noun*
Preaching, giving sermons.

To improve your HOMILETICS, try putting in an hour of preparation for each minute of spoken sermon.

homogenous *(ho-moj-en-us), adjective*
Consistent in composition or uniform in structure.

"By the mere act of watching television, a heterogeneous society could engage in a purely HOMOGENEOUS activity." —William J. Donnelly, American media critic

homunculus *(ho-MUN-cue-lluss), noun*
A perfectly formed miniature human being.

Harlan Ellison won a Hugo Award for his short story about an artificial HOMUNCULUS.

honorific *(on-err-IF-ik), adjective*
A tribute or reward given in an effort to honor someone as a sign of deep respect.

Lifetime achievement awards aren't for any single work, but an HONORIFIC for long service and a track record of excellence.

The Big Book of Words You Should Know to Sound Smart

hoplite *(HAHP-lyte), noun*
A foot soldier in ancient Greece, armed with spear and shield, usually fighting in a phalanx formation.
> *The phalanx of HOPLITES who fought the Persians at Thermopylae were responsible for one of the great military legends of the ancient world.*

horripilation *(haw-ri-puh-LEY-shun), noun*
Bristling of hair from fear; goosebumps.
> *During the shower scene in* Psycho, *I was seized with such a HORRIPILATION that my companion thought I had received an electrical shock.*

hortatory *(WHORE-tah-tor-ee), adjective*
Encouraging laudable behavior.
> *The teacher's HORTATORY classroom manner made her students near-perfect angels in school.*

hosel *(HO-zull), noun*
On a golf club, the part of the club head that acts as a receptacle for the shaft.
> *When the HOSEL contacts the ball instead of the club head, a shank is the result.*

hubris *(HYOO-briss), noun*
To possess pride, arrogance, or conceit not justified by reality.
> *Those who accuse us of HUBRIS are simply unaware of the efforts our families have made to perfect our bloodlines.*

humanism *(HEW-man-iz-um), noun*
The philosophy or belief that the highest ideals of human existence can be fulfilled without regard to religion or supernatural intervention.
> *"The four characteristics of HUMANISM are curiosity, a free mind, belief in good taste, and belief in the human race." —E.M. Forster, English novelist*

humectant *(hue-MEK-tant), noun*
A substance that absorbs moisture or retains water.
> *Sorbitol, a HUMECTANT, is used in the processing of dried fruit.*

humgruffin *(HUM-gruff-in), noun*
A terrible or repulsive person.
> *Bernie Madoff is the ultimate HUMGRUFFIN.*

hussy *(HUH-see), noun*
A loose woman.
  Monica was a HUSSY—and I liked it.

hygroscopic *(high-grow-SKOP-ick), adjective*
Capable of absorbing moisture from the air.
  Prescription pills are often packed with a container of HYGROSCOPIC material to keep the drugs dry.

hylogenesis *(hi-loh-JEN-eh-sis), noun*
A theory about the nature and origins of dark matter.
  The proposed theory of HYLOGENESIS purports to explain why there is more mass in the universe than can be visually accounted for.

hypactic *(hi-PAK-tik), adjective*
Purgative; cathartic.
  The storm of weeping, although not lasting long, was extremely HYPACTIC for Dorothy; she felt as if she had purged herself of all emotion.

hyperbaric *(hi-per-BARE-ik), adjective*
Related to artificially high atmospheric pressure, used to treat certain diseases.
  Divers who ascend to the surface too rapidly may be placed in a HYPERBARIC chamber to prevent the bends.

hyperbole *(high-PERR-buh-lee), noun*
An overexaggeration made for effect.
  "The final key to the way I promote is bravado. I play to people's fantasies. People may not always think big themselves, but they can still get very excited by those who do. That's why a little HYPERBOLE never hurts." —Donald Trump, American entrepreneur

hyperborean *(high-per-BORE-ee-an), noun*
A person or animal who lives at or near the North Pole.
  The polar bear, one of the great HYPERBOREANS, is in danger of extinction as the melting of the polar cap makes the ice floes on which they live disappear.

hypercritical *(high-purr-KRIT-ih-kuhl), adjective*
Excessively or meticulously critical.

"Good writers have two things in common: they would rather be understood than admired, and they do not write for hairsplitting and HYPERCRITICAL readers." —Friedrich Nietzsche, German philosopher

hyperextend *(high-per-ek-stend), verb*
To extend beyond the normal.

A clumsy swing caused him to HYPEREXTEND his back.

hypnopompic *(hip-nuh-PAHM-pick), adjective*
Having to do with the semiconscious state that precedes wakefulness.

With all of her partying at exclusive clubs, Madison spends most of her life in a HYPNOPOMPIC state.

hypothecation *(hi-poth-ih-KAY-shun), noun*
The practice of using property or other assets as the collateral for a loan.

Buying stock on margin is a useful form of HYPOTHECATION that encourages unsophisticated individual investors to buy more stock than they can afford.

hypothesis *(high-POTH-uh-sis), noun*
A principle derived from limited evidence, seen as sensible based on an analysis of available data, but not proven to the point where it is an accepted theory, rule, or law.

"In order to shake a HYPOTHESIS, it is sometimes not necessary to do anything more than push it as far as it will go." —Denis Diderot, French philosopher

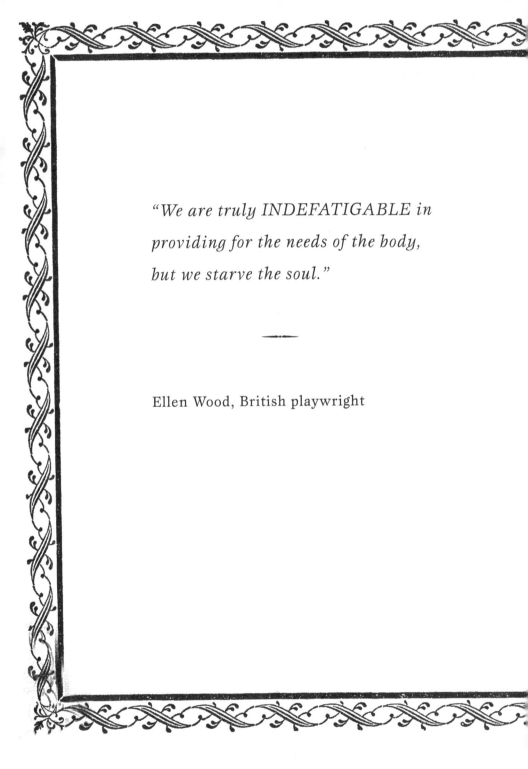

*"We are truly INDEFATIGABLE in
providing for the needs of the body,
but we starve the soul."*

———

Ellen Wood, British playwright

I, J, K

iamatology *(ey-am-uh-TAHL-uh-jee), noun*
The branch of medicine that studies remedies.
Doctors devoted to IAMATOLOGY have carefully examined homeopathic remedies but have found most do not work.

iatramelia *(ey-a-tra-MEHL-ee-ah), noun*
Neglect by a medical professional or institution.
The commission found a shocking number of cases of IATRAMELIA in which large hospitals had put patients' lives and health at risk for the sake of profits.

iatrophobia *(ey-a-troh-FOH-bee-ah), noun*
The fear of going to the doctor.
My IATROPHOBIA is well founded, since whenever I see my doctor he tells me there's something wrong with me.

ibis *(AYH-bis), noun*
A large, tropical wading bird with a long, curved bill.
In the tropical rainforest exhibit at the aquarium, we saw an IBIS and several parrots.

ichneumon *(ik-NEW-mun), noun*
An Egyptian mongoose.
Some families kept ICHNEUMONS as pets to ward off cobras.

ichnite *(IK-nyte), noun*
A fossil footprint.
Anthropologists have discovered human ICHNITES crossing a river in the Rift Valley in East Africa, proving an early presence of man there.

ichthyoid *(IK-thee-oyd), adjective*
Fish-like; having a fish-like appearance.
Many of H.P. Lovecraft's characters have a degenerate, ICHTHYOID appearance.

ichthyology *(ik-thee-AH-lah-gee), noun*
The study of fish.
After majoring in ICHTHYOLOGY as an undergraduate, he took a PhD in marine biology.

ichthyomorphic *(ik-thee-oh-MORE-fik), adjective*
Fish-like in shape.
> *H.P. Lovecraft's most famous ICHTHYOMORPHIC character is Dagon.*

ickle *(IK-uhl), adjective*
Ironic word for "little."
> *"Ahhh. Does ICKLE Ronnie have somefink on his nosie?" —Fred Weasley in J.K. Rowling's* Harry Potter and the Sorcerer's Stone

iconoclast *(eye-KAHN-uh-clast), noun*
An individual who is contrarian in thought, rebellious in spirit, oppositional, and who applies himself to battling established institutions, existing governments, religious doctrine, and popular notions and beliefs.
> *The late George Carlin saw the role of the comic in society as one of an ICONOCLAST.*

iconoclastic *(ey-kon-uh-KLAS-tik), adjective*
Characterized by attacks on institutions or long-held beliefs.
> *During the 1960s, ICONOCLASTIC student activists challenged the government's war in Vietnam.*

icterine *(IK-ter-eyn), adjective*
Yellow; marked with yellow.
> *The bird was small, and the ICTERINE markings on its wings matched the sunflower on which it was sitting.*

ideogeny *(ih-dee-AH-jen-ee), noun*
The study of the origin of ideas.
> *Historians of philosophy have long studied the IDEOGENY of the Greek schools of Epicureanism and Stoicism.*

ideologue *(EYE-dee-oh-log), noun*
A person who rigidly adheres to an ideology with a closed mind regarding other points of view.
> *"An IDEOLOGUE may be defined as a mad intellectual." —Clifton Fadiman, American critic*

idiomorphic *(id-ee-uh-MAWR-fik)*, *adjective*
Having its own, characteristic shape.
> *The tree is easily recognizable by its IDIOMORPHIC peculiarities, since the bulk of the branches grow only at its top.*

idioticon *(ih-dee-OH-tih-kan)*, *noun*
The glossary of a language or vocabulary of a particular group of people.
> *My son is a computer scientist, and they have an IDIOTICON my wife and I do not understand.*

ignavia *(ihg-NAY-vee-uh)*, *noun*
Laziness; sloth.
> *My teenage son suffers from an acute case of IGNAVIA; he won't even bother to pick up his clothes when he takes them off at night.*

ignominious *(ig-no-MIN-ee-us)*, *adjective*
Marked by failure or humiliation in public.
> *After his IGNOMINIOUS defeat in the election, Frank never ran for Congress again.*

ilk *(ILK)*, *noun*
Of a kind.
> *Fine wine is wasted on those of my ILK.*

illaudable *(ih-LAW-dih-bull)*, *adjective*
Not admirable.
> *Free college, paid for with tax dollars, is an ILLAUDABLE notion to many childless adults.*

illutation *(ihl-you-TAY-shun)*, *noun*
A mud bath.
> *As part of our time at the spa, we enjoyed a soothing ILLUTATION, after which the mud was hosed from our bodies by the attendants.*

imbroglio *(im-BRO-lee-oh), noun*
Colloquially referred to as a "sticky situation"—a predicament that is difficult to get out of.

Our inability to decide which New Year's Eve party to attend created an IMBROGLIO that disrupted our social calendar for months.

imbrue *(im-BREW), verb*
To moisten.

A small water well on my dad's desk enables him to IMBRUE postage stamps without licking them.

immunoelectrophoresis *(ihm-yoo-noh-ih-leck-tro-for-EE-sis), noun*
The separation and identification of proteins based on differences in electrical charge and reactivity with antibodies.

The police scientist uses IMMUNOELECTROPHORESIS to positively identify substances in forensic investigations.

immure *(ih-MYOOR), verb*
To confine, imprison, or enclose behind walls.

Whitney remained IMMURED in her room as she pondered the itinerary for her luxury vacation to Italy.

immutable *(im-MYOO-tuh-bull), adjective*
Unable, or unwilling, to change.

"I don't know what IMMUTABLE differences exist between men and women apart from differences in their genitals." —Naomi Weisstein, American feminist

impalpable *(im-PAL-puh-bull), adjective*
Difficult to understand easily; intangible.

"The soul is so IMPALPABLE, so often useless, and sometimes such a nuisance, that I felt no more emotion on losing it than if, on a stroll, I had mislaid my visiting card." – Charles Baudelaire, French poet, critic, and translator

imparity *(ihm-PAR-ih-tee), noun*
Inequality or disparity.

There is little, if any, IMPARITY between the chateaubriand offered at the two bistros.

impasto *(im-PAHS-toe), noun*
Paint that has been laid thickly onto a canvas as with a palette knife.
"By 1887, Vincent van Gogh abandoned heavy IMPASTO and reveled in an impressive range of dots and dashes, lattice lines, and basket-weave patterns." —Michael Kimmelman, art critic

impavid *(im-PAH-vid), adjective*
Unafraid, uncowed.
An IMPAVID Larry Holmes made short work of Muhammad Ali in the ring.

impecunious *(im-puh-KYOON-ee-us), adjective*
To be poor or broke; to have little or no money.
Alex has been raving about his IMPECUNIOUS state ever since his trust fund was cut from $25,000 to $20,000 per month.

impetrate *(IM-pih-trayt), verb*
To get by begging.
Appealing to my boss's good nature isn't going to work, so I'll have to IMPETRATE him to give me some extra time off for the birth of my daughter.

implausible *(im-PLAWZ-ih-bull), adjective*
Difficult to believe; highly unlikely to be true.
"At first glance, most famous fairy tales seem so IMPLAUSIBLE and irrelevant to contemporary life that their survival is hard to understand." —Alison Lurie, American novelist and academic

impleach *(im-PLEECH), verb*
Entwine.
The fish became IMPLEACHED in the Portuguese man-of-war's tentacles.

implicit *(im-PLIH-set), adjective*
Something that is understood or implied but not stated directly.
"The vanity of men, a constant insult to women, is also the ground for the IMPLICIT feminine claim of superior sensitivity and morality." —Patricia Meyer Spacks, American literary critic

implosion *(im-PLOH-shzin), noun*
Rapidly collapsing inward with great force.
Formation of a sudden vacuum results in an IMPLOSION if the vessel walls are weak enough.

impluvium *(im-PLOO-vee-uhm), noun*
Shallow basin, bowl, or pool.
Amateur detective Peter Wimsey once solved a mystery, the clue to which appeared on the bottom of a water-filled IMPLUVIUM.

importunate *(ihm-PORE-chuh-nitt), adjective*
Urgent and persistent in solicitation, to the point of annoyance.
"Sisters are always drying their hair. / Locked into rooms, alone, / They pose at the mirror, shoulders bare, / Trying this way and that their hair, / Or fly IMPORTUNATE down the stair / To answer the telephone." —Phyllis McGinley, American poet

imprecation *(im-pre-kay-shun), noun*
A curse spoken aloud.
Thomas muttered IMPRECATIONS as he circled the airfield, waiting for clearance to land his Airbus 380.

impresario *(im-preh-SAH-ree-oh), noun*
The producer or organizer of an opera, ballet, or concert.
He was an IMPRESARIO not because he loved opera, but because it gave him a nice tax write-off.

improvidence *(im-PRAH-vih-dense), noun*
A rash action performed without careful consideration or deliberation.
"This made him think of all the nights ... spending his youth with the casual IMPROVIDENCE of a millionaire." —Richard Matheson, American science fiction writer

impugn *(ihm-PYOON), verb*
To attack as false or wrong.
"I do not IMPUGN the motives of any one opposed to me. It is no pleasure to me to triumph over any one." —Abraham Lincoln

impunity *(im-PEW-nih-tee), noun*
With abandon; without concern for punishment, harm, loss, or other consequences.

Driving his wife in labor to the hospital, he disobeyed traffic regulations with IMPUNITY.

impute *(im-PYOOT), verb*
To attribute something; to assign responsibility or blame.

"The sin I IMPUTE to each frustrute ghost / Is—the unlit lamp and the ungirt loin, / Though the end in sight was a vice, I say." —Robert Browning, British poet and playwright

incandescent *(inn-can-DEH-sent), adjective*
Glowing with intense heat.

LEDs last many times longer than INCANDESCENT light bulbs.

incede *(in-SEED), verb*
To advance in a stately manner.

The coronation procession will INCEDE up the center aisle of the cathedral to the throne.

inchoate *(inn-KOH-ate), adjective*
Not fully developed.

The press grew weary of listening to the major's INCHOATE ramblings.

incipient *(in-SIH-pee-ent), adjective*
In the early stages of development; developing but not fully formed.

The chef's INCIPIENT cuisine already surpasses the fare of other, more established, culinary artists.

incommensurable *(in-co-MEN-ser-uh-bull), adjective*
Two things that cannot be measured or judged by the same standards.

"Two men who perceive the same situation differently but employ the same vocabulary in its discussion speak from INCOMMENSURABLE viewpoints." —Thomas Kuhn, American philosopher

incongruous *(in-KAHNG-grew-us), adjective*
Describes something that does not belong in its current place, setting, or role; out of place; not fitting in.

> *"The taste for quotations (and for the juxtaposition of INCONGRUOUS quotations) is a Surrealist taste." —Susan Sontag, American literary theorist, philosopher, and political activist*

incontrovertible *(in-kahn-trah-VER-tih-bull), adjective*
Beyond question or dispute.

> *"Some minds are as little logical or argumentative as nature; they can offer no reason or "guess," but they exhibit the solemn and INCONTROVERTIBLE fact." —Henry David Thoreau, American author and transcendentalist*

inculcate *(IN-kul-kate), transitive verb*
To impress an idea or belief upon someone by repeating it to that person over and over until the idea is firmly lodged in his brain.

> *New cult members are quickly INCULCATED with the cult leader's beliefs and world view.*

inculpate *(in-KOOL-pate), verb*
To incriminate, blame, or charge with a crime.

> *Thanks to our connections, none of us were INCULPATED in the nightclub melee.*

indefatigable *(in-deh-fah-tih-gah-bull), adjective*
Capable of continuing along one's current course of action without wavering, tiring, or faltering.

> *"We are truly INDEFATIGABLE in providing for the needs of the body, but we starve the soul." —Ellen Wood, British playwright*

indite *(in-DITE), verb*
To write or compose a literary work.

> *"But if, both for your love and skill, your name / You seek to nurse at fullest breasts of Fame, / Stella behold, and then begin to INDITE." —Sir Philip Sidney, English courtier, soldier, and poet*

indurate *(in-der-et), verb*
To establish or confirm something.

> *In my speech, I'll attempt to INDURATE to the audience that lowering taxes raises revenues.*

ineffable *(in-EF-uh-bull), adjective*
Something so fantastic, incredible, or difficult to grasp it cannot be described in words.
> *Poet Ezra Pound wrote of "the infinite and INEFFABLE imbecility of the British Empire."*

ineluctable *(in-eh-LUCK-tah-bull), adjective*
Unavoidable; inevitable; with a sense of being unfortunate, sad, or even tragic.
> *Our inability to procure Pratesi linens for our Colorado ski lodge created an INELUCTABLE sadness among the members of our family.*

inexorable *(in-eks-or-ah-bull), adjective*
Inevitable; unavoidable; relentless; persistent; unstoppable.
> *"I know enough to know that most of the visible signs of aging are the result of the INEXORABLE victory of gravity over tissue." —Isaac Asimov, Russian-born American author and biochemist*

inexpiable *(in-EKS-pee-ah-buhl), adjective*
Something that is unforgiveable, that cannot be atoned for.
> *Most people regard the Holocaust as an INEXPIABLE crime against the Jewish people.*

inextricably *(in-eks-TRIK-uh-blee), adverb*
Something that is strongly linked to something else, with the bond between quite difficult to break.
> *"At its best,[Japanese cooking] is INEXTRICABLY meshed with aesthetics, with religion, with tradition and history." —M.F.K. Fisher, American author*

inference *(IN-fer-ence), noun*
The process of reaching a logical conclusion by examining and analyzing the evidence.
> *Watson solved cases through INFERENCE, while Sherlock Holmes was seemingly gifted with flashes of brilliant insight.*

infinitesimally *(inn-fin-ih-TESS-ih-mull-ee), adverb*
A small fraction or quantity.
> *His chances of victory are INFINITESIMALLY better than his chances of losing.*

ingle *(ING-guhl)*, *noun*
A fire in a fireplace.
> *Beneath the mantle, there was a brightly burning INGLE that shed warmth and light throughout the room.*

inimical *(ih-NIM-ih-kull)*, *adjective*
Something working in opposition to your goal; having a harmful effect, particularly on an enterprise or endeavor.
> *Clarissa's decorating sense is INIMICAL to producing a successful soiree.*

inkhorn *(INGK-hawrn)*, *noun*
A small container used to hold ink.
> *The author had before him pen, paper, INKHORN, and blotting paper—all the tools of his craft—set out for use.*

inkometer *(ingk-AHM-uh-ter)*, *noun*
An instrument that measures the stickiness of ink that can damage the surface of paper.
> *The INKOMETER showed that the ink's excessive tack would pull fibers off the paper's surface.*

innocuous *(ih-NAHK-yew-us)*, *adjective*
Not harmful or offensive; innocent, incidental, and hardly noticeable.
> *"I know those little phrases that seem so INNOCUOUS and, once you let them in, pollute the whole of speech." —Samuel Beckett, Irish writer, dramatist, and poet*

inscrutable *(in-SKROO-tuh-bull)*, *adjective*
Mysterious and not easy to understand.
> *"I suppose I now have the reputation of being an INSCRUTABLE dipsomaniac. One woman here originated the rumour that I am extremely lazy and will never do or finish anything." —James Joyce, Irish author and playwright*

insouciant *(in-SOO-see-unt)*, *adjective*
Acting as if one has not a care in the world; free of worry and angst.
> *We are never INSOUCIANT about our wealth because we must work at all times to ensure its protection.*

instanter *(in-STAN-ter), adverb*
Instantly; at once.
> *I know this is of importance to you, so I'll see it's done INSTANTER.*

I

insular *(INN-suh-ler), adjective*
Self-contained and therefore isolated from the world and unaffected by outside influences, usually to one's detriment.
> *The Pricewaters moved from the family's traditional enclave to a more INSULAR compound further up the coast.*

insuperable *(in-SOO-per-uh-bull), adjective*
Not possible to overcome or surmount.
> *"Conceit is an INSUPERABLE obstacle to all progress." —Ellen Terry, British actress*

intelligentsia *(in-tell-ih-GENT-see-uh), noun*
The class of people who are cultured, educated, intellectual, and interested in art and literature.
> *"You see these gray hairs? Well, making whoopee with the INTELLIGENTSIA was the way I earned them." —Dorothy Parker, American author and poet*

intemperate *(in-TEM-prit), adjective*
Refers to a person who indulges his own whims and fancies without regard to other people's feelings or inconvenience.
> *"Certainly it was ordained as a scourge upon the pride of human wisdom, that the wisest of us all, should thus outwit ourselves, and eternally forego our purposes in the INTEMPERATE act of pursuing them." —Laurence Sterne, Irish-born English novelist and Anglican clergyman*

intercloud *(INN-ter-clowd), adjective*
Lightning that goes from cloud to cloud instead of from cloud to ground.
> *During the rainy season in Tucson, Arizona, summer thunderstorms can generate more than 10,000 lightning strikes per night, many of them INTERCLOUD.*

intermediation *(inn-ter-me-dee-AYE-shin), noun*
The normal flow of funds to a financial intermediary.
> *Savings and loan associations enjoy INTERMEDIATION from loan repayments.*

interminably *(in-TUR-min-uh-blee), adverb*
Seemingly without end or going on for an indeterminate period of time.
"The body dies; the body's beauty lives. / So evenings die, in their green going, / A wave, INTERMINABLY flowing." —Wallace Stevens, American Modernist poet

interpellation *(inn-ter-peh-LAY-shin), noun*
To question someone formally.
INTERPELLATION of the Supreme Court nominee took two full days.

interpolate *(in-TER-poh-late), verb*
To introduce something—often something unnecessary—between other things or parts.
Dexter could not help but continuously INTERPOLATE unnecessary criticism into the discussion of the latest Parisian designs.

interpose *(in-ter-POZ), verb*
To aggressively insert your unsolicited opinion, assistance, or presence into a situation where it is not particularly wanted.
"I hope I am not INTERPOSING," Eileen said as she walked in on our meeting—which of course, she was.

intractable *(in-TRACK-tuh-bull), adjective*
Difficult to control or manage.
"It is precisely here, where the writer fights with the raw, the INTRACTABLE, that poetry is born." —Doris Lessing, British author

intranet *(IN-trah-net), noun*
An internal Internet-like computer network created for one organization's use.
INTRANET developers have a lower status in IT than developers of external websites.

intransigent *(in-TRANZ-ih-gent), adjective*
Stubborn; refusing to consider opinions other than one's own.
"Lamont stared for a moment in frustration but Burt's expression was a clearly INTRANSIGENT one now." —Isaac Asimov, Russian-born American author and biochemist

intrinsic *(in-TRIN-zick), adjective*
Of, or related to, something's essential nature.
> *"We are the men of INTRINSIC value, who can strike our fortunes out of ourselves, whose worth is independent of accidents in life, or revolutions in government: we have heads to get money, and hearts to spend it." —George Farquhar, Irish dramatist*

introit *(IN-troh-it), noun*
A response sung by the choir at the beginning of a religious service.
> *As the congregation settled in their seats, the choir began the INTROIT that initiated Sunday's service.*

inurement *(inn-UR-meant), noun*
Acceptance without resistance or fighting back of punishment, poor treatment, or unpleasant circumstances or conditions.
> *"Perhaps others might respond to this treatment with INUREMENT," Eloise hissed, "but I will buy my diamonds at another boutique from this point forward."*

invective *(inn-VEK-tiv), noun*
Criticism or negative observations expressed in the strongest, harshest possible terms.
> *"The art of INVECTIVE resembles the art of boxing. Very few fights are won with the straight left. It is too obvious, and it can be too easily countered." —Gilbert Highet, Scottish-born American biographer and essayist*

inveigle *(in-VAY-gull), verb*
To convince or persuade someone through trickery, dishonesty, or flattery.
> *Craig INVEIGLED the dean to allow him to graduate even though he failed to meet the foreign language requirement of the university.*

inveterate *(in-VET-uh-rett), adjective*
A pattern of behavior or habit that never changes.
> *"Take all the garden spills, / INVETERATE, / prodigal spender / just as summer goes." —Hilda Doolittle, American poet and memoirist*

invidious *(in-VID-ee-us), adjective*
Designed to give offense or to create ill will.
> *"In the name of all lechers and boozers I most solemnly protest against the INVIDIOUS distinction made to our prejudice." —Aldous Huxley, British author and humanist*

inviolate *(inn-VY-oh-late), adjective*
Without restriction, violation, supervision, or fear of punishment.
> *"INVIOLATE, he could rupture wires, mangle flaps, destroy the balance of the ship." —Richard Matheson, American science fiction writer*

invious *(IN-vee-uhs), adjective*
Unwalked, and thus pristine.
> *The Wallenstones' new compound contains many INVIOUS tracts perfect for hiking or fox hunting.*

irascent *(ih-RAA-sent), adjective*
Becoming angry.
> *IRASCENT is a synonym for irascible or darn close to it.*

irascible *(ih-RASS-uh-bull), adjective*
Easily irritated or annoyed; prone to losing one's temper; quick to anger.
> *"I have never known anyone worth a damn who wasn't IRASCIBLE." —Ezra Pound, American expatriate poet*

iridescent *(ear-ih-DES-uhnt), adjective*
Showing luminous colors that seem to change depending upon the angle from which they are viewed.
> *"We passed…broken shells and the IRIDESCENT film of egg splatter reflected under streetlights where a battle had taken place." —Jeffrey Ford, American fantasy author*

irradiate *(ih-RAD-ee-ayt), verb*
Subjected to or bathed in radiation.
> *Gamma-ray IRRADIATION turned Bruce Banner into the Hulk.*

irredentist *(ir-ih-DEN-tist), noun*
Someone who advocates recovering a lost cultural or political heritage.
The advent of Black History departments in the 1970s was the action of IRRE-DENTISTS who sought to uncover a lost African American cultural heritage.

irremediable *(ihr-ree-MEE-dee-uh-bull), adjective*
Impossible to cure or remedy.
Sylvia's outdated concept of couture is completely IRREMEDIABLE.

irrevocable *(ear-reh-VOK-uh-bull), adjective*
Incapable of being revoked.
The bank issued an IRREVOCABLE letter of credit.

irruent *(o-ROO-ent), adjective*
Running rapidly.
The police mistook the IRRUENT teenager for a vandal.

isagogic *(eye-sa-GO-jik), adjective*
Introductory, especially in relationship to Bible study.
I've created an ISAGOGIC analysis of the Pentateuch that will allow young people to understand the importance of these five books of the Bible.

isobar *(EYE-sah-bar), noun*
A line on a meteorological map indicating barometric pressure levels.
The weatherman pointed out that the ISOBARS on his map showed a line of low pressure moving into the area.

isochronous *(eye-sok-ruh-nus), adjective*
Occurring consistently at regular intervals.
The ticking of a clock is ISOCHRONOUS, but the arrival of the elevator at different floors is not.

isolationism *(eye-so-LAY-shin-iz-um), noun*
A foreign policy in which a country deliberately keeps its relationships and interactions with other nations to a bare minimum, effectively isolating itself from world affairs.
In the early twentieth century, American ISOLATIONISM stopped the U.S. from joining the League of Nations.

iteration *(ih-ter-AYE-shun), noun*
The process of performing a series of instructions or steps repeatedly; also refers to one repetition of those repeated steps.
"Thou hast damnable ITERATION, and art indeed able to corrupt a saint."
—William Shakespeare, English playwright

itinerant *(eye-TIN-err-uhnt), adjective*
Aimless; shiftless; traveling from place to place.
Jack Reacher is the quintessential ITINERANT wanderer.

izzat *(IZ-uht), noun*
Honor or prestige.
Being appointed governor of this territory has substantially increased his IZZAT among his subjects.

jabot *(zah-BOW), noun*
A trimming of lace around the neck of a garment.
Judge Judy wears a white JABOT on her black robe.

jacquerie *(zak-REE), noun*
A peasant's revolt.
Les Misérables *is the story of a JACQUERIE.*

jactitation *(jak-ti-TAY-shun), noun*
A false boast, especially one that is harmful to others.
Beatrice tried impress her classmates by telling them her last name was Kennedy. However, her JACTITATION was discovered and her peers returned to ignoring her.

jannock *(JAN-uhk), adjective*
Honest; straightforward.
Old Benson is a JANNOCK sort of chap who'd tell us if anything were wrong.

jaraca *(jah-RACK-ah), noun*
A venomous pit viper found in South Africa.
The bite of the JARACA can be fatal if the victim is struck repeatedly.

jark *(JAHRK), noun*
Insignia on a counterfeit document.
> *The JARK on the fake certificate of authentication was what tipped off investigators that the Mark Twain manuscript was a fake.*

jaundiced *(JAWN-dist), adjective*
Demonstrating prejudice, due to envy or resentment.
> *The Blythingtons' view of our dinner parties is JAUNDICED by the fact that our personal chef is superior to theirs.*

jaunt *(JAWNT), noun*
A short journey taken for pleasure.
> *Nicole plans to take a JAUNT across the southern tip of Africa next year.*

javelot *(JAHV-eh-loh), noun*
A small javelin.
> *At the Junior Olympics, the javelin toss used a JAVELOT instead of a full-sized javelin.*

jawbone *(JAW-bon), verb*
To attempt to get someone to do something through persuasion rather than by force.
> *No matter how much he JAWBONED, Karl could not get Alison to sell her stock prior to the unveiling of the company's disastrous new line of parvenu fashion.*

jejune *(jih-JUNE), adjective*
Thoughts and actions that are not well thought out or fully formed; a poor performance or inferior work.
> *Samantha snidely informed Blake that her JEJUNE entertaining efforts might someday grow to maturity.*

jerboa *(jer-BOW-ah), noun*
A type of nocturnal rodent.
> *Some JERBOA resemble small kangaroos.*

jeremiad *(jer-uh-MY-uhd), noun*
A document or speech in which the author bitterly rails against the injustices of society or warns of impending death, destruction, or doom.
> *The Unabomber's manifesto was an intelligently written JEREMIAD.*

jeroboam *(jer-uh-BOH-um), noun*
A large wine bottle, holding about the equivalent of four ordinary bottles.
Anticipating heavy drinking on the part of his dinner guests, Jeremy sent to the cellar for a JEROBOAM of his best wine.

jess *(JES), noun*
In falconry, a short strap that is fastened around the bird's leg and then attached to a leash.
The falconer undid the merlin's JESSES, preparatory to sending the bird on a hunting flight.

Jesuitical *(jez-yoo-iht-ih-kull), adjective*
Relating or pertaining to the Jesuit order.
The young man's strict adherence to religious observance lead some to characterize his life as JESUITICAL.

jigger *(JIH-ger), noun*
A small container for measuring and pouring liquor.
The secret to my special drink is a JIGGER of vanilla liqueur.

jihad *(jee-HOD), noun*
Striving toward an important goal; in modern usage, a holy war conducted in the name of Islam.
"The tradition I cherish is the ideal this country was built upon, the concept of religious pluralism, of a plethora of opinions, of tolerance and not the JIHAD. Religious war, pooh. The war is between those who trust us to think and those who believe we must merely be led." —Anna Quindlen, American author and opinion columnist

jimmy *(JIM-ee), verb*
To force open a door or window.
The burglars proceeded to JIMMY open the window and make off with the family jewels.

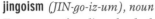

jingoism *(JIN-go-iz-um), noun*
Extreme nationalism, backed up by the explicit or implied threat of military force; more broadly, extreme enthusiasm and support for an idea or position without being open to contrary arguments or notions.
We cannot countenance JINGOISM, especially since it has such a negative impact on overseas markets.

jinn *(JIN), noun*
A mythical creature created from fire long before man inhabited the earth.
Failing in their rebellion against God, the JINN were banished to the deserts.

jobbernowl *(JOB-err-nowl), noun*
A stupid person.
I do not suffer JOBBERNOWLS with joy.

jocose *(joe-KOSS), adjective*
Humorous, playful, and characterized by good humor.
The pony's JOCOSE antics marked it for a career in polo, rather than on the racetrack.

jocund *(JOE-kund), adjective*
Having a lust for life; possessing a positive attitude and desire to enjoy life to the fullest.
Ron's JOCUND façade shattered when he found himself the victim of identity theft.

Jod-Basedow phenomenon *(yohd-bahs-eh-dof), noun*
Iodine-induced hyperthyroidism.
Jod-basedow PHENOMENON is like taking amphetamines.

joists *(joysts), noun*
Horizontal beams supporting a floor.
The contractor found a box of silver coins hidden below the floor JOISTS.

jollyboat *(JAHL-ee-boat), noun*
A larger vessel's small boat, usually carried on the stern.
We kept extra cases of beer stowed aboard the JOLLYBOAT.

jongleur *(zhawn-GLUR), noun*

A medieval strolling minstrel.

The twelfth-century court of Eleanor of Aquitaine was a popular venue for JON-GLEURS to perform their songs.

jordan *(JAWR-dn), noun*

A chamberpot.

If you need to go to the bathroom during the night, you'll find a JORDAN underneath your bed.

journeyman *(JUR-nee-man), noun*

A person who, although not a top master of his profession, has become extremely competent through long years of practice at a particular craft or skill.

"So this is happiness, / that JOURNEYMAN." —Anne Sexton, American poet and author

judder *(JUHD-er), verb*

To vibrate violently.

Experiencing severe turbulence, the old airplane JUDDERED and shivered as if it was falling apart.

jugate *(JEW-gayt), adjective*

Locked together, or marked by ridges.

The jaws of the two pit bulls were JUGATE.

juggernaut *(JUG-er-nawt), noun*

A large, overpowering, destructive force.

Once he begins arguing about the superiority of Maseratis, Jefferson becomes a JUGGERNAUT, capable of deflating anyone else's arguments.

juggins *(JUHG-inz), noun*

Idiot; simpleton.

Forest may be very nice, but he's a bit of a JUGGINS, so don't expect him to understand anything complicated.

julep *(JOO-lip), noun*

A sweet drink, traditionally Southern and made with bourbon.

For our Kentucky Derby party, I've made a big pitcher of mint JULEPS.

jurisprudence *(joor-iss-PROO-dense), noun*
The philosophy and methodology behind the practice of law.
> *The study of JURISPRUDENCE was interminably dull to John; he longed to work with real clients and real court cases.*

jussive *(JUHS-iv), adjective*
Expressing a command.
> *Marie's request, given in a JUSSIVE tone, spurred Justin to hurry to the house to fetch her drink.*

juvenescent *(jew-ven-ESS-ent), adjective*
Growing or becoming younger.
> *The main character in the film* The Curious Case of Benjamin Button *was literally JUVENESCENT.*

juvenilia *(joo-vuh-NILL-yuh), noun*
Early work by a creative artist, typically produced when the artist or writer was young.
> *Lorna turned toward the stock market and away from poetry after we read her JUVENILIA and laughed uproariously.*

juxtaposition *(juhk-stuh-puh-ZISH-uhn), noun*
The observation of the differences between two items being compared side by side.
> *"A manic JUXTAPOSITION turned Hill House into a place of despair."*
> *—Shirley Jackson, American author*

kabbalism *(KAH-bah-liz-um), noun*
A Jewish mystical tradition, based on revelation instead of reason, in which mystical feats can be performed by manipulating the letters of the Hebrew alphabet.
> *Through meditation, KABBALISM enables practitioners to become one with God.*

kaffeeklatsch *(CAW-fee-klatch), noun*
An informal social gathering, typically including coffee and gossip.
> *Jeanette is not welcome at our KAFFEEKLATSCH because she refuses to gossip about her social contacts.*

kakidrosis *(kah-KID-row-sis), noun*
Sweat that smells bad.
Deodorant fights KAKIDROSIS.

kalology *(kahl-OHL-oh-jee), noun*
The study of beauty.
This weekend on the beach, amid gorgeous women in skimpy swimsuits, was the best time for a session of KALOLOGY.

K

kamagraphy *(kahm-AH-graf-ee), noun*
The practice of making copies of paintings, using canvas.
The forger was particularly good at KAMAGRAPHY, and made many copies of paintings by Renoir and Cézanne.

kantikoy *(CAN-tih-koi), noun*
Dancing as an act of worship.
Being unable to dance, the thought of attending the tribe's KANTIKOY fills me with anxiety.

Kapellmeister *(kuh-PELL-my-ster), noun*
The director of a choir or orchestra.
Ever since the Prithingtons hired a personal KAPELLMEISTER for their Christmas parties, everyone else has had to follow suit.

karezza *(kahr-EDZ-zah), noun*
The practice of having prolonged sex without experiencing orgasm.
My lover and I spent many hours on the beach, engaging in KAREZZA, which drove him wild.

karyotype *(CARE-ee-oh-type), noun*
The chromosomal characteristics of a cell.
All of an organism's physical traits are determined by KARYOTYPE.

kasha *(KAH-shuh), noun*
Soft food derived from buckwheat.
Given my dental problems, we had KASHA for breakfast, and I had little difficulty in chewing it.

kebbie *(KEB-ee), noun*
A rough-headed Scottish walking stick.
  I would like to take a KEBBIE with us for walking in the Highlands; it would help to get over the rough patches.

keck *(kek), verb*
To retch.
  The choppy boat ride made his stomach KECK.

kelvin *(KEL-vin), noun*
A temperature scale in which absolute zero is zero degrees, and there are no negative values.
  When we questioned Rachel about her purse, suggesting that it is a knockoff, she gave us a stare cold enough to register on the KELVIN scale.

kemp *(KEMP), noun*
Coarse strand of wool.
  I've woven the KEMP into a rough blanket for us.

kenning *(KEN-ing), noun*
A metaphorical compound word or phrase, used often in epic poetry.
  Cliff's letter to Natasha included such KENNINGS as "pearl-eyed dove" and "crinkly-gowned angel." It's no wonder she broke up with him soon after.

kep *(KEP), verb*
To catch; especially Scottish.
  I KEP the ball when he tosses it to me.

kephalonomancy *(keh-fal-oh-no-man-cee), noun*
To divine the future over the roasted or boiled head of a donkey—believe it or not.
  KEPHALONOMANCY is an art little practiced in a country where the Society for the Prevention of Cruelty to Donkeys holds sway.

kerasine *(KER-ah-syn), adjective*
Made of horn.
  The KERASINE lamp had been fashioned from the antlers of a deer.

kerf *(KERF), noun*
The cut channel made by a saw.
> *You make a small KERF, place the saw blade in it, and then start sawing vigorously to cut wood.*

kerfuffle *(ker-FUF-uhl), noun*
Disorderly behavior, acting out of confusion.
> *"KERFUFFLE" is one of Judge Judy's favorite words.*

kerning *(KER-ning), noun*
In typography, the amount of spacing between letters in a word or line of type.
> *If the KERNING is too large or too small, words are difficult to read.*

ketch *(kech), noun*
A small sailing vessel with a mizzenmast stepped aft of a taller mainmast.
> *He kept his KETCH moored at the town dock.*

keyline *(KEE-lyn), noun*
In graphic design, a line separating areas of color from monochromatic sections.
> *The KEYLINE between the color and the black and white areas needs to be moved two ems to the right.*

khor *(KOR), noun*
A dry ravine.
> *When thunderstorms blow up, water comes down from the mountain and fills up the KHOR really fast; stay alert.*

kibe *(KAYB), noun*
A sore, usually on the heel.
> *After walking fifteen miles today, I've got a KIBE on my heel that needs to be soaked.*

kibosh *(KY-bosh), noun*
Something that serves to stop something else.
> *Father put the KIBOSH on my plans to extend my summer trip to Europe by another three months.*

kiddle *(KID-uhl), noun*
A barrier built in a river with a net stretched across an opening to catch fish.
> *Early native Americans build a KIDDLE near where the Passaic River runs close to my childhood home.*

kilter *(KIL-tur), noun*
Good condition.
> *I'm in a KILTER right now, since I've just managed to balance my checkbook.*

kine *(KYN), noun*
The plural of cow.
> *Jacob tended his KINE and sheep on the slopes of the mountain.*

kinesiology *(kih-nee-see-OL-uh-jee), noun*
The science of muscles and their function, physical movement, and muscular development.
> *As a body builder, he studied both nutrition and KINESIOLOGY.*

kinetics *(kin-EH-tiks), noun*
The science of motion; relating to motion.
> *The force of his punch could be measured by the use of KINETICS, something his trainer had studied extensively.*

kir *(KEER), noun*
A drink made from white wine and cassis.
> *Before the opening of the play the theater served its patrons KIRS and appetizers.*

kirtle *(CUR-till), noun*
A tunic, coat, dress, or skirt.
> *Muslim men sometimes wear KIRTLES.*

kismet *(KIHZ-met), noun*
Fate or destiny.
> *Elaine's parvenu background hardly seemed destined to make her part of our group, but KISMET has made her an important social contact.*

kitsch *(KIHCH), noun*
Art, artifacts, or other objects of a cheap or junky nature produced by the popular culture.
> *His room was filled with KITSCH: lava lamps, Farrah Fawcett and Cheryl Tiegs posters, and plastic models of Frankenstein and Dracula.*

klaxon *(CLACKS-on), noun*
An electric horn with a loud, shrill sound.
> *A blast from the KLAXON woke the troops.*

klezmer *(KLEZ-mir), noun, adjective*
A type of Jewish music.
> *KLEZMER prominently features clarinet.*

knavish *(NAY-vish), adjective*
Untrustworthy, dishonest, and mischievous.
> *Despite, or perhaps because of, his KNAVISH behavior, Jonathan is always a success at our society balls.*

knell *(NELL), noun*
The sound of a bell, especially when rung solemnly at a funeral.
> *"They are of sick and diseased imaginations who would toll the world's KNELL so soon." —Henry David Thoreau, American author and transcendentalist*

knitch *(NITCH), noun*
A bundle of objects tied together.
> *We made a KNITCH of sticks and tossed it on the fire, where it blazed brightly.*

knout *(NAUWT), noun*
A powerful whip, used by members of the Russian nobility.
> *All the serfs feared the punishment of the KNOUT and so did as their lord bade them.*

koan *(KOH-an), noun*
A paradoxical saying or question used as the object of a Zen Buddhist meditation.
> *"What is the sound of one hand clapping?" is an example of a KOAN.*

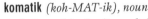

K

komatik *(koh-MAT-ik), noun*
A sled, used by Inuit, made by binding crossbars to runners and covering the frame with hide.
We crossed the ice using a KOMATIK, which we constructed according to instructions from our native guide.

kore *(KOHR-ee), noun*
An ancient Greek sculpture of a woman standing with her arms by her sides.
During the archaeological dig on Mycenae, excavators found many KORE, showing that an artistic civilization flourished there.

kouros *(KOO-ross), noun*
A statue of a nude young boy.
I hate water fountains with a peeing KOUROS.

kowtow *(KOW-tow), verb*
To give in to someone's every wish; to grovel and behave in a subservient manner.
Amy told Andrew that she was sick and tired of KOWTOWING to his every need.

kraken *(KRAH-ken), noun*
A gigantic creature, somewhat like the Loch Ness monster, reputedly sighted off the coast of Norway.
"Well, if you believe such things, there's a beast does the bidding of Davy Jones. A fearsome creature, with giant tentacles that'll suction your face clean off, and drag an entire ship down to the crushing darkness. The KRAKEN." —Joshamee Gibbs, Pirates of the Caribbean: Dead Man's Chest

kritarchy *(KRIT-ar-kee), noun*
The rule of judges.
The ancient KRITARCHY is described in the book of Judges in the Old Testament.

kummel *(KUM-uhl), noun*
A colorless, caraway-flavored liquor.
She was drinking a KUMMEL and soda on the rocks.

kvass *(KVAHS), noun*
A Russian beer made from fermented rye or barley.
> *Along with vodka, our Russian hosts plied us with plenty of KVASS, which was no less alcoholic and left us hung over the following day.*

Kwanzaa *(KWAN-zah), noun*
An African holiday observed by many African Americans from December 26 to January 1.
> *We feel we are doing our part to foster multiculturalism by allowing the stray KWANZAA decoration at our Christmas parties.*

kyloe *(KEYE-low), noun*
A breed of Highland cattle.
> *We raised KYLOE for the meat.*

kyphosis *(ki-FOE-sis), noun*
Excessive curvature of the spine suffered by hunchbacks.
> *After William's father forced him to help out the family gardener, William complained for weeks afterward that the outdoor work gave him KYPHOSIS.*

Kyrie *(KEE-ree-ey), noun*
A musical setting used within the Orthodox and Catholic Churches.
> *A high point of the service was the singing of KYRIE eleison, "Lord, have mercy upon us."*

"*I fear the popular notion of success stands in direct opposition in all points to the real and wholesome success. One adores public opinion, the other, private opinion; one, fame, the other, desert; one, feats, the other, humility; one, LUCRE, the other, love.*"

—

Ralph Waldo Emerson, American poet, essayist, and transcendentalist

labanotation *(la-bah-no-TAY-shun), noun*
A nomenclature used to choreograph ballets, modern dance, and other performances so the dancers can follow the steps.
> *Even with the best-available LABANOTATION, Walker was unable to adequately perform a Viennese waltz at Natasha's coming-out party.*

labefactation *(lab-ah-fact-AYE-shin), adjective*
Deterioration; worsening.
> *LABEFACTATION forced us to tear down the old barn.*

labiomancy *(LAB-ee-oh-man-see), noun*
Lip reading.
> *As George was skilled in LABIOMANCY, he was able to tell what Janet was saying to Walter, despite his distance from them.*

labret *(LEY-bret), noun*
A piece of jewelry worn in a lip piercing.
> *The goth woman wore black clothing, black lipstick, an eyebrow ring, and a large LABRET through her lower lip.*

labrose *(la-BROSS), adjective*
Having thick or large lips.
> *Many African Americans and Jews are LABROSE.*

labyrinth *(LAH-buh-rinth), noun*
A maze-like series of connected tunnels and passages through which it is difficult to find one's way.
> *He ran, terrified, as the Minotaur chased him throughout the LABYRINTH.*

lachrymiform *(lak-RIH-mih-form), adjective*
Tear-shaped.
> *Her LACHRYMIFORM silver earrings dangled and sparkled in the candlelight.*

lachrymose *(LAH-krih-mose), adjective*
Describes someone who cries at the drop of a hat.
> *She was so LACHRYMOSE, she cried at commercials for long-distance phone companies.*

lacis *(LAK-is), noun*
Network.
> *The agent maintained a LACIS of contacts across Europe that enabled him to know the political plans of any government.*

lackadaisical *(lack-uh-DAY-zih-kuhl), adjective*
Lazy and indolent; lacking determination.
> *No matter how many times a week her father allows her to go on a spending spree, Millicent is never LACKADAISICAL about her trips to Cartier.*

lackaday *(LAK-uh-dey), interjection*
An expression of dismay or disapproval.
> *"Hey-di, hey-di, misery me, LACKADAY-de!" —From* The Yeomen of the Guard, *by W.S. Gilbert and Arthur Sullivan*

laconic *(luh-KON-ik), adjective*
Being a person of few words; expressing oneself with an economy of words.
> *Harold may be LACONIC, but when he does speak, he is worth listening to.*

lactation *(lak-TAY-shun), noun*
The production of milk from the breasts of a mother mammal so her young can feed by sucking on the nipple.
> *When mother took us to visit the farm on one part of our property, she shielded our young eyes from the LACTATION of the various animals.*

lacteous *(LAK-tee-us), adjective*
Milky; pale and milky white.
> *His eyes, formerly clear, had turned LACTEOUS, and he stared at us blindly.*

lacuna *(lah-KOON-ah), noun*
A hole, gap, or space where something is missing.
> *Water spilled through a LACUNA in the dam.*

lagan *(LAG-uhn), noun*
An object that has been sunk in water, but is attached to a buoy for future recovery.
> *The LAGAN we observed being dropped from the boat proved, on closer examination, to be a lobster trap.*

lagerphone *(LAH-gur-fohn), noun*

A musical instrument, constructed by attaching bottle caps to a staff.

Along with a washboard and a cigar-box banjo, our backyard band included a LAGERPHONE.

laggard *(LAG-uhrd), noun, adjective*

A person who loiters; sluggish and reacting slowly.

"Reviewers…must normally function as huff-and-puff artists blowing LAG-GARD theatergoers stageward." —Walter Kerr, American theater critic

lagniappe *(lan-YAP), noun*

An unexpected bonus gift or extra benefit; the icing on the cake.

Frederick would have bought the Porsche Panamera, even without the LAGNIAPPE of a free voice-activated navigation system.

laissez faire *(lah-zay-FAIR), noun*

The belief that government should not interfere in economic affairs but should instead let the economy take its natural course.

Our family began to place most of its money in hedge funds when we became convinced that the government intended to forego LAISSEZ FAIRE and take a more active part in the nation's financial system.

lambaste *(lam-BAST), verb*

To berate or criticize harshly, especially in an unkind way.

We LAMBASTED Marla for not visiting Comme des Garçons during her recent weekender to Beijing.

lambent *(LAM-bent), adjective*

Flickering so as to give off a soft light.

The room was made peaceful by LAMBENT candles.

lamia *(LEY-mee-uh), noun*

A female vampire.

In Castle Dracula, Jonathan Harker is menaced by three LAMIA, who in the end devour a child instead of him.

laminar *(LAMB-en-are), adjective*
Smoothly flowing; nonturbulent.
The plant's inline mixers could mix fluids at LAMINAR flow rates.

lammergeyer *(LAM-er-guy-er), noun*
A large black bird of the vulture family.
"The world is just that LAMMERGEYER, or bearded vulture, in the sky."
—Pico Iyer, British-born essayist of Indian descent

lampion *(LAM-pee-yun), noun*
A small oil lamp with a tinted chimney.
On either end of the mantle sat a small LAMPION, which cast a gentle glow over the scene.

lampoon *(LAM-poon), noun or verb*
A mean-spirited satire directed at a person or institution; or, the act of submitting someone to a mean-spirited satire.
We LAMPOONED the nouveau riche attendees of our April Fool's Day party simply by dressing in the same overwrought couture favored by parvenus.

languid *(LANG-gwid), adjective*
Characterized by weakness and fatigue; or, lacking spirit and animation.
"In doing good, we are generally cold, and LANGUID, and sluggish; and of all things afraid of being too much in the right." —Edmund Burke, Anglo-Irish statesman, orator, and author

languor *(LANG-guhr), noun*
Feeling of torpidity or listlessness.
The warmth and humidity of the morning induced a state of LANGUOR in the children, which gave their parents the chance for much-needed rest.

lanyard *(LAN-yerd), noun*
A woven cord worn around the neck.
The coach wore a whistle suspended from a LANYARD round his neck, and he sounded this often.

lappet *(LAP-it), noun*
A flap hanging from a garment.
> *The coat's LAPPETS were so threadbare as to be practically worn through, making it seem even more ragged.*

lapping *(LAH-ping), noun*
The practice of falsifying accounting records to conceal a shortage caused by theft or loss, usually by posting a financial transaction to an accounting period other than the one during which it actually took place.
> *Even after Skyler was indicted, he could not accept that LAPPING was an objectionable practice.*

largesse *(lar-JESS), noun*
The generous bestowal of gifts; or, generosity in general.
> *"A LARGESS universal, like the sun, / His liberal eye doth give to everyone, / Thawing cold fear." —William Shakespeare, English playwright*

lascivious *(luh-SIV-ee-us), adjective*
Interested in and eager to engage in sexual activity; sexual in nature.
> *"An impersonal and scientific knowledge of the structure of our bodies is the surest safeguard against prurient curiosity and LASCIVIOUS gloating." —Marie Carmichael Stopes, British scientist and birth-control pioneer*

lassitude *(LAS-ih-tood), noun*
Having little energy or motivation; weariness.
> *"We know what boredom is: it is a dull / Impatience or a fierce velleity, / A champing wish, stalled by our LASSITUDE, / To make or do." —Richard Wilbur, American poet*

lateen *(la-TEEN), noun*
A triangular sail, often used by Mediterranean ships.
> *The Egyptian boats we saw in the harbor of Alexandria had LATEEN sails.*

latency *(LAY-ten-see), noun*
A period of dormancy that precedes a period of great growth or action.
> *We knew that Abigail's focus on extremely liberal causes was merely a LATENCY that would end with her focus solely on charitable giving to the proper charities.*

latifundia *(lah-ti-FUN-dee-uh), noun*
A large estate, plantation, or farm run by wealthy owners and staffed with underpaid or semi-servile workers.
Billings argued that his family's sugar cane plantation in the Caribbean is not a LATIFUNDIA because the factory pays its workers what is considered a living wage for the country.

latitant *(LAH-tih-tant), adjective*
Concealed or hidden.
A favorite technique of horror movie producers is to make deformed or frightening characters LATITANT.

laudable *(LAW-duh-bull), adjective*
Commendable; deserving of praise.
Rebecca's decision to tell her mother that she lost the emerald brooch she borrowed without permission was LAUDABLE.

laudanum *(LAWD-nuhm), noun*
A preparation of opium.
While under the influence of LAUDANUM, the poet Samuel Taylor Coleridge composed his poem "Kubla Khan."

lazar *(LEY-zer), noun*
Someone infected with leprosy.
LAZARS were shunned during the Middle Ages on account of their disease and often housed far away from towns and villages.

lector *(LEK-tohr), noun*
Lecturer at a university.
After passing his exams, Giles was offered a position as LECTOR at Trinity College, Cambridge.

legerdemain *(le-juhr-duh-MAYN) noun*
Magic tricks; or, generally speaking, trickery and deception.
The Wilkinsons are one of the few of our families whose initial wealth did not come as a result of financial LEGERDEMAIN.

L

leitmotiv *(LEET-mow-teef), noun*
A short, recurring musical phrase within a longer composition.
Beethoven's Fifth Symphony *has a four-note LEITMOTIV.*

leman *(LEE-muhn), noun*
Beloved; lover.
The king's favorite LEMAN was installed in a nearby palace so he might have ready access to her.

leonine *(LEE-oh-nine), adjective*
Having characteristics of a lion.
Cesar Romero's hair was distinctly LEONINE.

lepidopterist *(lep-ih-DOP-terr-ist), noun*
Someone who studies butterflies and moths.
The LEPIDOPTERIST designed the butterfly exhibit at the Bronx Zoo.

leprose *(LEP-rohs), adjective*
Suffering from leprosy.
The crowd of LEPROSE, sickened people, with scabby skin and gray faces, was both pitiable and horrifying.

lethargic *(luh-THAHR-jihk), adjective*
Drowsy and sluggish; lacking vigor.
"Great talents, by the rust of long disuse, / Grow LETHARGIC and shrink from what they were." —Ovid, Roman poet

lethe *(LEE-thee), noun*
Forgetfulness; named for the river surrounding Hades.
With the aid of this wine, I can commit the memory of this day to LETHE.

levant *(leh-VANT), noun*
The countries on the eastern coast of the Mediterranean Sea.
Ties between western Europe and the LEVANT were first established during the Crusades.

leverage *(LEH-veh-ridge)*, *noun*
Possessing an advantage or extra degree of influence in a given situation.
With his family's connections, Eldridge required no LEVERAGE to obtain a sinecure in the financial industry.

leviathan *(le-VY-ah-thun)*, *adjective*
A gigantic creature, structure, or thing, awe-inspiring in its sheer size.
"Wilson looked out through the window at the LEVIATHAN glitter of the terminal." —Richard Matheson, American science fiction writer

levity *(LEHV-ih-tee)*, *noun*
Lack of appropriate seriousness; or, inconstant in nature.
"Love, which is the essence of God, is not for LEVITY, but for the total worth of man." —Ralph Waldo Emerson, American poet, essayist, and transcendentalist

lexicon *(LEK-sih-kahn)*, *noun*
The language or vocabulary of a specialized discipline or profession.
"In the LEXICON of lip-smacking, an epicure is fastidious in his choice and enjoyment of food, just a soupçon more expert than a gastronome." —William Safire, American journalist and presidential speechwriter

liaison *(lee-ay-ZAWHN)*, *noun*
An adulterous relationship; or, a kind of illicit sexual relationship.
LIAISONS are much more common within our group than are stable marriages.

libation *(lye-BAY-shun)*, *noun*
An alcoholic beverage consumed at social gatherings, parties, and celebrations.
With the LIBATIONS flowing freely, each member of the winning team felt compelled to make a drunken speech.

libertine *(LIB-er-teen)*, *noun*, *adjective*
Licentious and free of moral restraint; or, a person so characterized.
"It is easier to make a saint out of a LIBERTINE than out of a prig." —George Santayana, author and philosopher

libration *(ly-BRAY-shun)*, *noun*
The oscillation of earth's moon around its axis.
LIBRATIONS are caused by changes in the intensity of earth's gravitational pull on the moon.

licentious *(ly-SEN-shus), adjective*
Promiscuous; slutty; someone who is sexually uninhibited and free.
Janine's LICENTIOUS behavior was really a cry for attention, the school psychologist was convinced.

L

lief *(LEEF), adjective*
Valued; adored.
My children are the most LIEF things in my life.

lien *(LEAN), noun*
A creditor's right to have debts paid out of the debtor's property, if necessary by selling it.
It's sad that we, at times, must place LIENS on our servants' automobiles, but that is why they are the servers and we the "servees."

ligniform *(LIG-nih-form), adjective*
Having the appearance of wood.
In the 1970s, some station wagons had LIGNIFORM side panels on the outside doors.

Lilliputian *(lil-ee-PEW-shun), adjective*
Small in stature; tiny in comparison to one's peers.
Jules Verne's LILLIPUTIAN appearance made people treat him like a child.

limn *(LIM), verb*
To paint or draw.
As a youth, my hobby was to LIMN cartoon characters.

limpid *(LIM-pid), adjective*
Clear and transparent; free from obscurity.
The Motsingers are fond of saying that they are capable of eschewing all of the most LIMPID tax dodges.

linchpin *(LYNCH-pin), noun*
The centerpiece; the most important element.
Direct mail is the LINCHPIN of our marketing campaign.

lineage *(LIN-ee-ij), noun*
Ancestry; your family tree.
> *We still consider Rachel nouveau riche because her family can only trace its American LINEAGE to the mid-eighteenth century.*

liquidity *(lih-KWI-dih-tee), noun*
The relative ease with which a person can sell an asset.
> *Despite a firm belief in wealth LIQUIDITY, Dotson continues to buy such depreciable items as yachts and Porsches.*

lissome *(LISS-um), adjective*
Lithe; supple; flexible.
> *Moira acquired her LISSOME frame from years of swimming in her family's Olympic-sized pool.*

litany *(LIT-n-ee), noun*
A prolonged and boring account.
> *"With the supermarket as our temple and the singing commercial as our LITANY, are we likely to fire the world with an irresistible vision of America's exalted purpose and inspiring way of life?" —Adlai Stevenson, American politician*

literati *(lih-ter-AH-tee), noun*
The segment of society comprised of learned or literary men and women.
> *We attract the LITERATI because of our constantly carefree and exciting exploits.*

literose *(LIT-air-ohs), adjective*
Affectedly literary; pretentious.
> *He was leaning against the bookcase in a deliberately LITEROSE fashion, trying to impress her.*

lithe *(LYTH), adjective*
Having a body and/or mind that is limber, flexible, and supple.
> *"The coconut trees, LITHE and graceful, crowd the beach … like a minuet of slender elderly virgins adopting flippant poses." —William Manchester, American historian*

litigious *(lih-TIJ-us), adjective*
Readily inclined to take someone to court; or, very argumentative.
> *"Our wrangling lawyers . . . are so LITIGIOUS and busy here on earth, that I think they will plead their clients' causes hereafter,—some of them in hell."*
> —Robert Burton, English scholar and vicar at Oxford University

littoral *(LIH-tore-el), adjective*
Found along the shore.
> *Tide pools are LITTORAL formations of shallow water.*

liturgy *(LIH-tur-jee), noun*
The performance of a Christian religious service in a church.
> *During the LITURGY, the singing of the Christmas hymns filled the church with the sound of joy.*

livid *(LIHV-id), adjective*
Enraged or extremely angry.
> *Jennifer was LIVID when we suggested that her new outfit was three weeks out of date.*

locative *(LOK-uh-tiv), noun*
Grammatical case indicating location.
> *To say, "We found the book in the bookcase" in Latin would require putting "bookcase" in the LOCATIVE case.*

locution *(low-KEW-shin), noun*
A person's manner and style of speaking.
> *Neil prides himself on his precise LOCUTION, but some of the guys think he sounds rather prissy.*

logarithmic *(log-ah-RITH-mick), adjective*
The exponent expressing the power to which a number must be raised to produce a given number.
> *The increase in population of the island was an almost LOGARITHMIC growth.*

loggia *(LOH-jee-uh), noun*
A covered passageway with one side open to the air.
> *Medieval monasteries centered on cloisters, with a LOGGIA running along each side where monks could walk in meditation.*

logocentric *(low-go-SEN-trik), adjective*
Based on reason.
> *Ayn Rand's novels are really LOGOCENTRIC tracts on libertarianism.*

logomachy *(luh-GOM-uh-kee), noun*
Antagonism expressed only in words.
> *LOGOMACHY guides my approach to debating politics.*

logos *(LOH-gos), noun*
A rational, governing principle.
> *In the Gospel according to John, God is defined as the LOGOS of the universe.*

logy *(LOW-gee), adjective*
Characterized by lethargy and sluggishness.
> *"To be scared is such a release from all the LOGY weight of procrastination, of dallying and pokiness! You burn into work. It is as though gravity were removed and you walked lightly to the moon like an angel." —Brenda Ueland, American author*

loquacious *(loh-KWAY-shus), adjective*
Verbose; chatty; the habit of talking nonstop.
> *Amy and Donna are each so LOQUACIOUS, their average phone call lasts ninety minutes.*

lorgnette *(lorn-YET), noun*
Eyeglasses attached to a handle.
> *LORGNETTES are favored by operagoers.*

lubricity *(lew-BRIH-sih-tee), noun*
A substance's effectiveness as a lubricant or its slipperiness.
> *Internal ball bearings have a high degree of LUBRICITY.*

luciferous *(loo-SI-fuh-ruhs), adjective*
Providing insight or enlightenment; illuminating.
> *Blake did not find the Ivy League LUCIFEROUS, so he decided to devote his life to world travel instead.*

lucre *(LOO-ker), noun*
Monetary reward or gain.
> *"I fear the popular notion of success stands in direct opposition in all points to the real and wholesome success. One adores public opinion, the other, private opinion; one, fame, the other, desert; one, feats, the other, humility; one, LUCRE, the other, love." —Ralph Waldo Emerson, American poet, essayist, and transcendentalist*

Luddite *(LUHD-eyt), noun*
A person who refuses to use or embrace modern technology.
> *We would not stop calling Annabel a LUDDITE until she finally got herself a Vertu cell phone like the rest of us.*

lugubrious *(loo-GOO-bree-us), adjective*
Pessimistic, emotionally downtrodden, spiritually low, sad, or depressed.
> *Prozac failed to ameliorate the patient's LUGUBRIOUS outlook on life.*

lumerpa *(loo-MER-pa), noun*
A mythological radiant bird from Asia that shines so brightly that it absorbs its own shadow.
> *The presence of numerous Waterford crystal chandeliers made the ballroom shine like a LUMERPA.*

luminary *(LOO-muh-nair-ee), noun*
A person recognized as an inspirational leader in his or her field.
> *Frederick's father is a LUMINARY in the field of circumventing most income tax.*

lumpenproletariat *(lum-pen-pro-lih-tear-ee-ut), noun*
Term used by Karl Marx to describe uneducated common people.
> *It's difficult to pretend to be a member of the LUMPENPROLETARIAT when your car costs more than your next-door neighbor's house.*

lunette *(loo-NET), noun*
An area framed or enclosed by an arch or vault.
> *The church's apse was a LUNETTE behind the high altar.*

lupine *(lew-pen), adjective*
Having characteristics of a wolf.
> *Children feared Fred because of his LUPINE appearance.*

lustration *(luh-STRAY-shun), noun*
Purification through symbolic or ceremonial means or remembrances.
After Melanie spent six months working with charities in third-world countries, we put her through LUSTRATION by reintroducing her to our favorite luxury boutiques.

lyceum *(LIE-see-um), noun*
A school or other place of learning.
"[Television] should be our LYCEUM, our Chautauqua, our Minsky's, and our Camelot." —E.B. White, American author

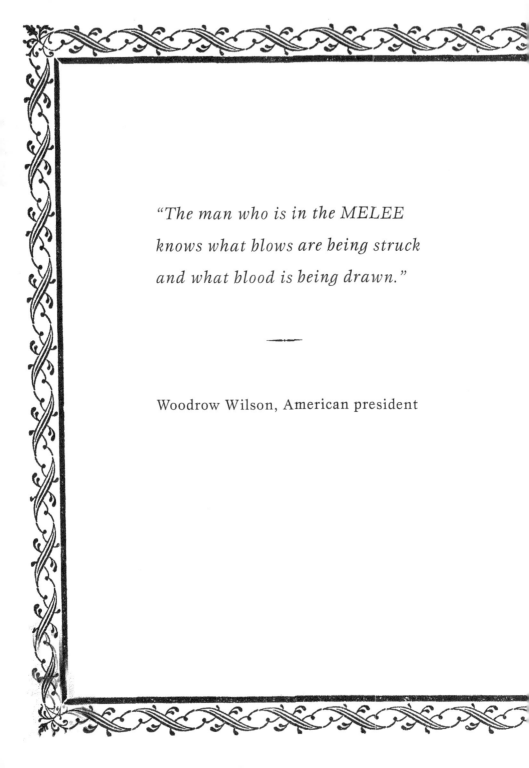

"The man who is in the MELEE
knows what blows are being struck
and what blood is being drawn."

Woodrow Wilson, American president

macarism *(mAA-ka-rih-zum), noun*
The practice of making others happy.
> *Santa Claus engages in MACARISM for one day a year; the other days, he just sleeps.*

macerate *(MASS-err-ayt), verb*
To soften or break down by placing in liquid.
> *I MACERATED the stale bagel by dunking it in my coffee.*

machair *(MAHK-eyr), noun*
In Scotland, a strip of sandy, grassy land just above high tide.
> *Aye, I've herded the cattle onto the MACHAIR above the loch; they'll be safe there for a wee while.*

Machiavellian *(mack-ee-uh-VEL-ee-uhn), adjective*
A somewhat unscrupulous and self-centered individual who is always looking out for his or her own good.
> *We can hardly be called MACHIAVELLIAN simply because we do what we need to do to hold onto the luxurious lifestyle to which we have become accustomed.*

machinations *(mack-in-AYE-shins), noun*
The plot of an evil scheme.
> *His boss saw through his MACHINATIONS to take over the company and promptly fired him.*

mackinaw *(MACK-in-awe), noun*
A coat made of a heavy woolen cloth.
> *A MACKINAW to wear outside can keep you snug and cozy in winter.*

macrobian *(mah-KRO-bee-ihn), adjective*
Long-lived.
> *Georgians, some of whom were said to live past 115, are a particularly MACRO-BIAN nation.*

macropicide *(mah-KRO-pih-side), noun*
The killing of kangaroos.
> *The slaughter in the outback was evidently a MACROPICIDE, given the large number of kangaroo carcasses.*

macrotous *(MAK-roh-tus), adjective*
Having large ears.
>*Barack Obama is, perhaps, our most MACROTOUS president, though he does not seem to have passed his ear size down to his children.*

madid *(MAD-did), adjective*
Moist; wet.
>*"His large deep blue eye, MADID and yet piercing" —Benjamin Disraeli, British statesman, author*

maelstrom *(MAIL-struhm), noun*
A situation marked by violence, turbulence, and uncertainty.
>*Many families who lost their fortunes during the MAELSTROM of the 1929 stock market crash are still trying to regain their social status today.*

maenadic *(men-AYE-dik), adjective*
Frenzied, in a rage.
>*Hell hath no fury like a MAENADIC woman.*

maffick *(MAF-ik), verb*
To celebrate with public events and demonstrations.
>*If the Red Sox win the pennant, the people of Boston intend to MAFFICK until the cows come home or the bars close—whichever comes first.*

Magna Carta *(MAG-nah-KAR-tah), noun*
Any constitution that guarantees rights and liberties.
>*The club's charter is a MAGNA CARTA that will ensure we are able to keep our tennis courts and swimming pools open only to our most significant social contacts.*

magnanimous *(mag-NAN-ih-mus), adjective*
A kind and generous act.
>*"In a serious struggle there is no worse cruelty than to be MAGNANIMOUS at an inopportune time." —Leon Trotsky, Bolshevik revolutionary and Marxist theorist*

magnate *(MAG-nayt), noun*
A wealthy and prosperous business leader; a tycoon.
>*Oil MAGNATE T. Boone Pickens is now investing in wind power.*

magniloquent *(mag-NILL-uh-kwuhnt), adjective*
Pompous, bombastic, and boastful.
> *The nouveau riche try to atone for their lack of polish with MAGNILOQUENT speech, but the result is ludicrous.*

magnum *(MAG-num), noun*
An extra-large wine bottle twice the size of a regular wine bottle; a powerful handgun firing large bullets.
> *We doubted the taste of the event planner when we saw that the tables were filled with distasteful MAGNUMS of wines of questionable vintage.*

magpiety *(mag-PI-uh-tee), adjective*
Loquaciousness; talkativeness.
> *The bar bore was distinguished by his misinformation and his MAGPIETY in spreading it.*

malapert *(MAL-ah-pert), adjective*
Saucy, impudent.
> *The king's mistress was a MALAPERT wench, whose wit as much as her body amused the ruler.*

malapropism *(MAL-ah-prop-iz-um), noun*
Deliberate misuse of a word or mangling of the English language, often done for comic effect.
> *Since Emily refused to take elocution lessons like the rest of us, her speech is constantly marred by ridiculous MALAPROPISMS.*

malar *(MEY-lehr), adjective*
Relating to the cheek.
> *Her MALAR muscles were damaged in the accident, impeding her ability to smile.*

maleferous *(mal-IFF-eh-russ), adjective*
Producing evil.
> *Hitler was the most MALEFEROUS villain of the twentieth century.*

maleficence *(muh-LEF-ih-sense), noun*
To act in a way that deliberately causes harm; behavior driven by evil intentions.
Our upstairs maid's various acts of MALEFICENCE finally caused her to be released from our family's employment.

malfeasance *(mal-FEE-zinss), noun*
Misbehavior; wrongdoing; illegal, unethical, or immoral conduct.
Gavin insists that insider trading is not MALFEASANCE; it's merely making good use of all available information.

malleable *(MAL-yah-bull), adjective*
Easily molded into different shapes; easily influenced to change one's opinion or actions.
"I did not know that mankind was suffering for want of gold. I have seen a little of it. I know that it is very MALLEABLE, but not so MALLEABLE as wit."
—Henry David Thoreau, American author and transcendentalist

malmsey *(MALM-zee), noun*
Sweet wine; sherry.
George, Duke of Clarence, is said to have been drowned in a butt of MALMSEY.

malware *(MAL-wear), noun*
Software designed to deliberately disable a computer.
My PC was shut down and the hard drive destroyed by MALWARE.

mammon *(mam-en), noun*
Items made secure through deposit.
We rented a safe deposit box to hold our gold coins and other MAMMON.

manciple *(MAN-sih-pull), noun*
A buyer or purchaser.
A purchasing agent is a professional MANCIPLE.

mandamus *(mahn-DAH-moos), noun*
A writ in which a higher court orders a lower court to do something.
The Supreme Court issued a writ of MANDAMUS to the First Circuit appeals court, ordering it to rehear the case.

M

mandarin *(MAN-dah-rin)*, *noun*
Influential or important government official.
> *The MANDARINS of the State Department are making things very difficult for the new secretary.*

Manichaeism *(man-ih-KEY-iz-um)*, *noun*
The belief that the world is characterized by a constant struggle between good and evil.
> *During the Cold War, many political philosophers took refuge in MAN-ICHAEISM as a framework for the conflict between America and the Soviet Union.*

manifest destiny *(MAN-ih-fest-DESS-tin-ee)*, *noun*
Expansion into foreign lands, justified as being necessary or benevolent.
> *"It's not greed and ambition that makes wars—it's goodness. Wars are always fought for the best of reasons, for liberation or MANIFEST DESTINY, always against tyranny and always in the best interests of humanity." —James Garner in* The Americanization of Emily

maniform *(MAN-ih-form)*, *adjective*
Having the form of a hand.
> *The claw in the arcade machine had a MANIFORM appearance.*

mansuetude *(MAN-swi-tood)*, *noun*
Gentleness.
> *The father's MANSUETUDE soothed his crying child.*

manumission *(man-you-MISH-in)*, *noun*
The act of freeing from slavery.
> *Thomas Jefferson has been criticized for not undertaking the MANUMISSION of his slaves.*

marginalize *(MAR-jin-ul-eyes)*, *verb*
To dismiss something as less important than it actually is.
> *Francine has too many connections for us to snub her completely, but we have done our best to MARGINALIZE her influence.*

marigraph *(MAR-ih-graf), noun*
An instrument for measuring the rise and fall of tides.
In order to correlate the motion of tides with the moon's orbit, we used a MARI-GRAPH to determine how high the water had risen.

marmoreal *(marr-MORE-ee-uhl), adjective*
Marble-like.
"He laid out every sentence as in a shroud—hanging, like a widower, long over its MARMOREAL beauty." —Max Beerbohm, writer

M

marshal *(MAR-shul), verb*
To gather all the resources at one's disposal to achieve a goal.
Patricia MARSHALED all of her social contacts to try to get a front-row ticket for fashion week.

marsupial *(mar-SOUP-ee-uhl), noun*
A mammal who carries its young with her after its birth in a pouch on the outside of her body, where the baby continues to develop.
The kangaroo is the best-known MARSUPIAL, but wombats also carry their babies in a pouch.

martinet *(mar-tin-ETT), noun*
A self-important, petty individual who demands obedience from others.
The chief engineer was a pompous little MARTINET.

marzipan *(MAR-zih-pan), noun*
A sweet confection made of almond paste, sugar, and egg white, used as a filling in candy or as icing for cake.
"American Danish can be doughy, heavy, sticky, tasting of prunes and is usually wrapped in cellophane. Danish Danish is light, crisp, buttery and often tastes of MARZIPAN or raisins; it is seldom wrapped in anything but loving care." —R. W. Apple Jr., American food critic

masticate *(MAS-tih-kate), verb*
To chew, especially to chew thoroughly.
The best way to appreciate the gustatory arts is to MASTICATE your personal chef's creations at as relaxed a pace as possible.

mastoid *(MAS-toid), adjective*
Resembling a breast or nipple.
> *The hill, with the small hillock on top of it, was so round that it had a MASTOID appearance.*

matin *(MAT-n), noun*
The first in a series of canonical hours.
> *The monks rose before daybreak to celebrate MATIN in the chapel.*

matriculate *(ma-TRIH-kyou-late), verb*
To be admitted to college.
> *I'm planning to MATRICULATE next year at Harvard.*

mattock *(MAH-tok), noun*
A tool for loosening the soil.
> *A hoe is a MATTOCK, as is a plough.*

maudlin *(MAWD-lin), adjective*
Foolishly and mawkishly sentimental or emotional.
> *"It is a MAUDLIN and indecent verity that comes out through the strength of wine." —Joseph Conrad, Polish-born English novelist*

maunder *(MAWN-dehr), verb*
To move, speak, or act in a random, meaningless manner.
> *Ricardo's speech MAUNDERS so much that you'd never know he was heir to one of Central America's largest fortunes.*

maundy *(MAWN-dee), noun*
A ceremony in which one washes the feet of the poor.
> *Next week, in celebration of MAUNDY Thursday, the priest will wash the feet of the neighborhood poor.*

maverick *(MAH-ver-ik), noun*
An unorthodox or unconventional person who does what it takes to get things done.
> *"The rugged individualist is too often mistaken for the misfit, the MAVERICK, the spoilsport, the sore thumb." —Lewis H. Lapham, former editor of* Harper's Magazine

mawkish *(MAW-kish), adjective*
Nauseating and sickly sentimental.

> *"I would jump down Etna for any public good—but I hate a MAWKISH popularity." —John Keats, English Romantic poet*

mean *(MEEN), noun*
In arithmetic, the average value of a series of numbers, determined by taking the sum of a series and dividing by the number of items in the series.

> *The MEAN of the Bakersfields' fortune is nowhere near that of ours, but we tolerate the family anyway because several members are excellent golfers.*

meander *(me-ahn-duhr), verb*
To wander aimlessly.

> *We fired that particular servant because he MEANDERED far too slowly from task to task.*

mechanism *(MEK-an-iz-em), noun*
An assembly of mechanical parts that performs a specific motion or function.

> *In my intro to mechanical engineering course, we had to create a MECHANISM for conveying a raw egg at high speed across the gym floor without breaking it.*

median *(MEE-dee-en), noun*
In arithmetic, the middle number in a series of numbers arranged in order from smallest to largest.

> *When philanthropists Brock, Cliff, and Edward were honored at a luncheon, Cliff was called upon to speak second as his donation was the MEDIAN of the three.*

meerkat *(MEER-kat), noun*
A burrowing mongoose found in southern Africa.

> *The plain was alive with MEERKATS, sitting by the sides of their burrows, long tails wrapped around them.*

megalopolis *(meg-ah-LAH-poe-liss), noun*
A large, sprawling urban area.

> *The northeastern coast of the United States is considered one big MEGALOPOLIS.*

M

megrim *(MEE-grim), noun*
Low spirits; depression.
  Ever since my dog died, I've been suffering from a MEGRIM.

melanin *(MEL-uh-nin), noun*
The pigment that determines the color of one's hair, eyes, and skin.
  Tamara is unwilling to accept that, no matter how much time she spends on the sunny beaches of the Mediterranean, she will not achieve her desired tan due to her lack of MELANIN.

melee *(MAY-lay), noun*
A confused struggle involving many people.
  "The man who is in the MELEE knows what blows are being struck and what blood is being drawn." —Woodrow Wilson, American president

meliorism *(meel-yor-iz-um), noun*
A philosophy of optimism that says the world is gradually improving through divine intervention or human effort—or both.
  Thomas Hardy's philosophy was distinctly MELIORIST because he believed ultimately in the goodness of humankind.

mellifluous *(meh-LIH-flu-us), adjective*
Music, speech, or other sound that is sweet and pleasant to listen to.
  The MELLIFLUOUS tones of his voice brought Martin many high-paying gigs for voice-overs.

melomania *(meh-loh-MAY-nee-ah), noun*
A passion for music.
  Since I can't be in my car or my home without music blasting from the stereo, some of my friends have accused me of MELOMANIA.

mendacity *(men-DAH-sit-tee), noun*
A tendency toward or habit of being a dishonest person.
  "The human condition is composed of unequal parts of courage, friendship, ethics, self-sacrifice, brutality, degeneracy, and MENDACITY." —Harlan Ellison, American author

mendicant *(MEN-dih-kant), noun, adjective*
A monk who does not own property or, more broadly, anyone who asks for alms and begs to support himself; in the act of begging.
"The woman who does her job for society inside the four walls of her home must not be considered by her husband or anyone else an economic 'dependent,' reaching out her hands in MENDICANT fashion for financial help." —Mary Gilson, American economist

mentat *(MEN-tat), noun*
A human being capable of performing mental tasks with the accuracy and speed of a computer.
Our accountant is a veritable MENTAT! Did you see how fast he determined all of our charitable deductions!

meracious *(mer-EY-shus), adjective*
Without adulteration; strong.
The gin and tonic you made me was among the most MERACIOUS I've had for a while.

mercantile *(MIR-kan-teel), adjective*
Characteristic of merchants or trading.
Options trading is a MERCANTILE activity.

mercurial *(mer-KYOOR-ee-uhl), adjective*
Volatile, fickle, and erratic.
Men always tolerate Natasha's MERCURIAL nature due to her beauty and her family's great fortune.

meretricious *(mer-i-TRISH-us), adjective*
Anything done to attract attention in an unseemly or inappropriate fashion.
His favorite brand of beer used MERETRICIOUS ads—TV commercials showing scantily clad young women—to attract more attention.

meridian *(mer-ID-ee-en), noun*
Any line that runs from north to south on a map or globe.
He sailed his yacht straight along a MERIDIAN to the Arctic Circle.

M

meritocracy *(mer-ih-TOK-ruh-see), noun*
Government or leadership by people with great merit, rather than by people with great wealth.
> *Corporate leadership in a family-owned business is determined by nepotism, not MERITOCRACY.*

meritorious *(mair-uh-TORE-ee-uhss), adjective*
Worthy of praise or reward.
> *"Arrogance on the part of the MERITORIOUS is even more offensive to us than the arrogance of those without merit: for merit itself is offensive." —Friedrich Nietzsche, nineteenth-century German philosopher*

mesotherm *(MEZ-oh-thirm), noun*
A plant that successfully grows in moderate temperatures.
> *Rosemary flourishes in mild weather, making it an excellent example of a MESOTHERM.*

metachromasis *(meh-tah-CROWM-ah-sis), noun*
The phenomenon of different substances becoming different colors and shades when stained by the same dye.
> *An identical cotton blend was used in the entire lot of shirts to avoid META-CHROMASIS ruining the color.*

metadata *(meh-tah-DAY-tah; also MEH-tah-dah-tah), noun*
Data that provides information about other data.
> *"The government takes the view that we have no privacy interest at all in our METADATA."—Kenneth Roth, political activist*

metallurgy *(meh-tul-err-jee), noun*
The science of metals.
> *As a chemical engineering student, I was required to take one course in METALLURGY.*

metamerism *(meh-TAM-err-iz-um), noun*
The phenomenon of an object appearing to be different colors depending on the lighting and the angle of viewing.
> *Owing to METAMERISM, no one could agree whether the car was green or blue.*

metanoia *(met-uh-NOI-uh), noun*
Change in one's basic beliefs, usually spiritual and profound.
As a result of my incarceration I've undergone a METANOIA regarding prison-ers' rights and am now an advocate for the interests of convicts.

M

metaphor *(MEH-tah-for), noun*
A sentence or phrase in which a word ordinarily associated with one thing is applied to something else, to indicate that in some way they are similar.
"If we are a METAPHOR of the universe, the human couple is the metaphor par excellence, the point of intersection of all forces and the seed of all forms."
—Octavio Paz Lozano, Mexican writer, poet, and diplomat

metaphysics *(met-a-fiz-iks), noun*
The study of arguments, thoughts, and principles based primarily on thinking and abstract reasoning rather than hard facts that can be demonstrated through physical evidence.
"During my METAPHYSICS final, I cheated by looking into the soul of the person sitting next to me." —Woody Allen, American film director, writer, and comedian

metastasize *(meh-TA-sti-size), verb*
The tendency of cancer cells to spread from a tumor throughout the body.
Byron's ugly nature quickly METASTASIZED in our group, as he spread lies and gossip among more and more of our social contacts.

metallism *(MEH-tah-liz-um), noun*
The belief that money must either be made of precious metal or backed by pre-cious metal held in reserve—usually gold or silver.
Richard Nixon abolished the gold standard for U.S. currency, and METALLISM declined as a result.

mete *(MEET), verb*
To distribute or allot.
After Elyssia ran up several of her father's platinum cards, he METED out sub-stantial punishment for her by not allowing her to shop at exclusive boutiques for an entire week.

methysis *(meh-THEE-sis), noun*
Drunkenness.
> *Alexander's METHYSIS was probably caused by the three bottles of wine, two six-packs, and a fifth of vodka he had consumed.*

M

meticulous *(meh-TICK-yuh-luhss), adjective*
Extremely precise; fussy.
> *The overly METICULOUS maitre d' made us self-conscious and detracted from our enjoyment of the meal.*

métier *(meh-tyeeay), noun*
One's occupation, profession, field of work, etc.
> *Since her family started one of Wall Street's most profitable houses, it's only natural that Ellen's MÉTIER would be finance.*

metonymy *(meh-TOHN-uh-me), noun*
A figure of speech, using one part of something as a symbol of it.
> *The phrase "To count noses" is an example of METONYMY, since we're counting people, not noses.*

mewl *(MYOOL), verb*
To whimper; to speak in a whimpering tone.
> *Rather than being strong and assertive, you MEWL your request as if you were a ten-year-old.*

miasma *(my-AZ-mah), noun*
An unhealthy atmosphere or environment; an unpleasant feeling pervading the air.
> *"These appearances, which bewilder you, are merely electrical phenomena not uncommon—or it may be that they have their ghastly origin in the rank MIASMA of the tarn." —Edgar Allan Poe, American author and poet*

microcosm *(my-kruh-kahz-uhm), noun*
A representation of something on a very small scale.
> *"Each particle is a MICROCOSM, and faithfully renders the likeness of the world." —Ralph Waldo Emerson, American poet, essayist, and transcendentalist*

mien *(MEEN), noun*
A person's look or manner.
> *Dan's country-bumpkin MIEN effectively hides his shrewd business tactics.*

milieu *(mill-YOU), noun*

Surroundings, especially surroundings of a social or cultural nature.

Poetry readings and coffee shops are not Andrew's MILIEU of choice.

millenarianism *(mil-uh-NAIR-ee-uhn-ism), noun*

Any apocalyptic religious, philosophical, or social movement that predicts radical disaster, particularly at the end of the current millennium or the beginning of the new one.

As they worried about the impact of computer errors on the family fortune during the change from 1999 to 2000, the Cadburys briefly believed in MILLENARIANISM.

millenium *(mil-EN-ee-um), noun*

A period of a thousand years.

Millicent takes a MILLENIUM to get ready for society balls, but the results, typically, are worth the wait.

milline *(mill-EYNE), noun*

A measure of advertising space in a newspaper.

The MILLINE rate is used to compare the cost of advertising between different newspapers.

milquetoast *(MILK-toast), noun*

A mild-mannered person, a wimp.

Walter Mitty is a Caspar MILQUETOAST.

minatory *(MIN-ah-tawr-ee), adjective*

Threatening.

The bill collector took on a MINATORY tone when Sheila explained she could not pay the amount due.

minimalism *(MIN-ih-mull-iz-um), noun*

A school of art in which "less is more"—clean and uncluttered paintings; sculpture with simple lines; fiction written in a lean and spare style; and music with uncomplicated scores and minimal instruments.

John Cage's MINIMALIST composition 4'33" consists of four and a half minutes of silence.

minion *(MIN-yuhn), noun*
A follower of someone in an important position.
> *"I caught this morning morning's MINION, king- / dom of daylight's dauphin, dapple-dawn-drawn Falcon, in his riding." —Gerard Manley Hopkins, English poet and Jesuit priest*

minutiae *(mih-NOO-shuh), noun*
Small, trifling matters that one encounters on an average day.
> *The MINUTIAE of golf, tennis, and spa treatments at the club can become utterly tiresome.*

mirador *(mir-u-DAWR), noun*
A balcony overlooking a courtyard, especially in Spanish architecture.
> *From the MIRADOR, the señoritas hid behind their fans and sent flirting glances into the crowd of men below.*

misanthrope *(MISS-anne-throwp), noun*
A person of anti-social nature who dislikes other people and thinks poorly of them until they give him reason not to.
> *Harold has become a veritable MISANTHROPE since Anabelle refused to attend the regatta with him.*

misconstrue *(miss-kuhn-STROO), verb*
To misinterpret or to take in a wrong sense.
> *The disagreement over the price of the yacht was due merely to the fact that David MISCONSTRUED the terms of the offer.*

misericord *(miz-er-ih-kawrd), noun*
Room in a monastery for monks where they can temporarily be free of the monastic rule.
> *Brother Samuel, while in the MISERICORD, cursed his ill fortune, something that would have been forbidden by his vows elsewhere in the monastery.*

misogyny *(mih-SAHJ-uh-nee), noun*
An intense hatred of women.
> *A lifetime of rejection had transformed him from a loving person into a rabid MISOGYNIST.*

missive *(MISS-iv), noun*
An official or formal letter.
> *He sent out a MISSIVE informing all employees that, henceforth, there would be no smoking in their quarters—but he forgot to remove the ashtrays.*

mixen *(MIKS-en), noun*
Dunghill.
> *After dinner, we cleaned the kitchen and tossed leftover scraps on the MIXEN.*

mizzle *(MIZ-ill), verb*
To rain lightly in a fine mist.
> *There's really no difference between MIZZLE and drizzle.*

mnemonic *(neh-MON-ik), adjective, noun*
A rhyme, sentence, or other word pattern designed to help one memorize facts.
> *Roy G. Biv is the MNEMONIC for the colors of a rainbow: red, orange, yellow, green, blue, indigo, violet.*

modernism *(MOD-er-nih-zum), noun*
Describes a modern avant-garde style of painting, sculpture, or architecture.
> *"Postmodernism is MODERNISM with the optimism taken out." —Robert Hewison, British historian*

modicum *(MOD-ih-kuhm), noun*
A modest amount; a small quantity.
> *"To be human is to have one's little MODICUM of romance secreted away in one's composition." —Mark Twain, American author*

moiety *(MOY-ih-tee), noun*
A part, portion, or share.
> *When I go out to dinner with my wife and kids, I don't order a meal for myself, as my dinner is a MOIETY from each of theirs.*

moilsome *(MOYLE-sum), adjective*
Involving toil and labor.
> *Putting in a pond is a MOILSOME task, involving a lot of digging and hauling dirt.*

M

monandry *(mahn-ANN-dree), noun*
Having only one male sex partner over a period of time.
> *I prefer MONANDRY as a way of life, but my last girlfriend was polyamorous, which made things awkward.*

monastic *(moh-NAS-tik), adjective*
Relating to the practice of withdrawing from society to live a quiet, contemplative life, often dedicated to religious faith.
> *Saint Pachomius founded the first organized Christian MONASTIC community.*

monistic *(moh-NIS-tik), noun*
The idea that everything—including philosophy, religion, and mysticism—can be reduced to a single substance or explained by a single principle.
> *Of course we believe the world is MONISTIC. Wealth is the source of everything in the universe.*

monotheism *(MOH-no-THEE-iz-um), noun*
A belief in one omnipotent, omniscient God who is actively involved in the workings of both the physical universe that He created and the society of men who dwell in it.
> *Christianity, Judaism, and Islam are all MONOTHEISTIC.*

monticle *(MON-tih-kuhl), noun*
Small hillock.
> *We'll raise the flag on that MONTICLE, where it will be easy for people to see it.*

monture *(mon-TOOR), noun*
Mounting; frame.
> *We set the picture in an elaborate MONTURE, which accentuated its beauty.*

moot *(MOOT), adjective*
A fact or point that is uncertain or no longer relevant.
> *Whether to continue injecting growth hormones became a MOOT point as Alex grew from five feet to five feet nine in eighteen months.*

morass *(muh-RASS), noun*
A confusing or troublesome situation from which it is difficult to disentangle oneself.
"One idea is enough to organize a life and project it / Into unusual but viable forms, but many ideas merely / Lead one thither into a MORASS of their own good intentions." —John Ashbery, American poet

mordantly *(MORE-dant-lee), adverb*
To behave in a negative, malicious, or damaging fashion.
"The ocean looked dead too, dead gray waves hissing MORDANTLY along the beach." —John Fowles, British novelist and essayist

mores *(MORE-ayz), noun*
The accepted norms of social behavior for the time and society in which you live.
Grant learned the hard way that MORES vary from country to country when he made the faux pas of trying to shake the hand of the Thai businessman.

moribund *(MOR-ih-bund), adjective*
Lacking vigor; soon to be dead or defunct.
Ever since its head chef left for the Food Network, that gourmet restaurant has become MORIBUND and is likely to close soon.

morient *(MORE-ee-ent), adjective*
Dying.
My father was MORIENT from cancer for eighteen long months.

morose *(muh-ROHSS), adjective*
Gloomy and ill-humored.
Now that his parents have taken away his private plane, Anthony has become positively MOROSE.

morsitation *(mor-si-TAY-shun), noun*
The act of biting or gnawing.
The foundation of the building shows the MORSITATION of rodents, making it necessary to replace many of the wooden beams.

motif *(mow-TEEF), noun*
A dominant or frequently repeated theme, design, image, or idea.
> *The Whittingtons' china has a diamond-shaped MOTIF that is a testament to how the family made its fortune.*

M

mot juste *(MOW-zshoost), noun*
The perfect word or phrase to communicate precisely what you mean to say.
> *Years of elocution lessons have left Paulina capable of leavening every occasion with a suitable MOT JUSTE.*

mountenance *(MAWN-ten-ans), noun*
Distance.
> *It is no great MOUNTENANCE to the next town as the crow flies, but the road winds a great deal.*

mulct *(mulct), verb*
To punish with a fine or by taking something away.
> *The judge threatened to MULCT the building's owner substantial damages if he did not compensate his tenants for their loss in the fire.*

mulligan *(MULL-ih-gihn), noun*
Taking a shot over in golf.
> *"I'll take a MULLIGAN," Jeff said cheerily after whiffing his first drive.*

multifarious *(mull-tih-FAIR-ee-us), adjective*
Varied; wide-ranging; versatile; covering many different areas or fields.
> *Yvonne's MULTIFARIOUS talents include showing horses, lacrosse, and opera singing.*

multilateral *(mull-tih-LAH-terr-ul), adjective*
An agreement or accord requiring two nations or states to take the same position or action on an issue or problem.
> *A pacifist, he frequently spoke out for MULTILATERAL nuclear disarmament.*

mundify *(MUHN-duh-fy), verb*
To clean; to disinfect.
> *Now that the patient has finally left, we'll have to MUNDIFY his room before the next occupant shows up.*

munificent *(myoo-NIFF-uh-suhnt), adjective*
Characterized by great generosity.
> *The Pattersons are so MUNIFICENT that they give to charity year-round rather than merely at times when giving offers tax benefits.*

muse *(MEWS), noun*
The source of one's creative or artistic inspiration, named after the mythical Greek *Muses* said to be patrons of the fine arts.
> *"O for a MUSE of fire, that would ascend / The brightest heaven of invention."*
> *—William Shakespeare, English playwright*

mutable *(MYOO-tuh-bull), adjective*
Subject to change at a moment's notice.
> *"For is the same! For, be it joy or sorrow, / The path of its departure still is free: / Man's yesterday may ne'er be like his morrow; / Nought may endure but MUTA-BILITY"* *—Percy Bysshe Shelley, English Romantic poet*

myriad *(MIR-ee-ud), noun*
An abundance of possibilities, selections, choices, or options.
> *The MYRIAD possibilities inherent in selling her ex-husband's family diamonds for ten million dollars boggled Elizabeth's mind.*

"The comic spirit is given to us in order that we may analyze, weigh, and clarify things in us which NETTLE us, or which we are outgrowing, or trying to reshape."

———

Thornton Wilder, American playwright and novelist

nabalitic *(nah-buh-LIH-tik), adjective*
Churlish or miserly.
> *Scrooge may be the most NABALITIC character in all of fiction.*

N

nacelle *(NAY-sell), noun*
The pod-shaped outer hull of an airplane engine.
> *Bentley always has his family crest imprinted on the NACELLE of each of his private planes.*

nadir *(NAY-der), noun*
Rock-bottom, the lowest of the low, the worst a thing can get or become.
> *We always have to attend the Wallingtons' Christmas party, due to their standing, but, in truth, that boringly dreadful event is always the NADIR of our social calendar.*

naevous *(NI-vus), adjective*
Spotted or freckled.
> *The redhead's skin was NAEVOUS, but the freckles added to her attractiveness.*

nankeen *(nan-KEEN), noun*
A buff-colored cotton cloth.
> *NANKEEN originated in China, and many Chinese clothes were made from it.*

nanosecond *(NAN-oh-sek-uhnd), noun*
A time period equal to one billionth of a second.
> *Amanda's new diamond-encrusted watch not only has a second hand but also a NANOSECOND hand.*

nappe *(NAP), noun*
A mass of rock extending along a horizontal fault.
> *Our hike took us to a NAPPE that, from our geologic map, we knew was poised directly over the San Andreas Fault line.*

narcolepsy *(NAR-ko-lep-see), noun*
A disease that causes you to fall asleep rather suddenly.
> *NARCOLEPSY caused him to nod off frequently in social situations.*

narcose *(NAHR-kos), adjective*
Characterized by stupor.
> *The students sank into their usual NARCOSE state as soon as the teacher began talking.*

narrowback *(NAIR-oh-bak), noun*
Someone of slight build, unsuited to manual labor.
> *The 162-pound man applied for the position on the loading dock, but the supervisor deemed him too much of a NARROWBACK to handle it.*

narthex *(NAR-theks), noun*
An enclosed lobby between the entrance and the nave of a church.
> *The bride and her father waited in the NARTHEX to begin their journey up the aisle.*

nascent *(NAY-sent), adjective*
Having just been born or invented and still in the early stages of growth and development.
> *It's always amusing to watch the nouveau riche during the NASCENT period of their adjustment to luxury.*

natation *(ney-TEY-shun), noun*
The act of swimming.
> *The track meet included running events and a significant amount of NATATION for the athletes to prove their all-around skills.*

nationalism *(NAH-shin-ul-iz-um), noun*
The idea that citizens should take great pride in their country and support it to the hilt; extreme patriotism.
> *Albert Einstein called NATIONALISM "the measles of mankind."*

natter *(NAH-ter), verb*
To talk ceaselessly; babble.
> *The way Emily NATTERS endlessly about her family's new yacht is revolting to those of us who have owned several yachts over the years.*

naucify *(NAW-sih-fy), verb*
To despise.
> *Although he had been her mentor, Arlene could not help but NAUCIFY Mr. Peterson after he made an unwanted advance to her.*

naufrageous *(nah-FREY-jus), adjective*
In a state of ruin.
> *The NAUFRAGEOUS old house was slowly collapsing under its own weight.*

naupathia *(nuh-PATH-ee-uh)*, *noun*
Seasickness.
> *My mother inevitably gets NAUPATHIA on boats.*

naze *(NEZ)*, *noun*
Cape or headland.
> *Looking ahead, they could see the NAZE stretching out from the mainland in a long curve.*

neap *(NEEP)*, *noun*
Tides between spring tides, in which water level is lowest.
> *The line of rocks and shells showed the line of the NEAP tide on the beach.*

nebbish *(NEB-ish)*, *noun*
Mocking term for a pitiful, inadequate person.
> *In his early movies, Woody Allen often played a NEBBISH who was afraid of everything, especially women.*

Nebuchadnezzar *(neb-uh-ked-NEZ-er)*, *noun*
A king mentioned in the Old Testament of the Bible who destroyed Jerusalem and exiled the Israelites to Babylonia.
> *"And NEBUCHADNEZZAR was driven from men, and did eat grass as oxen, and his body was wet with the dew of heaven, till his hairs were grown like eagles' feathers, and his nails like birds' claws." —Daniel 4:33*

nebulous *(NEB-yoo-luhs)*, *adjective*
An idea or plan that is vague and not well thought out; ill-defined; lacking concretes.
> *Jay's plans for what he would do when he graduated college were NEBULOUS at best.*

necessitate *(nuh-SESS-ih-tate)*, *verb*
To make necessary; to obligate.
> *"Each coming together of man and wife, even if they have been mated for many years, should be a fresh adventure; each winning should NECESSITATE a fresh wooing." —Marie Carmichael Stopes, British scientist and birth-control pioneer*

necrogenic *(nek-ruh-jen-ik)*, *adjective*
Living in or originating in dead matter.
> *Maggots are a NECROGENIC life form, since they live and multiply in rotten meat.*

necromancy *(NEHK-roh-man-see), noun*
The ability to gain new knowledge by communicating with the dead; magic and trickery in general.
"The so-called science of poll-taking is not a science at all but mere NECRO-MANCY." —E.B. White, American author

necrotomy *(neh-KROHT-uh-me), noun*
The dissection of a corpse.
The class requiring NECROTOMY gave him the creeps; he hated dead bodies.

nefandous *(neh-FAN-dus), adjective*
Something about which it's forbidden to speak.
The NEFANDOUS deeds to the villain remained unrecounted until long after his death.

nefarious *(nih-FARE-ee-us), adjective*
Inherently evil, malicious, and unjust.
"You were preceded by your NEFARIOUS reputation," the sheriff said to the gunslinger who had just sidled up to the bar.

nemaline *(NEH-muh-leen), adjective*
Thread-shaped.
The NEMALINE fibers of the sea creature extended several feet from its body, where they trapped unwary fish.

nemesis *(nem-UH-sis), noun*
An opponent one is unable to defeat.
"How wonderful to live with one's NEMESIS! You may be miserable, but you feel forever in the right." —Erica Jong, American author and teacher

nemesism *(NEH-meh-sih-zum), noun*
Frustration directed against yourself.
As an expression of my NEMESISM, I beat my head against the wall.

nemoral *(neh-MORE-uhl), adjective*
Living in the woods.
Nymphs and satyrs are NEMORAL, being rarely found outside sylvan glades.

neoconservative *(nee-oh-kon-SERVE-ah-tiz-um)*, *noun*
A liberal who has become a conservative.
> *We've removed Bradley from our list of social contacts because he has become such a NEOCONSERVATIVE.*

neogamist *(nee-AH-guh-mist)*, *noun*
Someone who's recently married.
> *The young man was a NEOGAMIST and could scarcely be out of the sight of his new bride.*

neologism *(nee-AHL-uh-jiz-um)*, *noun*
A new word, or an "old" word used in a new way.
> *William Shakespeare coined such NEOLOGISMS as "gossip," "swagger," and "domineering."*

neomort *(NEE-oh-mort)*, *noun*
Someone who is brain dead.
> *The family made the painful decision to disconnect the breathing apparatus from their NEOMORT grandfather.*

neonatal *(nee-oh-NAY-tul)*, *adjective*
Of, or relating to newborn children.
> *Honestly, the Atkinsons treat their grown children as though they still require NEONATAL care. No wonder they never get invited to any of our galas.*

neophyte *(NEE-uh-fight)*, *noun*
A beginner or novice.
> *"Like footmen and upstairs maids, wine stewards are portrayed as acolytes of the privileged, ever eager to intimidate the NEOPHYTE and spurn the unwary."*
> *—Frank J. Prial, former* New York Times *wine columnist*

neoteny1 *(nee-OH-ten-ee)*, *noun*
Keeping an ancestral physical feature.
> *This nose of mine has been passed down through the generations, the result of NEOTENY.*

neoteny2 *(nee-OH-ten-ee)*, *noun*
Retention of juvenile characteristics in an adult.
> *In* Mad Max, *Mel Gibson fights a huge man suffering from NEOTENY.*

nephology *(neh-FOL-uh-jee), noun*
The study of clouds.

> *The meteorologist had specialized in NEPHOLOGY, so he always knew what weather the clouds signified.*

nepotism *(NEH-poh-tiz-um), noun*
The practice of a business owner or manager giving favorable treatment to his family; e.g., hiring his son for a summer job, giving the company's advertising work to his wife's ad agency, etc.

> *Rampant NEPOTISM in the company prevented most of the employees from rising very far up the ranks.*

nether *(NETH-uhr), adjective*
Located below or under something else.

> *"I know a lady in Venice would have walked barefoot to Palestine for a touch of his NETHER lip." —William Shakespeare, English playwright*

nettle *(NET-uhl), verb*
To provoke, irritate, or annoy.

> *"The comic spirit is given to us in order that we may analyze, weigh, and clarify things in us which NETTLE us, or which we are outgrowing, or trying to reshape." —Thornton Wilder, American playwright and novelist*

nettlesome *(NET-l-suhm), adjective*
Irksome; irritating.

> *I find the waiting for word of my promotion extremely NETTLESOME; why don't they just tell me and get it over with?*

neuropathy *(noo-RAH-pah-thee), noun*
Pain in nerve endings, most often caused by diabetes.

> *There is no cure for NEUROPATHY.*

nexus *(NEK-sus), noun*
A linkage or connection between two or more things.

> *"Every time a message seems to grab us, and we think, 'I just might try it,' we are at the NEXUS of choice and persuasion that is advertising." —Andrew Hacker, American media critic*

N

niaiserie *(nye-zree), noun*
Simplicity; foolishness.
> *She was stunned by the uncharacteristic NIAISERIE she found in the intellectual's latest book.*

niblick *(NIH-blik), noun*
Wooden golf club for playing shots from bad lies.
> *A NIBLICK is equivalent to a nine iron.*

nidamental *(nih-duh-MEN-tul), adjective*
Pertaining to eggs.
> *The platypus is unique among mammals in that it is NIDAMENTAL in the bearing of its young.*

nidify *(NIH-dih-fie), verb*
To build a nest.
> *Most, but not all, birds NIDIFY to create a place of safety in which to bear their young.*

niggling *(NIG-ling), adjective*
Demanding a great deal of care, attention, or time; or, trifling and insignificant.
> *People just don't understand how difficult it for us to attend to all the NIGGLING needs of our servants.*

nihilism *(NIE-uh-lizz-uhm), noun*
The belief that nothing can be known with absolute certainty, resulting in an intense skepticism of almost everything, especially religion and moral principles.
> *"NIHILISM is best done by professionals." —Iggy Pop, American singer and songwriter*

nimbose *(NIM-bows), adjective*
Cloudy; stormy.
> *The NIMBOSE weather kept most of us indoors.*

nimbus *(NIM-bus), noun*
A halo of light surrounding the head of a saint or other holy person.
> *"Sally is such a goody two-shoes, you'd think she would have a NIMBUS on top of her head," Nancy said to the girls.*

nitid *(NIT-id), adjective*
Bright and lustrous.
>*Brock and Jenny flew through NITID moonbeams in Brock's new Gulfstream GIV personal jet.*

nivellate *(NIH-vel-ate), verb*
To level by planing.
>*Since the wood's surface was rough-hewn, the carpenter found it necessary to NIVELLATE it before using it.*

nixie *(NICK-see), noun*
A direct-mail piece that is undeliverable usually because the address is incorrect or the person has moved.
>*Most mailing-list brokers guarantee no more than 7 percent NIXIES when you rent a list from them.*

noblesse oblige *(no-BLESS-oh-BLEEZH), noun*
An act of generosity, charity, or kindness performed by a rich person for the benefit of someone less fortunate than himself, viewed by the giver as paying the universe back for his good fortune.
>*Donald gave the young man a job not out of a sense of pity or guilt, but out of a sense of NOBLESSE OBLIGE.*

noctivagant *(knock-TIH-vih-gant), adjective*
Night wandering.
>*NOCTIVAGANT animals include raccoons and bats.*

noctuary *(NOK-tchoo-air-ee), noun*
A journal of nightly occurrences.
>*In light of the disturbing events of the past few nights, I've decided to keep a NOCTUARY.*

noisette *(nwah-ZET), noun*
A loin or fillet of meat.
>*For dinner tonight we're having NOISETTES of lamb with truffled mashed potatoes.*

nomenclature *(NO-men-klay-cherr), noun*
A labeling or naming system used in a specialized field or industry.
>*Even an activity as seemingly simple as macramé has a NOMENCLATURE all it's own, indecipherable to the layperson or newbie.*

nominal *(NAHM-ih-nl), adjective*
A thing of relatively minor importance; an insignificant amount or volume of something.

> *For a NOMINAL fee, the store delivers your new widescreen TV to your home and sets it up for you.*

nominalism *(NAHM-ih-nl-iz-um), noun*
A philosophy that denies the existence of universal truths.

> *Some scientists suspect that, rather than being universal, the laws of physics may vary in different regions of the universe—a strong supporting argument for NOMINALISM.*

nominative *(NAHM-ih-na-tiv), noun*
Grammatical case used to express the subject of a sentence.

> *In "John throws the ball," "John" is in the NOMINATIVE.*

nonagenarian *(none-uh-jen-AIR-ee-en), noun*
A person in his or her nineties.

> *When you're a NONAGENARIAN, it begins to occur to you that you could in fact live to be one hundred.*

non compos mentis *(NAHN-KAHM-pohs-MEN-tiss), adjective*
Crazy; insane; not in one's right mind.

> *When Bryce suggested he was considering the ministry rather than joining the family bond business, we were certain he was NON COMPOS MENTIS.*

nondescript *(non-dih-SKRIPT), adjective*
Lacking distinction; ordinary.

> *"Actors ought to be larger than life. You come across quite enough ordinary, NONDESCRIPT people in daily life and I don't see why you should be subjected to them on the stage too." —Donald Sinden, British actor*

nonentity *(non-EN-tih-tee), noun*
A person or thing considered completely unimportant.

> *Ever since Cassandra scorned us at the Brackingtons' Thanksgiving gala, we have taken to treating her as a NONENTITY.*

nonpareil *(non-pah-RAYLE), adjective*
Without equal or peer.
We could tell Jeanette was a typical parvenu when she attempted to convince us that Bennington Posh Couture golf bags are NONPAREIL.

nonpartisan *(non-PAHR-tih-zuhn), adjective*
Not in support of a particular political party or special interest group.
The Vallinghams pride themselves in being NONPARTISAN, but they have never been known to vote even for a moderate Democrat.

nonplussed *(non-plust), adjective*
In modern usage, not being bothered by commotion; undisturbed by what is happening around you; in traditional usage, the opposite of the modern definition.
The construction on the bridge left him NONPLUSSED, because he enjoyed listening to books on tape in his car.

non sequitur *(nahn-SEH-kwit-ur), noun*
A conclusion or statement that does not seem to follow from that which preceded it.
Hilary's belief that she was now welcome in our group was, clearly, a NON SEQUITUR on her part.

noosphere *(NO-oh-sfear), noun*
The part of the biosphere affected by humans.
In the movie Total Recall, *ancient machines were used to manipulate the NOOSPHERE by enriching the Martian atmosphere with oxygen.*

nootropic *(new-oh-TROH-pick), noun*
A medication, vitamin, herb, or mineral that can improve cognition.
Many popular NOOTROPIC supplements contain B vitamins.

normalize *(NORM-ah-lyze), verb*
To make normal, or correct a defect.
Diplomats NORMALIZE relations between adversarial nations.

nosology *(no-ZAH-low-gee), noun*
Classification of diseases.
NOSOLOGY gives doctors a standard way of referencing illnesses.

nostrum *(NAH-strum), noun*
An ineffective solution that is a quick fix or Band-Aid, covering up a problem or masking its symptoms but never addressing its root cause for a permanent fix.
  "America's present need is not NOSTRUMS but normalcy." —Warren G. Harding, American president

nougat *(NEW-git), noun*
A candy made from sugar or honey, nuts, and egg white.
  NOUGATS are delicious but rarely included in boxes of mixed candies.

nouveau riche *(noo-voh-REESH), adjective, noun*
A person who has recently acquired wealth.
  The most distinguished families in the club snubbed him because he was NOUVEAU RICHE.

novation *(no-VAY-shin), noun*
The release of one party from a contract with another party being added to the contract as a substitute.
  When Eric defaulted on his rent, a NOVATION was made when his dad cosigned the rental agreement.

novity *(NAH-vih-tee), adjective*
Newness.
  The NOVITY of the experience had worn off, and I was now bored.

noxious *(NOCK-shuss), adjective*
Morally harmful and pernicious.
  Even with his wealth, good looks, and charm, Steven has such a NOXIOUS personality that we always feel awful after spending time with him.

nuance *(NOO-ahnts), noun*
A subtle difference in meaning, expression, or tone.
  "[Venice] in winter is rich with the bittersweet NUANCE and somber beauty of the once-was." —Terry Weeks, American travel writer

nubile *(NOO-bile), adjective*
Of sexually developed and attractive youth.
  We have explained time and again to Melinda that she must get a personal trainer like the rest of us to be truly NUBILE.

nuchal *(NEW-chul), adjective*
Relating to the nape of the neck.
NUCHAL hairs stood on end when he became frightened.

nuciferous *(noo-SIH-fir-us), adjective*
Nut bearing.
The nutmeg is a NUCIFEROUS plant whose nuts are ground to make spice.

nugatory *(NOO-guh-tore-ee), adjective*
Trifling, worthless, and ineffective.
We spend our time like most, with the NUGATORY pastimes of polo, tennis on grass courts, and weekends in Europe.

nullify *(NUHL-uh-fie), verb*
To make something valueless or ineffective.
We keep our collections under lock and key because, sometimes, merely breathing on them NULLIFIES their value.

nuncio *(NUN-see-oh), noun*
Diplomatic representative of the pope.
The papal NUNCIO expressed His Holiness's thoughts on the subject of global warming.

nutant *(NOO-tunt), adjective*
In botany, drooping.
The branches of the weeping willow are NUTANT, some of them even brushing the ground.

nyctograph *(NIK-tow-graf), noun*
A card containing a grid of cells that guides you in writing in the dark, using a peculiar alphabet invented for that purpose.
Lewis Carroll invented the NYCTOGRAPH.

nymph *(NIMF), noun*
A spirit linked to a particular place or element.
"Reason is a supple NYMPH, and slippery as a fish by nature." —D.H. Lawrence, British author

"The bottom of being is left logically OPAQUE to us, as something which we simply come upon and find, and about which (if we wish to act) we should pause and wonder as little as possible."

———

William James, American psychologist and philosopher

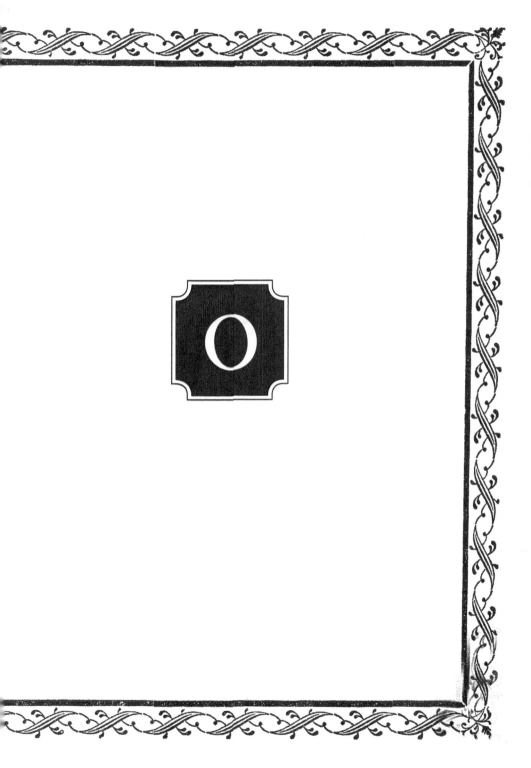

oakum *(OH-come), noun*
A stringy fiber made by pulling apart old ropes.
A mixture of OAKUM and tar is good for caulking.

obambulate *(ohb-AM-byoo-leyt), verb*
To wander about.
To kill time, I decided to OBAMBULATE around the hotel lobby.

obedible *(oh-BE-dih-bl), adjective*
Able to obey.
She's an OBEDIBLE child who always does what she's told. I'm a bit worried about her.

obelisk *(OB-uh-lisk), noun*
Four-sided vertical construction, tapering toward the top.
Near Hagia Sophia, in Istanbul, there stands an ancient Egyptian OBELISK brought by the Romans.

obdurate *(OB-doo-rit), adjective*
Stubborn and unyielding.
"The fates are not quite OBDURATE; / They have a grim, sardonic way / Of granting them who supplicate / The thing they wanted yesterday." —Roselle Mercier Montgomery, American poet

obeisance *(oh-BEE-sance), noun*
Deferential respect or homage, or an act or gesture expressing the same.
Rachael practiced OBEISANCE by allowing the elderly woman to sit in her plush opera box rather than in the mezzanine.

obelize *(OH-bel-eyes), verb*
To mark noteworthy passages in a book or other reading material.
College students OBELIZE textbooks with yellow highlighters.

obfuscate *(OB-few-skate), verb*
To talk or write about a subject in a way that deliberately makes it unclear, selectively omits certain facts, or communicates wrong ideas or impressions, so that the listener or reader does not grasp the whole truth of the situation.
Despite his Ivy League education, Alexander seems able only to OBFUSCATE any subject upon which he touches.

obi *(OH-bee), noun*
Sash tied around a kimono.
> *The colorfulness of the kimono was emphasized by the plain black OBI she wore around it.*

objectify *(ob-JEK-tih-fie), verb*
To treat as an object.
> *Many have said that our culture tends to OBJECTIFY women by not treating them as fully human.*

objectivism *(ub-JEK-tih-vi-zim), noun*
A philosophy espoused by author Ayn Rand in which people should act in their own self-interest rather than in the interest of the collective or group.
> *In direct opposition to OBJECTIVISM, Spock in* Star Trek *said the needs of the many outweigh the needs of the few—or the one.*

objurgatory *(ahb-jer-ga-tor-ee), adjective*
A critical attitude voicing or implying an objection or complaint.
> *"I can to some extent sympathize with the OBJURGATORY tone of certain critics who feel that I write too much." —Joyce Carol Oates, American author*

oblique *(oh-BLEAK), adjective*
Indirectly or deviously achieved.
> *If direct appeals do not work, Amanda is always quick to use OBLIQUE methods in order to get her father to buy her whatever luxury item she wants.*

oblong *(AHB-long), adjective*
Elongated.
> *Plastic Man was an OBLONG superhero.*

obloquy *(AHB-luh-kwee), noun*
Verbal abuse; insult; vehement criticism.
> *My mother, herself a painter, heaped OBLOQUY upon abstract art.*

obnubilate *(ob-NOO-buh-leyt), verb*
To obscure; to cloud over.
> *I won't let you OBNUBILATE the purpose of this discussion by trying to divert my attention.*

obsecrate *(OB-se-kreyt), verb*
To beg; beseech.
His attempts to OBSECRATE for the life of his sister were in vain.

obsequious *(uhb-SEE-kwi-us), adjective*
Subservient; eager to listen and to please others to an excessive degree; behaving in the manner of a servant or slave.
"[The political mind] is a strange mixture of vanity and timidity, of an OBSEQUIOUS attitude at one time and a delusion of grandeur at another time.
—*Calvin Coolidge, American president*

obsign *(ob-SINE), verb*
To confirm by signing or sealing.
In the name of the king, I OBSIGN this decree and order it made known throughout the land.

obsolescence *(ob-suh-LESS-uhnts), noun*
The state of being no longer useful.
Roderick found, to his dismay, that some of the new Maserati models had lapsed into OBSOLESCENCE almost as soon as they hit the showroom floor.

obstinate *(AHB-stih-nit), adjective*
Inflexible in one's opinions and attitudes; refusing to change or accede to the wishes of others.
"The male sex still constitutes in many ways the most OBSTINATE vested interest one can find." —Francis Pakenham, British social reformer

obstreperous *(ob-STREP-er-us), adjective*
Describes a troublemaker who is noisy, unruly, or otherwise attracts attention in his endeavor to be difficult.
Two OBSTREPEROUS employees made the training class a nightmare for the instructor.

obtenebrate *(ob-TEN-uh-breyt), verb*
To cast a shadow over.
The evil fairy's threat to the baby OBTENEBRATED the celebration of the child's christening.

obtuse *(ahb-TOOS), adjective*
Lacking understanding, intelligence, and perception; unable to comprehend; having a dense mind.
Thomas was so OBTUSE, he didn't realize his inappropriate behavior was making his friends uncomfortable.

obvallate *(OB-va-leyt), adjective*
Surrounded by a wall.
York is one of the few OBVALLATE cities left in England; one can walk large portions of its medieval wall.

obvert *(ob-VURT), verb*
Turn something to show a different surface.
Rather than repair the furniture, the homeowner merely chose to OBVERT it while showing the house to prospective buyers.

obviate *(OB-vee-ate), verb*
To anticipate, and therefore prevent, difficulties or disadvantages.
We changed the location of our fall gala at the last minute, OBVIATING the need to cut anyone from our ever-expanding guest list.

ocarina *(ok-uh-REE-nuh), noun*
A type of musical wind instrument.
Harpo Marx was fond of playing the oboe and the OCARINA in his movies.

occlude *(oh-KLOOD), verb*
To block or obstruct; to close off a passage or entranceway.
Debris from the second-floor construction OCCLUDED the entryway to the laundry room in Linda's beach house.

occultation *(ahk-uhl-TAY-shin), noun*
The act of hiding or blocking from view.
With disguises offering a bit of needed OCCULTATION, we were able to hit Manhattan's hot spots away from the glare of the dreaded paparazzi.

odal *(OH-dull), noun*
Absolute ownership of a property that is beyond dispute and can never be revoked.
> *Among the Norse, land allotted to a warrior at the time of conquest became ODAL after his family had held it for three generations.*

odalisque *(OH-dah-lisk), noun*
A female slave in a harem.
> *Liam Neeson's daughter is kidnapped to be used as an ODALISQUE in the movie* Taken.

odious *(OH-dee-us), adjective*
To be so offensive or disgusting that people are repulsed or experience revulsion.
> *"To depend upon a profession is a less ODIOUS form of slavery than to depend upon a father." —Virginia Woolf, British essayist and novelist*

odoriferous *(oh-duh-RiF-err-us), adjective*
Bad smelling; foul.
> *Eleanor believed she would enjoy her weekend trek through the South American rainforest, but she found the animals too noisy, the constant rain unpleasant, and the forest's ODORIFEROUS vegetation distasteful.*

oeniphile *(EE-nuh-file), noun*
A connoisseur of wines.
> *Despite his relatively young age, Brad's family has brought him up to be a consummate OENIPHILE.*

oeuvre *(OO-vruh), noun*
An artist's, writer's, or composer's body of work, treated as a whole.
> *Esmerelda is familiar with and adores all of Puccini's OEUVRE, but many find his operas overly mawkish.*

offal *(OH-full), noun*
Rotting waste; decaying organic matter. In general, anything considered garbage or refuse.
> *"I have often told you that I am that little fish who swims about under a shark and, I believe, lives indelicately on its OFFAL." —Zelda Fitzgerald, American author*

officious *(oh-FISH-ee-us), adjective*
Asserting authority or power in an obnoxious, overbearing, or pompous manner.

> *"There is immunity in reading, immunity in formal society, in office routine, in the company of old friends and in the giving of OFFICIOUS help to strangers, but there is no sanctuary in one bed from the memory of another." —Cyril Connolly, British literary critic and writer*

ogle *(OH-guhl), verb*
To look at in an amorous or impertinent way.

> *No one would want to trade places with us if they only knew how tiresome it becomes to have the paparazzi constantly OGLING you.*

oikology *(oy-KAH-loh-jee), noun*
The study of housekeeping.

> *The university is considering endowing the Betty Crocker Seat of OIKOLOGY.*

oleaginous *(oh-LIG-in-us), adjective*
Having an offensively ingratiating manner.

> *Politicians often display OLEAGINOUS behavior in election years.*

olfactory *(ole-FAK-tore-ee), adjective*
Related to the sense of smell.

> *Miranda and Jonathan savored the OLFACTORY pleasures wafting from early-opening bakeries on the Upper West Side.*

oligarchy *(OH-lih-gar-kee), noun*
A nation, state, or other place where the population is governed by a relatively small group of people, especially when all are members of the same family.

> *Most family-owned businesses are OLIGARCHIES, not democracies.*

oligomania *(oh-lih-go-MEY-nee-ah), noun*
Obsession with a few thoughts or ideas.

> *That Russell is obsessive-compulsive resulted in a university career characterized by OLIGOMANIA.*

O

oligopoly *(oh-lih-GAH-poll-lee), noun*
Control of an industry, sector, or market by a small number of companies dominating that particular niche.
> *One can argue that Intel and Microsoft collectively are an OLIGOPOLY in personal computing.*

olio *(OH-lee-oh), noun*
A mix of unrelated ingredients.
> *For supper, mother tossed everything she could find in a pot and boiled it, then dished out the unappetizing OLIO for us to eat.*

ombudsman *(ohm-budz-min), noun*
A person who is charged with mediating disputes between businesses and consumers, students and a university, etc.
> *All it took to get Brock off academic probation at UPenn was to have his father remind the OMBUDSMAN of how much money the family had donated to the university over the years.*

omnipotent *(ahm-NIP-uh-tuhnt), adjective*
All powerful.
> *"An OMNIPOTENT God is the only being with no reason to lie." —Mason Cooley, American author*

omniscient *(ahm-NIH-shent), adjective*
Describes someone who knows everything.
> *"The god of love, if omnipotent and OMNISCIENT, must be the god of cancer and epilepsy as well." —George Bernard Shaw, Irish playwright*

omnium-gatherum *(om-nee-uhm-GATH-er-um), noun*
A miscellaneous collection.
> *The hoarder's piles of possessions seemed to represent a kind of OMNIUM-GATHERUM of the previous half century.*

omnivore *(AHM-nih-vore), noun*
An animal that eats both plants and other animals.
> *I ordered a delicious steak salad with crumbled blue cheese—an OMNIVORE'S delight.*

onanism *(OH-nuh-nihz-um), noun*
Masturbation.

Like most teenage boys, Jason engaged in regular ONANISM in his bedroom, until he was caught by his mother.

onerous *(OH-nerr-us), adjective*
Describes a difficult task or heavy responsibility that one does not desire.

Caring for his son's large aquarium quickly went from an interesting hobby to an ONEROUS burden.

onomastics *(oh-nuh-MAS-tiks), noun*
The study of proper names.

ONOMASTICS often gives historians valuable clues about the geographic spread of various ethnic groups.

onomatopoeia *(on-uh-ma-tuh-PEE-uh), noun*
Words that sound like, or suggest, their meaning.

The spring gala, with its popping corks, fizzing champagne glasses, and thumping music, was a cornucopia of ONOMATOPOEIA.

onus *(OH-nuss), noun*
Obligation; responsibility; duty; burden.

The ONUS for choosing the color scheme for our new lacrosse uniforms fell ultimately to Tabitha, who had previously chosen the design for our polo uniforms.

onymy *(ON-ih-me), noun*
A system of scientific nomenclature.

Physics has, over the course of many centuries, developed a complex ONYMY to explain the universe.

oose *(ooss), noun*
A piece of link or fuzz.

Because of our pets, our living room coach is covered with OOSE.

opaque *(oh-PAYK), adjective*
Hard to understand; obscure.
> *"The bottom of being is left logically OPAQUE to us, as something which we simply come upon and find, and about which (if we wish to act) we should pause and wonder as little as possible."* —William James, American psychologist and philosopher

operose *(OP-uh-roass), adjective*
Hard-working and industrious.
> *What's the point of being OPEROSE when our social connections help us to achieve success with little effort?*

opine *(oh-PYNE), verb*
To give your opinion.
> *The way that Charlotte OPINES about fashion, you'd think she created couture rather than just purchasing it.*

opiniaster *(oh-PIN-ee-as-tur), adjective*
Opinionated.
> *The OPINIASTER character of most political discourse makes civilized debate difficult.*

opinionee *(oh-pin-yin-EE), noun*
One who receives or purchases an option.
> *By paying for the right to purchase a property within the next year, you become an OPINIONEE.*

oppidan *(OP-ih-dun), adjective*
Urban.
> *The OPPIDAN setting for the conflict ensured that it would involve a very large number of people—cities being more populated than the countryside.*

opprobrium *(uh-PRO-bree-uhm), noun*
Disgrace incurred by outrageously shameful conduct.
> *Natasha incurred OPPROBRIUM when, in a fit of anger, she deliberately smashed her Waterford crystal wine glass at the Smythingtons' annual Thanksgiving gala.*

The Big Book of Words You Should Know to Sound Smart

oppugn *(uh-PYOON), verb*
Attack with criticism.
> *You have OPPUGNED my character and that of my family, something that goes beyond the boundaries of acceptable behavior.*

opsimath *(OHP-see-math), noun*
A person who begins to learn or study later in life.
> *After founding a software company, he became an opsimath and earned an MD.*

opulent *(AHP-yoo-lent), adjective*
Reflecting wealth and affluence.
> *Donald Trump showcases his OPULENT lifestyle by wearing designer suits, drinking Cristal champagne, and traveling in private airplanes.*

opus *(OH-puss), noun*
A major work of music written by a composer.
> *The Breckinridges commissioned the composer's next OPUS, which will be debuted at the family's fall ball.*

oragius *(o-REY-jus), adjective*
Stormy.
> *The onset of ORAGIUS weather meant we were forced to remain indoors for much of the summer.*

orator *(OR-ah-ter), noun*
A skilled and persuasive public speaker.
> *Tom overestimated his abilities as an ORATOR and, consequently, stayed at the podium far longer than the audience wanted him to.*

oratory *(ORE-uh-tawr-ee), noun*
Skill in public speaking.
> *William Jennings Bryan, Woodrow Wilson's secretary of state, was known for his golden-tongued ORATORY.*

ordinance *(OR-dih-nance), noun*
A specific law or regulation.
> *The lavish tree house Roger built for his kids was in clear violation of at least half a dozen local ORDINANCES.*

ordinate *(OR-dih-nut), noun*
On a plane, a point's distance from the x-axis measured in relation to the y-axis.
The ship's ORDINATE was measured by the navigator, using a grid representing the area of ocean.

O

orgiastic *(or-jee-AS-tick), adjective*
Arousing unrestrained emotional release.
William becomes loathsomely ORGIASTIC when he attends and bids at art auctions.

oriflamme *(ORE-ih-flaym), noun*
A symbol of courage or devotion.
In The Wizard of Oz, *the wizard gives the lion a medal as an ORIFLAMME.*

orison *(OR-ih-sun), noun*
Prayer.
"Only the stuttering rifles' rapid rattle / Can patter out their hasty ORISONS." —Wilfred Owen, English poet, "Anthem for Doomed Youth"

orotund *(OR-uh-tund), adjective*
Characterizes a voice distinguished by strength, fullness, and clearness.
In a beguilingly OROTUND voice, the conductor offered a synopsis of the evening's opera.

orphrey *(AWR-free), noun*
An ornamental band on an ecclesiastical vestment.
The bishop accused the vicar of having too many ORPHREYS on his chasuble.

orthodox *(OR-thuh-docks), adjective*
Mainstream; conventional; adhering to the strictest interpretation of a law or religion.
ORTHODOX medicine has long ignored the obvious effect diet and nutrition have on health and illness.

orthography *(or-THAG-ruh-fee), noun*
The practice of good spelling.
The boy's ORTHOGRAPHY was impeccable—hardly surprising since he had won the school spelling bee three years running.

orthoscopic *(or-tho-sckop-ik), adjective*
Showing a true flat image with no distortion.
The binoculars gave an ORTHOSCOPIC view of the distant town and lake.

oscillate *(AHSS-uh-layt), verb*
To change one's mind frequently about beliefs and opinions.
We can hardly keep up with Lydia's choices regarding the quality of luxury jewelers because she OSCILLATES from week to week.

oscilloscope *(ah-SILL-ih-skope), noun*
An instrument for measuring sound, electricity, and other forces and substances that propagate in waves.
An OSCILLOSCOPE is a vital bench instrument for scientists.

oscitant *(AHS-ih-tent), adjective*
Yawning; drowsy.
The long, warm afternoon made him OSCITANT, and he paid little attention to the teacher's droning voice.

osculant *(OS-kyuh-lunt), adjective*
Describes a passionate kiss.
"He planted a hell of a kiss on me: lips, tongue, the entire OSCULANT assemblage." —Charlaine Harris, New York Times *bestselling mystery writer*

osmosis *(oz-MOW-sis), noun*
A subtle and gradual assimilation of new knowledge based on one's proximity to another with greater knowledge.
Just hanging out with Bob, who was an A student, seemed to help Vincent improve his grades, as if he was learning what Bob knew through OSMOSIS.

ossify *(OS-ih-fahy), verb*
To harden like bone.
The loaf of bread had been left unwrapped for a week, causing it to OSSIFY until it was hard as a rock.

ostensibly *(ah-STEN-sih-blee), adverb*
Something that exists or has been done for what would seem an obvious reason.

The nouveau riche always seek to spend time with us, OSTENSIBLY to be absorbed into our world, but they will never fully be a part of our community.

ostentatious *(ah-sten-TAY-shus), adjective*
Pretentious; presented in a showy manner so as to impress others; visibly flaunting one's wealth or success.

"The man who is OSTENTATIOUS of his modesty is twin to the statue that wears a fig-leaf." —Mark Twain, American author

ostracize *(OS-truh-size), verb*
To exclude from society, friendship, community, etc.

Once we learned that Sasha had been planting stories about us in the society pages, we, of course, had to OSTRACIZE her permanently from our group.

outré *(oo-TRAY), adjective*
Radically unconventional; outside the limits of expected conduct or behavior.

"One of life's intriguing paradoxes is that hierarchical social order makes cheap rents and OUTRÉ artists' colonies possible." —Florence King, American author

overweening *(oh-ver-WEE-ning), adjective*
Extremely presumptuous, arrogant, and overconfident.

"Golf is an open exhibition of OVERWEENING ambition, courage deflated by stupidity, skill soured by a whiff of arrogance." —Alistair Cooke, British-born American journalist and broadcaster

oxidation *(oks-ih-DAY-shin), noun*
A chemical reaction that increases the oxygen content of a compound or material.

When Carlton viewed the wreck of the Titanic *from the window of a submersible, he was shocked to see how OXIDATION had ravaged the ship.*

oxymoron *(ok-see-MORE-on), noun*
A phrase made by combining two words that are contradictory or incongruous.

> *Melissa sheepishly used the OXYMORON "accidentally on purpose" to explain to her father why her emergency credit card included a charge for $500 Manolo Blahnik heels.*

oxyphonia *(oks-ee-FON-ee-ah), noun*
A high-pitched voice.

> *Tiny Tim was famous for his OXYPHONIA.*

"I want to kiss God on His nose
and watch Him sneeze / and so do
you. / Not out of disrespect. / Out
of PIQUE. / Out of a man-to-man
thing."

———

Anne Sexton, American poet and author

P

pabulous *(PAB-you-lus), adjective*
Pertaining to nourishment.
> *I could have wished for a more PABLOUS meal than Twinkies and artificial fruit juice.*

pabouche *(puh-boosh), noun*
A slipper or soft shoe.
> *Men in Persia and Turkey often wear a PABOUCHE.*

pacable *(PAK-uh-bul), adjective*
Easily appeased.
> *I'm far more PACABLE than my partner, who doesn't want to forgive your embezzlement.*

pachyderm *(PAK-ih-derm), noun*
Member of the elephant family including rhinoceros and hippopotamus.
> *The mighty PACHYDERM has often been illegally hunted for its ivory tusks.*

pachynsis *(pa-KIN-sis), noun*
In medicine, a thickening of an organ or tissue.
> *A symptom of diabetes is the PACHYNSIS of the walls of blood vessels, inhibiting the flow of blood.*

padella *(pa-DEL-uh), noun*
A large cup containing fatty material and a wick, used as a lamp.
> *The cathedral of St. Peter's in Rome uses PADELLAS to illuminate the darker corners of the church.*

padrone *(pa-DRONE-eh), noun*
Italian term for landowner, especially one who hires laborers.
> *The PADRONE kept his workers busy on his estate during the harvest season.*

paduasoy *(PAJ-oo-uh-soi), noun*
Fabric made of strong silk.
> *"When gentlemen wore ruffles, and gold-laced waistcoats of PADUASOY and taffeta." —Beatrix Potter, British author,* The Tailor of Gloucester

paedophobia *(pi-doh-FOH-be-uh), noun*
Fear of children.
Allison's stint as a volunteer at a childcare facility was enough to instill a lifelong PAEDOPHOBIA; she couldn't even stand to be in the same room with a child.

paginal *(PAJ-uh-nul), adjective*
Of or relating to pages.
The PAGINAL arrangement of the book seemed strange, since pages appeared to be numbered backwards.

paideutic *(pi-DOO-tik), adjective*
Having to do with educational theory.
John Dewey's PAIDEUTIC approach was revolutionary for its time, and he founded a school in Chicago to illustrate its practice.

paisley *(PEYZ-lee), noun*
A pattern made up of colorful, detailed figures.
In a throwback to the early 1970s, Mark wore bell-bottom jeans and a PAISLEY shirt.

palaeosophy *(pey-lee-AH-so-fee), noun*
Ancient philosophy or thought.
In our study of PALAEOSOPHY, we will include not only the Greeks but Zoroastrianism and ancient Eastern philosophers.

palamate *(PAL-uh-mayt), adjective*
Web-footed.
In the movie Waterworld, *Kevin Costner was a PALAMATE mutant with gills.*

palatine *(PAL-uh-tayn), noun*
An official of an imperial court.
The other courtiers observed the PALATINE to see how he reacted to the emperor's mood.

palaver *(pa-LAH-ver), noun*
A rambling, meandering stream-of-consciousness conversation spoken to prove or make a point.
Don't ask Eileen about collecting art. The result will be twenty minutes of mind-numbing PALAVER.

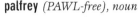

palfrey *(PAWL-free), noun*
A riding horse for a woman.
> *Lady Godiva rode a white PALFREY on her legendary journey through the streets of Coventry.*

palimpsest *(PAL-imp-sest), noun*
A parchment manuscript on which the text is written over older, earlier text, much like an oil portrait or landscape painted over another painting.
> *The newest addition to the Pattersons' rare manuscript collection turned out to be a PALIMPSEST, covering a text nearly 1,000 years old.*

palindrome *(pal-in-DROHM), noun*
A word or sentence that reads the same forwards as backwards.
> *At private school, Evelyn learned about PALINDROMES, including, "Madam, I'm Adam."*

palinode *(PAL-uh-node), noun*
A poem in which the poet retracts something said in an earlier poem.
> *The poet Chaucer wrote a PALINODE as part of* The Canterbury Tales, *in which he apologized for his vulgarity.*

palisade *(PAL-ih-seyd), noun*
A defensive fence of pointed stakes set close together.
> *The pirates stormed the stockhouse's PALISADE but were unable to cross over it.*

palliate *(PAL-ee-ate), verb*
To treat a patient so that his symptoms abate even though he still has the disease.
> *We introduced Amanda to Roberto in an attempt to PALLIATE the broken heart that Amanda suffered over her breakup with one of the scions of the Chesterfield family.*

pallid *(PAL-id), adjective*
A wan, sickly, washed-out appearance indicating illness or weakness, or lack of energy, strength, and vitality.
> *Many of us maintain a PALLID complexion because we want to make it clear that we do not need to go outdoors unless we so choose.*

palpable *(PAL-pah-bull), adjective*
Refers to something so strong or intense that its presence is impossible to ignore.
When Alistair did not give Lorissa the luxury watch she was expecting for her birthday, the silence was PALPABLE.

palter *(PAHL-tur), verb*
To lie; to be deceitful in speech.
I have no wish to PALTER with you; I'll give you the unvarnished truth, and you can make of it what you will.

panacea *(pan-uh-SEE-uh), noun*
A universal solution for all problems, diseases, or woes.
Parents today see buying their kids everything they want as a PANACEA for misery, boredom, and unhappiness.

pandation *(pan-DEY-shun), noun*
Warping.
Unfortunately, because of the damp, the floor has been subject to PANDATION and is a bit uneven.

pandect *(PAN-dekt), noun*
Body of laws.
The Code of Justinian largely revised the PANDECT of Roman laws that had been developed during the Roman Empire.

pandemic *(pan-DEM-ik), noun*
An outbreak of a disease that threatens to spread rapidly and endanger the population of an entire nation or planet.
Many scientists feared that Asian bird flu would become a PANDEMIC.

panegyric *(pan-uh-JIR-ik), noun*
A formal speech praising a person or event.
Natalie Portman delivers a PANEGYRIC at the end of Mars Attacks!

Pangaea *(pan-GEE-uh), noun*
A single massive continent that comprised all the land on the earth before the crust shifted and the Pangaea divided into many smaller continents.
The PANGAEA existed until Mesozoic times, when it divided into two separate continents.

Panglossian *(pan-GLOSS-ee-an), adjective*
Unrealistically optimistic.
Pollyannas are PANGLOSSIAN.

pangram *(PAN-grum), noun*
A sentence containing all the letters of the alphabet.
A famous PANGRAM is "The quick brown fox jumped swiftly over the lazy dog."

pannikin *(PAN-ih-kin), noun*
Small metal cup.
The water fountain had a PANNIKIN attached to it so everyone who wanted could get a drink.

panoply *(PAN-oh-plee), noun*
A complete or impressive collection; a splendid or abundant array.
The gallery offered a PANOPLY of African face masks.

panoptic *(pan-OP-tik), adjective*
Considering all the parts.
In examining our foreign policy, I must take a PANOPTIC view of the international situation rather than focus on a single country.

pantheon *(PAN-thee-on), noun*
The group of all the gods of a particular religion or culture, or a group of important people in a particular field or region.
The sons of Odin, Thor and Loki, represent good and evil in the PANTHEON of the Norse gods.

papule *(PAP-yool), noun*
A small, inflamed pimple on the skin.
As a result of my allergy to asparagus, my chest broke out in PAPULES, which were both painful and embarrassing.

paradigm *(PAH-ruh-dyme), noun*
An observation or discovery in conflict with known facts, beliefs, and theories.
The new PARADIGM for fashion, according to Sasha, is extremely expensive clothes that look as inexpensive as possible.

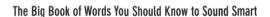

paradox *(PAIR-uh-doks), noun*
A seemingly absurd and self-contradicting situation that seems impossible but may in fact be true.

> *The article profiled a man who was a real PARADOX; he was grossly overweight, yet had tremendous athletic stamina.*

paralogism *(puh-RAL-uh-jih-zum), noun*
An argument that breaks the rules of logic.

> *Your PARALOGISM that the sun goes around the earth is an outstanding example of circular reasoning.*

parameter *(pah-RAM-ih-terr), noun*
A factor or variable that must be taken into account when solving a problem or understanding a situation.

> *The weight of Paul's grand piano is a PARAMETER that must be taken into account when building the mansion's new music room and ballroom.*

paravail *(par-uh-VEYL), verb*
To sublet; to rent from someone who is already a tenant.

> *Since I only need the apartment for a month, the existing tenant agreed to PARAVAIL to me while he's out of the country.*

parcenary *(PAHR-suh-ne-ree), adjective*
Holding of land by two joint heirs.

> *Rather than divide the family acreage, my father left it in a PARCENARY arrangement to both me and my sister.*

paregoric *(par-ih-GAWR-ik), noun*
A soothing medicine.

> *The children had diarrhea, so the doctor prescribed a PAREGORIC to settle their stomachs.*

parhelia *(par-HEEL-ee-uh), noun*
Bright spots of color in the sky.

> *"Sun dogs, also known as PARHELIA or mock suns, are halos that form to either side of the sun when sunlight passes through the faces of ice crystals suspended in the atmosphere."—Michael Carlowicz, science writer*

parisology *(pah-ris-AHL-ah-gee), noun*
The use of ambiguous language.
He employed PARISOLOGY as an obfuscation technique.

P

parity *(PAH-rih-tee), noun*
The condition of everyone being more or less equal.
The firemen received a raise to help them achieve pay PARITY with the sanitation workers and police department.

parlance *(PAR-lunss), noun*
To speak in the vernacular or jargon used by a particular industry, profession, or group.
By using the terms "discourse," "pedagogy," and "literary criticism," the professors spoke in the PARLANCE of academia.

paroexia *(pa-roh-EX-see-a), noun*
The desire to eat strange foods.
His PAROEXIA took the form of eating stuffed rattlesnake and pickled pigs' feet.

parsimonious *(par-sih-MOAN-ee-us), adjective*
To be conservative in spending and tight with a dollar; to agree to part with money or other resources only grudgingly and after much cajoling.
Esmerelda can be surprisingly PARSIMONIOUS, considering that her family's fortune is among the greatest possessed by our social contacts.

parvenue *(PAR-vuh-new), noun*
A woman who has suddenly come into some money.
Leona Helmsley became a PARVENUE when she married Harry.

pasticheur *(PAH-sti-chore), noun*
An artist whose work borrows from multiple sources thereby lacking originality.
"Pound was by nature a talentless PASTICHEUR." —Nicholson Baker, writer

pathological *(path-a-LODGE-ick-uhl), adjective*
Compulsive in nature; possessing a belief system or mindset that makes one unable to resist repetition of a particular type of behavior, e.g., a pathological liar.
Diane's PATHOLOGICAL need for attention has caused her, on more than one occasion, to plant lies about herself in the society pages.

patina *(puh-TEE-nuh), noun*
A film or surface coloring, often indicating great age.
> *The dust had been wiped away so we could see the statue's PATINA, showing it to be a work of antiquity.*

paucity *(PAW-sih-tee), noun*
A lack of something; a small supply or limited selection.
> *"It is very strange, and very melancholy, that the PAUCITY of human pleasures should persuade us ever to call hunting one of them." —Samuel Johnson, British moralist and poet*

pavid *(PAV-id), adjective*
Timid; fearful.
> *After his experience in the haunted house, Rex was understandably PAVID about entering the dark cave.*

peccadillo *(pek-ah-DILL-oh), noun*
A small problem that's trivial but irritating.
> *What started as a PECCADILLO evolved into a full-blown shouting match.*

peccavi *(peh-KEE-vey), noun*
Confession of a sin or sins.
> *Entering the confessional, the young woman made her PECCAVI to the priest on the other side of the curtain.*

pecuniary *(pih-KYOO-nee-air-ee), adjective*
Something related to money.
> *Because all of Craig's articles had a strong PECUNIARY slant, his editor moved him from the features page to the finance page.*

pedagogue *(PED-ah-gog), noun*
A strict, humorless, no-nonsense teacher.
> *"The negative cautions of science are never popular. If the experimentalist would not commit himself, the social philosopher, the preacher, and the PEDAGOGUE tried the harder to give a short-cut answer." —Margaret Mead, American cultural anthropologist*

pedantry *(PEHD-an-tree), noun*
An obsessive behavior of being proper and technically correct down to the last detail.
Samuel Taylor Coleridge defined PEDANTRY as "the use of words unsuitable to the time, place, and company."

pejorative *(pih-JOR-a-tiv), adjective*
Insulting; meant as a put-down or to belittle the other person.
"Wordsmith" is a corporate term used to denote someone who is a good writer, but professional writers see it as PEJORATIVE.

pelagic *(puh-LAJ-ik), adjective*
Relating to oceans or seas.
The area's PELAGIC character was indicated by scattered shells and the sound of breakers just beyond the dunes.

pellucid *(peh-LEW-sid), adjective*
Easy to understand because it is clearly expressed.
Isaac Asimov's science writing was particularly PELLUCID.

Penates *(peh-NAH-teys), noun*
Household gods worshipped by the Romans.
According to legend, Aeneas, founder of the Roman people, fled from Troy, bearing with him his PENATES as well as his aged father and young son.

penitent *(PEN-ih-tent), adjective*
Feeling sorry and regretful that you have done something wrong.
According to Ambrose Bierce's jaded view, the PENITENT are typically those undergoing or awaiting punishment.

penultimate *(pen-UHL-tah-met), adjective*
Next to last in importance.
The Whittingtons' Christmas gala is the PENULTIMATE party of the social season.

penury *(PEN-yuh-ree), noun*
The condition of extreme poverty.
PENURY permeates the city of my birth, Paterson, New Jersey.

per capita *(per-KA-pih-tah), adjective*
Per person; pertaining to a single individual.
We find it satisfying to mull over the fact that the PER CAPITA income among our social contacts is greater than that of many countries.

perdure *(per-DOOR), verb*
To endure.
Our people PERDURE through the ages because of our faith and our culture.

P

perfervid *(per-FUR-vid), adjective*
Overly intense and passionate; overblown and dramatic.
We laughed at the distastefully PERFERVID love letters that Roland sent to Germaine.

perfidious *(purr-FIH-dee-us), adjective*
Treacherous.
Captain Blight could not trust his PERFIDIOUS crew.

perfunctory *(per-FUNK-ter-ee), adjective*
Implemented or executed quickly, without much care or thought put into it.
"The tale is so contrived and PERFUNCTORY that many readers will be tempted to skip to the real story in the second half of the book." —Tim Parks, British novelist

peripatetic *(per-ih-pa-TET-ik), adjective*
Someone who wanders from career to career, job to job, company to company, or place to place, seemingly without a clear goal or definiteness of purpose.
While waiting to receive his trust fund at age thirty, Giles lived a PERIPA-TETIC lifestyle.

periphery *(puh-RIFF-uh-ree), noun*
The outermost part or boundary; the outside edge.
Craig's plans are always on the PERIPHERY of what could charitably be called normal behavior.

peristerophily *(per-iss-tare-oh-fil-ee), noun*
Pigeon collecting.
Daniel became unpopular with the building's other tenants because of his hobby of PERISTEROPHILY, leading to enormous numbers of pigeons on the roof.

permeate *(PUR-mee-ayt), verb*
To penetrate; to spread throughout.
> *The scent of Donna's exclusive perfume quickly PERMEATED the entrance hall of the Blakelys' stately home.*

pernicious *(purr-NISH-us), adjective*
Resulting in damage or harm; having a debilitating effect.
> *We believe that, once the producers of luxury items become publicly traded companies, the results will be PERNICIOUS.*

persiflage *(PURR-sih-flayshz), noun*
Speaking in a frivolous or flippant manner.
> *Our kids were often PERSIFLAGE when they were younger.*

pertinacious *(purr-tih-NAY-shus), adjective*
Holding firmly to an opinion or a course of action.
> *The attorney's PERTINACIOUS behavior contributed to his success.*

perturbation *(purr-ter-BAY-shun), noun*
Originally used to describe the phenomenon of one planet's gravitational field throwing another planet's orbit slightly out of kilter. Today, *perturbation* refers more generally to any disturbance that alters the normal state of function of a system, moving object, person, or process.
> *"O polished PERTURBATION! golden care! / That keep'st the ports of slumber open wide / To many a watchful night." —William Shakespeare, English playwright*

petulant *(PET-chew-lant), adjective*
Describes someone who sulks, complains, or whines because he or she is acting immaturely or is ill-tempered.
> *Emma was sick and tired of her husband's PETULANT pouting.*

phaeton *(FAY-ih-tun), noun*
A four-wheeled carriage.
> *In the movie* Witness, *Harrison Ford rides in a PHAETON.*

phalanx *(FAY-lanks), noun*
A large division or group of soldiers grouped closely together in an orderly fashion for marching or fighting.
> *Philip of Macedon armed each man with a long spear so the PHALANX bristled like a porcupine.*

P

Pharisee *(FAIR-ih-see), noun*
A person who is self-righteous and hypocritical.
> *The state attorney general was a PHARISEE who prosecuted others for the same crimes he was secretly committing himself.*

phenomenology *(fe-nahm-eh-NAHL-ah-gee), noun*
The study of phenomenon.
> *My great interest in PHENOMENOLOGY is gravity hills where cars in neutral roll up the hill instead of down.*

philanthropist *(fill-ANN-throw-pist), noun*
A person who generously gives of his or her time, energy, and money to charity.
> *Bill Gates is the most proactive PHILANTHROPIST out of all the billionaires who care to invest their time in contributing to charitable causes.*

philippic *(fil-IP-ik), noun*
Argument against someone or something.
> *The speaker launched into a PHILIPPIC against the practice of fox hunting.*

philistine *(FILL-ih-steen), noun*
A crude and ignorant person who is uninterested in and does not appreciate culture and the arts.
> *"A PHILISTINE is a full-grown person whose interests are of a material and commonplace nature, and whose mentality is formed of the stock ideas and conventional ideals of his or her group and time." —Vladimir Nabokov, Russian-American novelist*

philology *(fil-LOL-oh-jee), noun*
The study of languages.
> *Modern PHILOLOGY has uncovered the existence of families of languages descended from a single ancestral language.*

philter *(FILL-ter), noun*
A love potion.
A PHILTER is the subject of the song "Love Potion No. 9."

P

phoenix *(FEE-niks), noun*
A mythical bird about the size of an eagle, but with brilliantly colored plumage, that dies by fire and then is reborn from the ashes.
One day the PHOENIX appeared in the forests of France, and legend has it that all the other birds became instantly jealous.

phrenology *(fren-AH-lah-gee), noun*
The belief that you can discern a person's personality by the shape of his skull.
In the movie Django Unchained, *Calvin Candie was a believer in PHRENOLOGY, using it to conclude that African Americans were inferior.*

phrensis *(FREN-sis), noun*
Fury; frenzy.
The pair of excavators, at the sight of the buried chest, plunged into a PHRENSIS of activity.

pibroch *(PEE-brokh), noun*
A piece of music for bagpipes.
The piper at Glen Coe sounded a melancholy PIBROCH that resounded off the rocks and echoed through the glen.

pied-a-terre *(pyed-ah-TARE), noun*
A second home or apartment, usually small, used as a place to stay for short trips to the location in lieu of renting a hotel room.
We were amazed that Alison and her family could survive in a PIED-A-TERRE containing just 950 square feet.

pietà *(pyay-TAH), noun*
Depiction of the Virgin Mary holding dead Jesus in her arms.
Michelangelo's PIETÀ is among his most famous works of art.

pinion *(PIN-yin), noun*
A small gear that fits into a rack.
A widely advertised feature of automobiles is rack-and-PINION steering, whatever that means.

piquant *(pih-KANT), adjective*
Sharp or pungent.
> *Blue cheese is mildly PIQUANT.*

pique *(PEEK), noun, verb*
To generate interest or curiosity; a feeling of annoyance resulting from a perceived insult or injustice.
> *"I want to kiss God on His nose and watch Him sneeze / and so do you. / Not out of disrespect. / Out of PIQUE. / Out of a man-to-man thing." —Anne Sexton, American poet and author*

piscine *(pie-SEEN), adjective*
Resembling a fish.
> *H.P. Lovecraft had numerous PISCINE figures in* The Shadow over Innsmouth.

plauditory *(PLAW-dih-tore-ee), adjective*
Expressing approval.
> *The keynote speaker received a warm and PLAUDITORY response to his talk.*

plethora *(PLETH-uh-ruh), noun*
An excessive amount of something.
> *Agnes tried a PLETHORA of wines before she finally decided on her favorite vintage.*

pluralism *(PLOOR-al-iz-im), noun*
The understanding and tolerance of a diversity of differing cultures and views within a single society.
> *As long as someone comes from a family of high-standing, we wholeheartedly embrace PLURALISM.*

polemic *(pah-LEM-ik), noun*
A long, rambling speech or diatribe, the goal of which is to prove a point or sway the listener to see your point of view.
> *"He had a strong will and a talent for POLEMIC." —Saul Bellow, American author*

polymath *(POHL-ee-math)*, *noun*
A person with a wide range of intellectual interests or a broad base of knowledge in many different disciplines.

> *"I had a terrible vision: I saw an encyclopedia walk up to a POLYMATH and open him up."* —Karl Kraus, Austrian writer

polyphonic *(pahl-ee-FAHN-ik)*, *adjective*
Having many different sounds.

> *"The guitar is a small orchestra. It is POLYPHONIC. Every string is a different color, a different voice."* —Andres Segovia, Spanish classical guitarist

pontificate *(pahn-TIF-uh-kayt)*, *verb*
To hold forth on a topic in which one is knowledgeable.

> *"Maurice Evans PONTIFICATED two or three times, reminding us what the English language sounds like when spoken properly."* —Harlan Ellison, American author

populism *(POP-you-liz-um)*, *noun*
A political movement or policy that appeals to the masses—the average working man or woman—not the upper class.

> *"Being naked approaches being revolutionary; going barefoot is mere POPULISM."* —John Updike, American novelist and literary critic

portent *(poor-tent)*, *noun*
A warning sign that something bad is going to happen.

> *In Ray Bradbury's novel* Something Wicked This Way Comes, *the carnival coming to town is a PORTENT of evil things to come.*

posit *(PAHZ-it)*, *verb*
To suggest or propose a theory or explanation, especially one that represents new, unusual, or nonobvious thinking and conclusions.

> *Astronomers POSIT that Jupiter may sustain life in its clouds.*

postulate *(PA-stew-late)*, *verb*
To arrive at a theory, belief, hypothesis, or principle based upon an analysis of known facts.

> *"The primacy of human personality has been a POSTULATE both of Christianity and of liberal democracy."* —Julian Huxley, English evolutionary biologist

potentate *(POH-ten-tayt), noun*
A powerful dictator, king, leader, or ruler.
A much-feared POTENTATE, Victor Von Doom ruled Latvia with an iron fist.

poultice *(POLE-tiss), noun*
A home remedy for physical injuries.
Granny's homemade POULTICE stank to high heaven.

pragmatism *(PRAG-muh-tiz-um), noun*
The belief that one's actions should be guided primarily based on knowledge or opinion of what is likely to work best in a given situation; the imperative to always do what is practical and effective.
Our families have succeeded in amassing great wealth over many generations because we are all, at heart, practitioners of PRAGMATISM.

prattle *(PRAT-l), verb*
To babble; to talk nonstop without regard as to whether what you are saying makes sense or is of any interest to the listener.
"Infancy conforms to nobody: all conform to it, so that one babe commonly makes four or five out of the adults who PRATTLE and play to it." —Ralph Waldo Emerson, American poet, essayist, and transcendentalist

precarious *(prih-KAYR-ee-us), adjective*
Tenuous; positioned so as to be in danger of falling; unsecured.
"Existence is no more than the PRECARIOUS attainment of relevance in an intensely mobile flux of past, present, and future." —Susan Sontag, American literary theorist, philosopher, and political activist

precipitous *(pri-SIP-ih-tuss), adjective*
A steep drop, precarious position, unstable situation, volatile market, or rapid and sudden change.
Investors were stung Friday by a PRECIPITOUS drop in the Dow.

predestination *(pree-dess-tih-NAY-shun), noun*
The belief that we do not have free will, and that our lives and destinies are pre-ordained and beyond our control.
The problem with PREDESTINATION is that whatever happens, you can say that it was meant to be, and no one can prove you wrong.

premonitory *(PREH-mahn-ih-tor-ee), adjective*
Strongly indicative of or intuiting that something is going to happen.
> *The Harrisons sold their stock in that company because they had a PREMONI-TORY vision that the company would soon go bankrupt.*

prestidigitation *(press-tih-dih-ji-TAY-shun), noun*
The performance of sleight-of-hand magic tricks.
> *The New Year's Eve gala at the Worthingtons included sumptuous meals, a full orchestra, and even a practitioner of PRESTIDIGITATION who amazed the children with her performance.*

preternatural *(pree-tur-NACH-err-uhl), adjective*
Both *supernatural* and *preternatural* describe things that are out of the norm. But *supernatural* implies forces beyond understanding, while *preternatural* simply means abnormal or unnatural.
> *"I rested my knee against the cabinet for leverage and pulled hard, calling on PRETERNATURAL strength." —Mario Acevedo, American fantasy author*

prima facie *(pree-ma-FAY-shuh), adjective, adverb*
Something accepted upon the face of the evidence until further examination proves or disproves it.
> *We have PRIMA FACIE evidence that it was Evelyn who fed those lies to the society page gossip columnists.*

primordial *(pry-MORE-dee-ul), adjective*
Relating to the beginning of time or the early periods of the earth's developments.
> *The Summerfelds' fortune has been in the family for so long that many of us joke that it has PRIMORDIAL origins.*

proctor *(PROHK-ter), noun*
One who manages or supervises another person's activities and affairs.
> *A life of luxury would be so exhausting if it weren't for the many PROCTORS who take care of our mundane activities.*

procure *(pro-KYORE), verb*
To seek and eventually gain ownership of something.
> *My book dealer recently PROCURED, at considerable expense, a first edition of Great Expectations for our library.*

profligate *(PROF-lih-gayt), adjective*
Extravagant; wasteful; activity, expenditures, or indulgences beyond what any
reasonable person would desire.

> *"The official account of the Church's development viewed alternative voices as
> expressing the views of a misguided minority, craven followers of contemporary
> culture, PROFLIGATE sinners, or worse." —Harold Attridge, dean of Yale Uni-
> versity Divinity School*

pro forma *(pro-FOR-mah), adverb, adjective, noun*
Standard; following a commonly accepted format or process.

> *"Don't worry about reading the fine print," the manager told the young singer as
> he shoved the contract in front of him and put a pen in his hand. "It's just PRO
> FORMA."*

proletariat *(pro-leh-TARE-ee-uht), noun*
A class of society whose members earn their living solely by the exchange of
their labor for money.

> *Your average dentist thinks he is upper class, but in reality, he is just another
> member of the PROLETARIAT.*

prolixity *(pro-LICK-sih-tee), noun*
Refers to a speech or piece of writing that is deliberately wordy and long-
winded due to an ornate or formal style.

> *"The writer who loses his self-doubt, who gives way as he grows old to a sudden
> euphoria, to PROLIXITY, should stop writing immediately: the time has come for
> him to lay aside his pen." —Colette, French novelist*

promulgate *(PRAH-mull-gate), verb*
To elevate a behavior or action—or the prohibition of a particular behavior or
action—to the status of a law, rule, or regulation through public decree.

> *The Department of Public Works PROMULGATED mandatory recycling of all
> paper waste in Bergen County.*

propagate *(PRAH-pah-gayt), verb*
To grow, breed, or cause to multiply and flourish.

> *"The fiction of happiness is PROPAGATED by every tongue." —Samuel Johnson,
> British moralist and poet*

propensity *(pro-PEN-sih-tee), noun*
A tendency to behave in a certain way.
> *Despite her vehement denials, Virginia has shown us a PROPENSITY toward pomposity.*

propinquity *(pro-PIN-kwi-tee), noun*
Nearness in time or place.
> *The PROPINQUITY of the theft and Tony's being seen near the scene of the crime are unlikely to be a coincidence.*

propitiate *(pro-PISH-ee-ate), verb*
To win over; to gain the approval and admiration of.
> *"The life that went on in[many of the street's houses] seemed to me made up of evasions and negations; shifts to save cooking, to save washing and cleaning, devices to PROPITIATE the tongue of gossip." —Willa Cather, American author*

propitious *(pro-PEE-shus), adjective*
Favorably inclined or disposed.
> *"These conditions were so PROPITIOUS for absolute mobility that it felt as if the American dream was functioning at full capacity." —Nicholas Lemann, professor, Columbia University*

propriety *(pro-PRY-ah-tee), noun*
Behaving in a way that conforms to the manners and morals of polite society.
> *"PROPRIETY is the least of all laws, and the most observed." —François de La Rochefoucauld, French author*

proscribe *(pro-SCRIBE), transitive verb*
To forbid or prohibit; frequently confused with the word "prescribe."
> *State law PROSCRIBES the keeping of wild animals as house pets.*

proxy *(PRAHK-see), noun*
The authority, typically in writing, to represent someone else or manage their affairs; a person authorized to act on the behalf of others.
> *While his mother was ill, Larry acted as her PROXY and made hospitalization decisions on her behalf.*

puerile *(PYOO-er-ill), adjective*
Immature; babyish; infantile.
> *"An admiral whose PUERILE vanity has betrayed him into a testimonial…[is] sufficient to lure the hopeful patient to his purchase." —Samuel Hopkins Adams, American journalist*

P

pugnacious *(pug-NAY-shus), adjective*
Some who always wants to argue and debate every last thing.
> *Teenagers are PUGNACIOUS by nature: If I say "No," he invariably asks "Why?"*

purport *(per-PORT), verb*
Claiming to be something you are not; pretending to do something you aren't in fact doing.
> *"Doris Lessing PURPORTS to remember in the most minute detail the moth-eaten party dresses she pulled, at age thirteen, from her mother's trunk." —Tim Parks, British novelist*

pusillanimous *(pyoo-suh-LAN-ih-muss), adjective*
Being mild or timid by nature; a shrinking violet; a person who seeks to avoid conflict, challenge, and danger.
> *Frank L. Baum's most PUSILLANIMOUS fictional creation is the Cowardly Lion of Oz.*

putative *(PEW-tah-tiv), adjective*
Assumed to be true or right.
> *"The PUTATIVE merit of affirmative consent is that it removes from a rape victim any obligation to prove that she resisted her assailant." —Zoë Heller, author*

pyre *(PIE-err), noun*
A pile of wood and twigs, lit on fire to burn bodies during funerals.
> *Suzette was so devastated when her fiancé ran off with another socialite that she took his belongings and burned them on a metaphorical funeral PYRE.*

pyrrhic *(PIR-ick), adjective*
A prize or victory won at the cost of an effort that exceeds its value.
> *Spending $20 at the carnival game to win his child a stuffed animal worth $5 was a PYRRHIC victory at best.*

"O the orator's joys! / To inflate the chest, to roll the thunder of the voice out from the ribs and throat, / To make the people rage, weep, hate, desire, with yourself, / To lead America—to QUELL America with a great tongue."

———

Walt Whitman, American poet and humanist

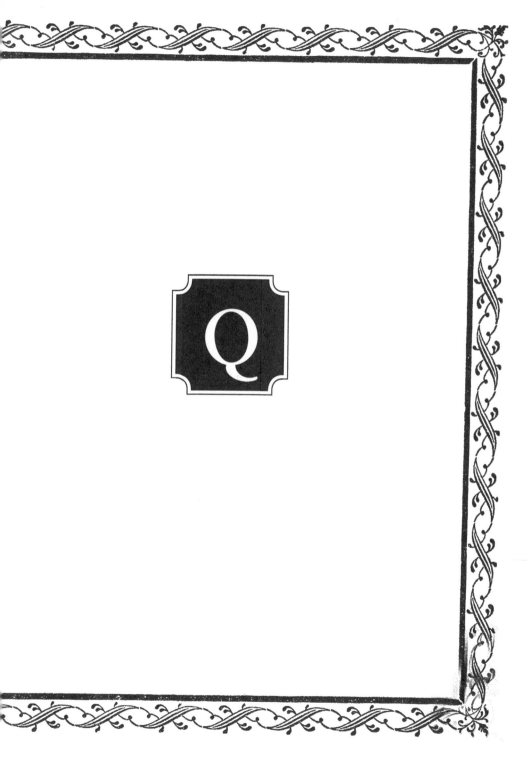

quackle *(KWA-kull), verb*
Choke.

> *Ironically, he QUACKLED on his duck dinner.*

quadrivoltine *(kwa-DRIV-ul-tyne), adjective*
Having four litters in one year.

> *QUADRIVOLTINE bitches overcrowded the puppy mill.*

quadrophonic *(kwa-droh-FON-ik), adjective*
Sound reproduction from speakers using four channels.

> *QUADROPHONIC stereos produce superior sound quality.*

quaff *(KWAF), verb*
To drink with gusto and in large volume.

> *"We QUAFF the cup of life with eager haste without draining it, instead of which it only overflows the brim." —William Hazlitt, English literary critic and philosopher*

quagmire *(KWAG-myer), noun*
A thorny problem for which there is no ready solution; a messy situation from which there is no expeditious means of escape.

> *"Your home is regarded as a model home, your life as a model life. But all this splendor, and you along with it . . . it's just as though it were built upon a shifting QUAGMIRE." —Henrik Ibsen, Norwegian playwright*

quahog *(KO-hog), noun*
An edible clam.

> *In* Family Guy, *the bar in the town of QUAHOG is called the Hungry Clam.*

qualm *(KWAHM), noun*
A sudden feeling of uneasiness, often linked to a pang in one's conscience.

> *Of course we feel no QUALMS about wanting the finest things in life; that is the legacy our forefathers bequeathed to us.*

quandary *(KWON-duh-ree), noun*
A state of uncertainty about one's next move.

> *Estelle realized that her unrestrained comments to the society pages had left the rest of us quite upset, and she was in a QUANDARY as to how to repair the situation.*

quash *(KWAHSH), verb*
To repress or subdue completely.
> *She quickly QUASHED the rebellion of the other members of the PTO by reminding them of the superiority of her social contacts.*

quatrefoil *(KAT-er-foyl), noun*
A flower with four petals.
> *The evening primrose is a QUATREFOIL.*

quaver *(KWAY-ver), verb*
To tremble and shake from fear, excitement, etc.
> *Eloise positively QUAVERED as she made her debut at her coming out party.*

quean *(KWEEN), noun*
A disreputable woman; a prostitute.
> *Esmerelda can act like such a QUEAN when her boyfriends do not automatically give her the luxury items she requires.*

quell *(KWELL), verb*
To suppress or extinguish; or, to quiet one's own or another's anxieties.
> *"O the orator's joys! / To inflate the chest, to roll the thunder of the voice out from the ribs and throat, / To make the people rage, weep, hate, desire, with yourself, / To lead America—to QUELL America with a great tongue." —Walt Whitman, American poet and humanist*

quercine *(kwer-SEEN), adjective*
From an oak.
> *Acorns are QUERCINE.*

querulous *(KWER-eh-luss), adjective*
Describes a person who continually whines and complains about practically everything.
> *Their QUERULOUS manner with the waiter made them unpleasant and embarrassing dinner companions.*

quibble *(KWIB-ul), noun*
To argue over a minor matter; to voice a niggling objection.
> *If you are not 100 percent satisfied, your money will promptly be refunded without question or QUIBBLE.*

quid pro quo *(kwid-pro-kwo), noun*
A fair exchange of assets or services; a favor given in return for something of equal value.

> *In a QUID PRO QUO, Stephen helped Alex with his math homework, while Alex did Stephen's chores.*

quiescent *(kwee-ESS-ehnt), adjective*
Being at rest, inactive, or motionless.

> *"There is a brief time for sex, and a long time when sex is out of place. But when it is out of place as an activity there still should be the large and quiet space in the consciousness where it lives QUIESCENT." —D.H. Lawrence, British author*

quietus *(kwy-EET-uhs), noun*
Something that ends or settles a situation.

> *"For who would bare the whips and scorns of time, / Th'oppressor's wrong, the proud man's contumely, / The pangs of disprized love, the law's delay, / The insolence of office, and the spurns / That patient merit of th'unworthy takes, / When he himself might his QUIETUS make / With a bare bodkin?" —William Shakespeare, English playwright*

quiff *(kwiff), noun*
A sexually promiscuous woman.

> *Sue shows no shame in being a QUIFF—in fact, she's proud of it.*

quinch *(kwinch), verb*
Start or stir up something.

> *He's good at QUINCHING, not so good at finishing what he quinched.*

quintessential *(kwin-tuh-sen-shul), adjective*
The most perfect or typical example of its category or kind.

> *"Craving that old sweet oneness yet dreading engulfment, wishing to be our mother's and yet be our own, we stormily swing from mood to mood, advancing and retreating—the QUINTESSENTIAL model of two-mindedness." —Judith Viorst, American author and psychoanalyst*

quirk *(KWIHRK), noun*
A peculiarity of one's personality or manner.

> *One of the most omnipresent QUIRKS of the nouveau riche is that they still ask the price of a luxury item, rather than simply offering to purchase it.*

quirt *(kwert), noun*
A type of riding whip.
He urged his horse onward with his QUIRT.

quisling *(KWIZ-ling), noun*
A traitor; a person who conspires with the enemy.
The top officials of Nazi collaborationist regimes were often executed after the war for being QUISLINGs.

quixotic *(kwik-SOT-ick), adjective*
A person or team pursuing a seemingly unreachable or at least extremely ambitious and difficult goal—one considered by many to be either idealist, impractical, or both.
"There is something QUIXOTIC in me about money, something meek and guilty. I want it and like it. But I cannot imagine insisting on it, pressing it out of people." —Brenda Ueland, American author

quizzacious *(kwi-ZAYE-shuss), adjective*
Mocking or satirical.
Jon Lovitz has a QUIZZACIOUS manner.

quizzical *(KWIHZ-ih-kuhl), adjective*
Unusual or comical; or, puzzled.
The QUIZZICAL look on Amanda's face, when David trailed a marriage-proposal banner behind his private plane, was absolutely priceless.

quondam *(KWAHN-dumm), adjective*
Former; at one time.
You should not hire the Wilkersons' QUONDAM servant because she has been known to break many objets d'art.

quotidian *(kwo-TID-ee-an), adjective*
Familiar; commonplace; nothing out of the ordinary.
Despite closets full of the latest Parisian couture, Alison's QUOTIDIAN complaint is that she has "nothing to wear."

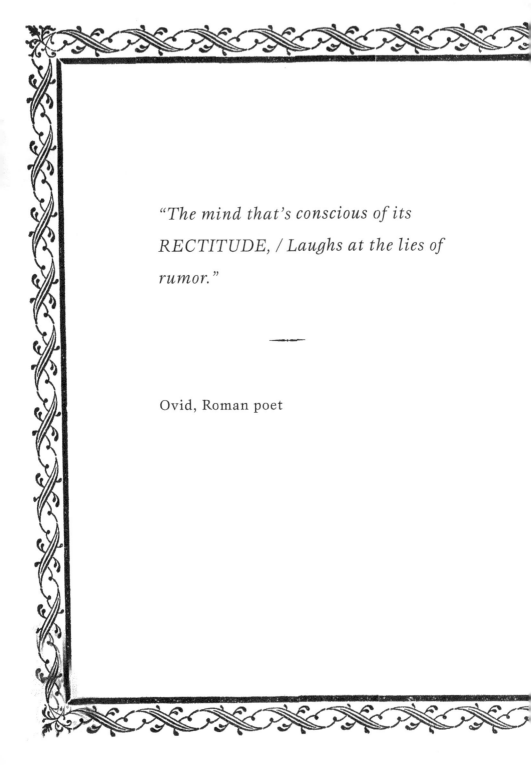

"*The mind that's conscious of its RECTITUDE, / Laughs at the lies of rumor.*"

———

Ovid, Roman poet

R

rabbet *(RAB-it), noun*
A deep notch cut in one end of a board so another piece can be fitted into it.
I've cut a RABBET in that piece so I can put this other side of the frame into it, securing it with a couple of brads.

R

Rabelaisian *(rah-bell-AYE-shzin), adjective*
Humorous or satirical.
We saw a RABELAISIAN comedy on Broadway.

rabulous *(RAA-bew-luss), adjective*
Vulgar and evil.
The new gentleman's club on 49th Street is RABULOUS.

raceme *(rey-SEEM), noun*
The central stem of a plant with small branches or florets extending from it.
The plant's RACEME was very straight and covered with small, white flowers.

rackrent *(RAK-rent), noun*
An excessively high rent.
My son is paying RACKRENT for a tiny apartment in Manhattan.

raconteur *(rah-kon-tour), noun*
Someone who enjoys telling stories, does so frequently, and is good at it.
"O'Hara writes as a poetic one-man band, shifting rapidly among his roles as RACONTEUR, sexual adventurer, European traveler. . . ." —Edward Mendelson, professor of English and comparative literature at Colombia University

radicated *(RAD-ih-key-ted), adjective*
Rooted; established.
His convictions were RADICATED in his experience as a teacher of young children.

radiotelegraphy *(ray-dee-oh-te-lehg-raf-ee), noun*
The use of a radio instead of a wire to communicate telegraphy messages over a distance.
My shortwave radio picks up RADIOTELEGRAPHY messages.

radula *(RAJ-oo-luh), noun*
A chitinous band in the mouths of mollusks that helps them break up food.
In examining the clam, the biologist was much struck by the large RADULA, indicating the creature must have had difficulty "chewing" its food.

raffish *(RAF-ish), adjective*
Mildly disreputable; rakish.
Her boyfriend was a RAFFISH character whom she'd picked up in a down-at-the-heels bar.

raillery *(RAIL-err-ee), noun*
Good-natured teasing.
"RAILLERY," said Montesquieu, is "a way of speaking in favor of one's wit at the expense of one's better nature."

raiment *(RAY-muhnt), noun*
Clothing or apparel of the finest quality.
When Priscilla entered the room attired in RAIMENT of pure gold, her guests gasped and more than one glass of wine was overturned on silken tablecloths.

raison d'être *(RAY-zohn-deh-truh), noun*
The core reason why something exists; its central purpose and mission in this world.
When Jane's children went off to college, her RAISON D'ÊTRE disappeared, and she fell into a deep depression.

ramage *(RAM-ij), noun*
A group of people descended from a single individual.
The RAMAGE of Queen Victoria is surprisingly large, since she had many children, most of whom married into European nobility.

rambunctious *(ram-BUHNGK-shuhss), adjective*
Difficult to handle; wild and boisterous.
"The golden age, when RAMBUNCTIOUS spirits were regarded as the source of evil." —Friedrich Nietzsche, nineteenth-century German philosopher

ramiferous *(ram-IH-fir-us), adjective*
Bearing branches.
> *Trees are, by definition, RAMIFEROUS, since all trees have branches.*

ramification *(ram-uh-fuh-KAY-shun), noun*
A natural consequence of an action or circumstance.
> *A RAMIFICATION of a prolonged stay in low or zero gravity would be loss of bone mass and lean muscle.*

rancescent *(ran-SEH-sent), adjective*
In the process of becoming rancid.
> *At three weeks old, the carton of milk was RANCESCENT, and Stephanie could see when she opened it and inhaled.*

rancor *(RANG-ker), noun*
Conflict between individuals or groups, usually resulting from disagreement over an action or issue, and accompanied by ill will, bad feelings, and an escalation of the dispute over time.
> *"They no longer assume responsibility (as beat cops used to do) for averting RANCOR between antagonistic neighbors." —Harlan Ellison, American author*

ranivorous *(ra-NIH-vir-us), adjective*
Frog eating.
> *The French are notoriously RANIVOROUS, enjoying frogs' legs as a great delicacy.*

rantipole *(RAN-tih-pole), noun*
A poorly behaved individual.
> *You can't take a RANTIPOLE anywhere.*

rapacity *(ruh-PAH-sih-tee), noun*
Greed for wealth, power, fame, and success, even at the expense of others.
> *An unquenchable desire for the finer things in life is not RAPACITY, as some have suggested. It is, instead, a mark of higher birth.*

rapprochement *(rah-PROWCH-ment), noun*
Re-establishment of friendly relations between nations following a period of hostility.
Lydia spoke at length about how RAPPROCHEMENT between the United States and some former Soviet nations has been a real boon to her family's prestige and wealth.

rapscallion *(rap-SKAHL-yin), noun*
Rascal; rogue.
"You RAPSCALLION, you," she said, but her eyes were admiring, not critical.

raptorial *(rap-TAWR-ee-ul), adjective*
Raptor-like; preying on others.
The man's arched nose and haughty bearing gave him a RAPTORIAL appearance, as if he were waiting for the youngest of us to stray from the herd.

rapturous *(RAP-chur-us), adjective*
Adoring, loving, obsessive admiration of something or someone.
"I got my first RAPTUROUS glance at Sheba Poe, who became the most beautiful woman in Charleston the moment she crossed the county line." —Pat Conroy, novelist

rarefied *(RARE-uh-fyed), adjective*
Lofty; exalted; of high class or caliber.
Most copywriters don't operate in the RAREFIED environment in which Clayton makes his millions.

rataplan *(RA-tah-plan), noun*
The sound a beating drum makes.
Gene Krupa's RATAPLAN for "Sing, Sing, Sing" is iconic in the jazz world.

rathe *(RAAYTH), adjective*
Quick; prompt.
The Flash is a RATHE superhero.

R

ratiocinate *(ray-shee-OSS-inn-ate), verb*
To work toward the solution of a problem through logical thinking and reason.
Since the dawn of humanity, our best minds have failed to RATIOCINATE a method of proving God's existence.

raze *(RAYZ), verb*
To tear down or demolish.
We had to RAZE our Cape Cod home and rebuild it entirely, due to some structural damage to the home caused by high winds.

rebarbative *(re-BAR-bah-tiv), adjective*
Repellant; objectionable.
A REBARBATIVE personality is the opposite of having charisma.

reboant *(re-BOW-ant), adjective*
Loudly reverberating.
The bass saxophone has a REBOANT sound.

recalcitrant *(rih-KAL-sih-trunt), adjective*
Unwilling to cooperate voluntarily; hesitant to step forward and do what one is asked or told to do.
On the witness stand, the mobster was RECALCITRANT and uncommunicative.

recant *(rih-KANT), verb*
To withdraw or disavow formally.
"I cannot and will not RECANT anything, for to go against conscience is neither right nor safe." —Martin Luther, the father of Protestantism

recapitulate *(ree-kah-PIT-chew-late), verb*
To repeat something, but in a more concise form.
"To RECAPITULATE: always be on time for my class," the professor told his freshman class on the first day of the semester.

recession *(ree-SESH-in), noun*
A troubled economy characterized by a decline in gross domestic product for two consecutive quarters; a period during which unemployment is on the rise, inflation is increasing, and consumer confidence and spending power is eroded.
The looming RECESSION has even hurt some of our families, who have had to let go of second yachts and one or two homes.

recherché *(ruh-SHAIR-shey), adjective*
Very rare; exotic; strange; foreign.
The bracelet was of a strange, RECHERCHÉ design, as if it had been created by an unknown civilization.

recidivist *(reh-SIH-dih-vist), noun*
One who chronically behaves antisocially.
"We have incapacitated those who would otherwise be RECIDIVISTS." —Judge Jed Rakoff

reciprocity *(res-uh-PROS-ih-tee), noun*
Doing business with—or a favor for—someone, because they have done a favor for, or bought from, you.
Giving customers free gifts increases sales because of the principle of RECIPROCITY.

recompense *(REK-um-pense), verb, noun*
To give someone cash or something else of value to make up for injury or inconvenience they suffered at your hands, either accidentally or deliberately.
"To be remembered after we are dead, is but poor RECOMPENSE for being treated with contempt while we are living." —William Hazlitt, English literary critic and philosopher

recondite *(REHK-un-dite), adjective*
Beyond typical knowledge and understanding.
For most people, opera, polo, and fine wine remain RECONDITE subjects.

recriminate *(rih-KRIM-uh-nayt), verb*
To bring up accusations against someone who has accused you.
After Natasha was snubbed by us for blabbing to the gossip pages, she RECRIMINATED by pointing out that some of us had leaked gossip ourselves.

rectitude *(REHK-ti-tood), noun*
Moral virtue; rightness.
> *"The mind that's conscious of its RECTITUDE, / Laughs at the lies of rumor."*
> —Ovid, Roman poet

recto *(REK-toh), noun*
In publishing terminology, the right-hand page of a book.
> *The chapters in this book all begin on RECTO pages.*

recumbent *(rih-KUHM-bent), adjective*
Inactive, idle; lying down.
> *During our Italian cruise, we spent most of our time RECUMBENT on the bow of the yacht, soaking up the sun's rays.*

recursive *(ree-KURSS-iv), adjective*
Pertaining to a process in which each step makes use of the results of the earlier steps.
> *The study of mathematics is a RECURSIVE learning experience.*

redact *(re-DAKT), verb*
To edit a comment, thought, or written document before going public with it.
> *"You may want to REDACT your opinion on your opponent's healthcare policies," his campaign manager warned him.*

redistributive *(ree-dih-STRIB-you-tiv), adjective*
To distribute again in a different way.
> *"The United States was able to confer the blessings of its growing economy widely across the population through a REDISTRIBUTIVE tax system."* —Nicholas Lemann, professor, Columbia University

redolent *(RED-oh-lent), adjective*
An object possessing a rich scent or alluring aroma; or, a situation with a hint or promise of rich possibilities.
> *Her rose garden was REDOLENT with the perfume of a thousand flowers.*

redoubt *(ri-DOWT), noun*
Military fortification consisting of an earthen wall and a fence.
> *The legion settled down within the REDOUBT to await the coming of the assault they were sure would occur next morning.*

redoubtable *(rih-DOW-tuh-bull), adjective*
The quality of being a formidable opponent.
> *Michael's REDOUBTABLE nature made him a successful negotiator and trial attorney.*

R

reflexive *(reh-FLEK-siv), adjective*
Something that happens through reflex rather than deliberate choice or effort.
> *We don't mean to act imperiously toward the nouveau riche; it's just a REFLEX-IVE and conditioned response.*

reflexogenic *(ree-fleks-oh-JEN-ik), adjective*
Producing a reflect action.
> *Stroking the knee with a small rubber mallet is REFLEXOGENIC.*

refluent *(REF-loo-unt), adjective*
Flowing back; ebbing.
> *As the tide ebbed, the REFLUENT waters drew back to reveal hidden rocks.*

reflux *(REE-fluks), noun*
Retreating; flowing back or away.
> *The REFLUX of activity gave us a few minutes in which to catch our breathe.*

refractory *(ree-FRAK-tore-ee), adjective*
Difficult to get someone or something to do what you want them or it to do.
> *Mules and children can be especially REFRACTORY.*

refulgent *(rih-FUHL-jent), adjective*
Radiant, gleaming; shining brightly.
> *When Anastasia moved her bejeweled hand while lounging in the midday sunshine, her sparkling diamonds were REFULGENT.*

reglementary *(REG-lem-en-ter-ee), adjective*
According to procedures.
> *Chemistry is a REGLEMENTARY activity.*

regorge *(re-GAWRJ), verb*
To cast out again; to vomit again.
> *Although George tried his quarter several times in the vending machine, the device REGORGED it each time.*

reguerdon *(ree-GWER-den), noun*
Reward.
> *Honesty is its own REGUERDON.*

rejoinder *(rih-JOIN-der), noun*
A clever or witty reply to a question or comment.
> *Lydia's often catty REJOINDERS quickly made her the bane of our group.*

religate *(ree-LIH-geyt), verb*
Tie together.
> *If you'll help me RELIGATE these two poles, we can raise the tent.*

reliquary *(REL-ih-kware-ee), noun*
A case in which relics are kept on display.
> *Objects from King Tut's tomb were displayed in a glass RELIQUARY.*

remiss *(rih-miss), adjective*
Negligent or careless.
> *Our servants know that if they ever are REMISS in their duties, then we will quickly fire them.*

remittance *(ree-MITT-inss), noun*
A payment for goods or services purchased on credit.
> *Lacking a credit card, he made a REMITTANCE on his account online using PayPal.*

remonstrate *(rih-MON-strate), verb*
To protest, object, or to show disapproval.
> *When Carlotta REMONSTRATED our snubbing of Julia, we simply began to snub Carlotta as well.*

remunerate *(rih-MYOO-nuh-rate), verb*
To settle a debt or other financial obligation by making a payment.
> *Peter's supervisor at the insurance company would do anything to avoid REMUNERATING policyholders for the claims they made.*

renaissance *(REN-ah-sonce), noun, adjective*
A period of great learning, thinking, and creativity—in art, literature, science, economics, and philosophy.
> *We were so pleased by the RENAISSANCE of wealth acquisition that arose during the closing years of the twentieth century.*

renal *(REE,nul), adjective*
Concerning or connected to the kidneys.
> *The patient's RENAL failure meant he had to be connected to a dialysis machine to keep his kidneys functioning.*

renunciation *(ree-nun-see-AYE-shun), noun*
To distance yourself from a position or belief; to publicly state a shift in ideals or position on an issue while criticizing your past stance as wrong.
> *"With RENUNCIATION life begins." —Amelia E. Barr, British novelist*

reparations *(reh-par-AYE-shins), noun*
Payments made by nations defeated in war to the victors, who impose these payments to recover some of the costs of battle.
> *After World War I, REPARATIONS of 132 billion gold marks were imposed on Germany by the French.*

repartee *(rep-er-TAY), noun*
Conversation characterized by witty banter.
> *Our galas and balls are always marked by delightful REPARTEE around the grand dinner table.*

repertoire *(REH-per-tware), noun*
A library of works that a group knows and regularly performs.
> *The philharmonic's REPERTOIRE includes most of the classical standards from Bach, Beethoven, Brahms, and Mozart.*

replete *(rih-PLEET), adjective*
Abundantly provided; complete.
> *"The highway is REPLETE with culinary land mines disguised as quaint local restaurants that carry such reassuring names as Millie's, Pop's and Capt'n Dick's." —Bryan Miller, American food critic*

repose *(rih-POHZ), noun*
To be in a position or state of rest.

> *The wholesome relief, REPOSE, content; / And this bunch, pluck'd at random from myself; / It has done its work—I tossed it carelessly to fall where it may.* —Walt Whitman, American poet and humanist

reprobate *(REP-ro-bait), noun*
A person who routinely commits illegal, immoral, or unethical acts without hesitation or remorse.

> *One reason that Anthony continues to be a REPROBATE is because his father, as well as his social contacts, keep bailing him out of jail.*

reprove *(ree-PROOV), verb*
To criticize and correct others.

> *We found it necessary to REPROVE Elyssia for some of her questionable fashion choices.*

repudiate *(reh-pew-dee-ayte), verb*
To dispute an idea, decision, or belief; to distance oneself and refuse to be associated with someone or something.

> *We repeatedly REPUDIATED James for his assertion that Rolex watches surpass those of Cartier.*

requiescat *(reh-kwee-ESS-kat), noun*
A prayer for the dead.

> *"Against the new masonry I re-erected the old rampart of bones. For the half of a century no mortal has disturbed them. In pace REQUIESCAT!"* —Edgar Allan Poe, "The Cask of Amontillado"

requisite *(REK-wiz-it), noun, adjective*
A mandatory action, requirement, or condition; or, necessary and mandatory.

> *Being physically fit is a REQUISITE to getting a job as a fireman.*

requite *(rih-KWYTE), verb*
To seek revenge for an actual or assumed wrong.

> *". . . Certain sets of human beings are very apt to maintain that other sets should give up their lives to them and their service, and then they REQUITE them by praise"* —Charlotte Brönte, British novelist

rescind *(ree-SINNED), verb*
Take away; revoke; cancel; withdraw; remove.
   Richard RESCINDED his order for a yacht, opting instead to purchase a private aircraft.

respite *(RESS-pit), noun*
A temporary delay from something distressing.
   "Sweet Flower of Hope! free Nature's genial child! / That didst so fair disclose thy early bloom, / Filling the wide air with a rich perfume! / For thee in vain all heavenly aspects smiled; / From the hard world brief RESPITE could they win . . ."
   —Samuel Taylor Coleridge, English poet

resplendent *(reh-SPLEN-dent), adjective*
Garbed or decorated in lush fabrics and rich, vibrant colors.
   The bride was RESPLENDENT in a beaded silk gown.

restive *(RESS-tihv), adjective*
Impatient and stubborn.
   Audrey was so worked up about her first summer abroad that her excitement came across as RESTIVE.

retainage *(ree-TAYNE-idge), noun*
Money earned by but not yet paid to a contractor.
   The developer held back a 10 percent RETAINAGE until the certificate of occupancy is issued.

reticent *(REH-tih-scent), adjective*
Reluctance to openly express one's thoughts, feelings, and personal business to other people; behaving like an introvert in social situations.
   "The shorter poems tend to be RETICENT, psychologically acute love poems about the shifting inequalities of love." —Edward Mendelson, professor of English and comparative literature at Colombia University

reticule *(REH-tik-yule), noun*
A small women's handbag made of netting.
   Few accessories are as ridiculous as RETICULES.

retinue *(RET-n-oo), noun*
A group of people who follow an important person either because they desire to do so or because it is their job to do so.

A Secret Service RETINUE follows the president wherever he goes, twenty-four hours a day.

R

retort *(rih-TORT), verb, noun*
To reply in a sharp, retaliatory manner.

Carl had to bite back a sharp RETORT when Sallee criticized the couture gown his mother wore to the soiree.

retrograde *(REH-trow-grayed), adjective*
Reverting to an earlier state, condition, or style; harkening to an earlier time and place.

My favorite diner is decorated in a RETROGRADE art deco style.

retroussé *(reh-true-SAY), adjective*
Turned up at the tip.

Rhinoplasty took care of his RETROUSSÉ nose.

revelry *(REV-uhl-ree), noun*
Boisterous festivity and merrymaking.

"Midnight shout and REVELRY, / Tipsy dance and jollity." —John Milton, English poet

revirescent *(reh-veer-ESS-sent), adjective*
Growing young again.

His extensive spa treatments as well as his facelift gave him a REVIRESCENT appearance, despite his age.

rhabdoid *(RAB-doyd), adjective*
Rod-shaped, esp. in medicine.

Microscopic examination disclosed RHABDOID growths on his heart, endangering his life.

rhapsodize *(RAP-sih-dize), verb*
To speak or write about someone or something with great enthusiasm and delight or in a gushing manner.

My ex-boss, David Koch, RHAPSODIZED about the virtue of libertarian philosophy.

rhematic *(ri-MAT-ik), adjective*
Having to do with the formation of words.
> *Her interest in the development of English led her to a RHEMATIC examination of early English words.*

rheostat *(REE-uh-stat), noun*
A current resistor that can change its resistance without interrupting the flow of electricity.
> *The RHEOSTAT allowed electricians to create the dimmer switch for chandeliers.*

rhetoric *(REH-tore-ik), noun*
Artful use of language to get other people to see your point of view; making a persuasive case more through persuasive speech or writing than with actual facts and evidence.
> *Plato called RHETORIC "the art of ruling the minds of men."*

rheum *(ROOM), noun*
A discharge of mucus during a cold.
> *Linda was miserable with her cold, coughing up RHEUM into a handkerchief.*

rhinoplasty *(RYE-no-plah-stee), noun*
Nose surgery.
> *South Park residents get their nose jobs at Tom's RHINOPLASTY.*

ribald *(RIB-uld), adjective*
Lewd; off-color; somewhat dirty and inappropriate.
> *"It is . . . useful to distinguish between the pornographic, condemned in every society, and the bawdy, the RIBALD, the shared vulgarities and jokes, which are the safety valves of most social systems." —Margaret Mead, American cultural anthropologist*

rictus *(RIK-tuhs), noun*
The opening of the mouth.
> *The lips were drawn back from the RICTUS, distorting the face into a horrid grin that seems to show the man's last moments had been painful.*

rife *(RIFE), adjective*
Prevalent; abundant; abounding.
   The hotel was RIFE with tourists, so we quickly went upstairs to the penthouse.

R

rigadoon *(rig-ah-dune), noun*
A lively dance for couples.
   Square dancing and RIGADOONS have similar energy.

rigmarole *(RIG-muh-roll), noun*
Absurdly complicated procedures and instructions; a bunch of unnecessary
baloney.
   *The club had some value to him in business, but he quickly grew tired of all the
   RIGMAROLE at meetings.*

rimple *(RIM-puhl), noun*
A wrinkle.
   *A RIMPLE showed on the smooth surface of the pond, and a moment later the
   head of an otter appeared.*

riparian *(rih-PAIR-ee-un), adjective*
Relating to the bank of a river.
   *The erosion of the river bank and other RIPARIAN concerns led those owning
   waterside houses to meet regularly.*

riposte *(rih-POST), noun*
A quick, often witty or cutting, response to a comment or question.
   *Eileen was unable to offer one of her usual RIPOSTES when we descried her deci-
   sion to eschew the season's fashion.*

risible *(RIZZ-uh-bull), adjective*
Capable of causing laughter due to its ludicrous nature.
   *Janine's decision to summer in the Hamptons instead of on the French Riviera
   was deemed RISIBLE by the rest of us.*

robinet *(rah-bi-NET), noun*
Small cannon.
   *The company, surrounded by the enemy, had only their firearms and a comple-
   ment of ROBINETS to defend themselves.*

Roentgen *(RENT-jen), noun*
A measure of exposure to x-ray or gamma radiation.
> *The doctor and his assistant wore lead aprons to limit the ROENTGENS they would be exposed to during the radiation therapy.*

roisterers *(ROY-stir-ers), noun*
Partiers, celebrators, or an individual or group having a good time in a loud and boisterous manner.
> *The ROISTERERS' enjoyment of the party was so infectious their neighbors joined them instead of complaining about the noise.*

Ronstadt *(RON-stadt), noun*
In golf, a longer drive than others you are playing with.
> *Eddie hit a RONSTADT and blew by me on the fifteenth hole.*

rood *(ROOD), noun*
Cross; crucifix.
> *The Anglo-Saxon poem "The Dream of the ROOD" tells the story of the crucifixion from the point of view of the cross.*

rota *(ROH-tuh), noun*
Rotation, as in job or assignment.
> *Since I was new to the job, they didn't immediately place me in the ROTA for the night shift but let me learn my duties first.*

roué *(roo-AY), noun*
A dissolute man in fashionable society; a rake.
> *"A pretty wife is something for the fastidious vanity of a ROUÉ to retire upon."*
> *—Thomas Moore, Irish poet and songwriter*

rubeus *(ROO-bee-us), adjective*
Reddish.
> *Jimmy Olsen had a RUBEUS head of hair.*

rubigo *(ROO-bih-go), noun*
Mildew; blight.
> *The dampness of the spring resulted in basement walls covered in RUBIGO, which had to be cleaned before it spread.*

rubric *(ROO-brick), noun*
A class, category, title, or heading.
We decided to place Natasha's ball gown under the RUBRIC of "failed fashion choices."

rubricate *(ROO-brih-keyt), verb*
To color red.
The signs were RUBRICATED so their scarlet color would catch the attention of passersby.

ructation *(ruk-TEY-shun), noun*
The act of burping.
Like all small boys, he found RUCTATION funny, though everyone else thought belching was gross.

rue *(ROO), verb*
To repent of and regret bitterly.
Elliott knew he would RUE the day that he decided to sell his Maserati, but he did so at his father's urging.

rugose *(rue-GOS), adjective*
Full of wrinkles.
Collagen injections can make a RUGOSE face smooth again.

rumbustious *(ruhm BUS-chus), adjective*
Overactive; disruptive.
The RUMBUSTIOUS boys running to and fro made all normal conversation impossible.

rumination *(roo-muh-nay-shun), noun*
The act of thinking about something in great detail, weighing the pros and cons over and over in your mind.
For busy people under stress, RUMINATION after going to bed is a frequent contributor to insomnia.

ruptile *(RUP-tyl), adjective*
Easily breakable; fragile.
The glasses are RUPTILE; don't squeeze them too hard or you'll break them.

ruritanian *(roor-ih-TAYNE-ee-in), adjective*
Anything related to a romantic adventure or its environment.
  The two lovers found Barbados to be a RURITANIAN paradise.

rusticate *(RUSS-tuh-kayt), verb*
To live in the country.
  RUSTICATING is the unspoken dream of many a city dweller.

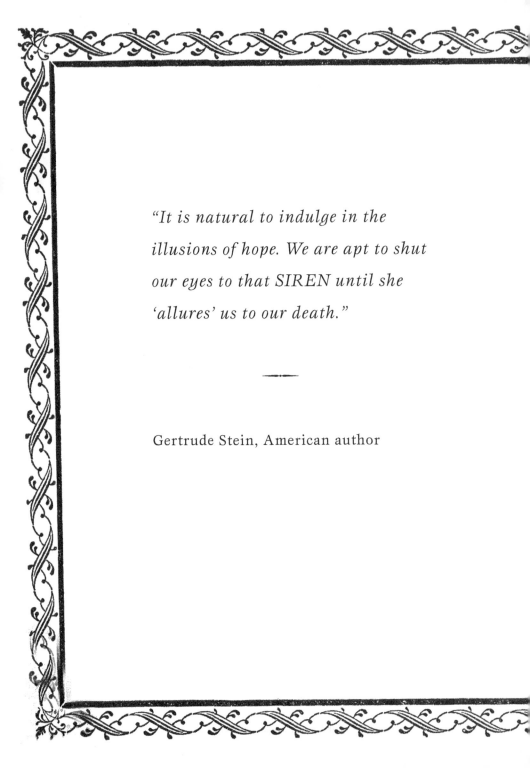

"*It is natural to indulge in the illusions of hope. We are apt to shut our eyes to that SIREN until she 'allures' us to our death.*"

———

Gertrude Stein, American author

sabbatarian *(sahb-ah-TARE-ee-un), noun*
A person who observes the Sabbath.
Religious people are SABBATARIANS.

sable *(SAY-bul), adjective*
Black.
Her SABLE cloak and long dress matched the blackness of her heart.

saccadic *(sah-KAD-ik) adjective*
Eye movement while reading.
His SACCADIC reading patterns made him a fast reader.

sacerdotal *(sas-err-DOUGH-tuul), adjective*
Priestly.
Being SACERDOTAL, he believes priests have divine authority.

sachet *(sa-SHAY), noun*
A small bag or sack containing perfume or pot pourri.
He bore a small SACHET in an attempt to mask his foul odor, but it was unsuccessful.

sackbut *(SAK-buht), noun*
A medieval trombone.
The medieval musical ensemble included one member who played the SACKBUT, drowning out the other instruments with its blare.

sacrilegious *(sack-reh-LIIH-juss), adjective*
Openly insulting or disrespectful to the beliefs, religion, ideas, and practices of others—especially the ones they hold most sacred.
Bryson's insistence that Miró is more collectible than Warhol is positively SACRILEGIOUS.

sacristan *(SAK-rih-stun), noun*
The person in charge of sacred items in a church.
The SACRISTAN removed the reliquary from its accustomed place above the altar and bore it away to be hidden.

sacrosanct *(SACK-roh-sankt), adjective*
Beyond criticism because it is considered sacred.
> *"If men could get pregnant, maternity benefits would be as SACROSANCT as the G.I. Bill." —Letty Cottin Pogrebin, American editor and writer*

saffron *(SAF-rahn), noun*
A spice made from the dried stigmas of the crocus flower.
> *A little SAFFRON in the rice will give it an unusual flavor and color.*

sagacity *(suh-GASS-ih-tee), noun*
Wisdom; soundness of judgment.
> *"Our minds are endowed by nature with such activity and SAGACITY that the soul is believed to be produced from heaven." —Quintilian, Roman rhetorician*

salacious *(suh-LAY-shuss), adjective*
Having an unhealthy, obsessive, or addictive interest in sex.
> *For weeks, the society pages were rife with SALACIOUS gossip, which turned out to originate from Mallory, who had lost her beau to Jeannette.*

salient *(SALE-yent), adjective*
Relevant; germane; important; something that stands out and gets noticed.
> *The pond in the front yard is the most SALIENT feature of our new home.*

salify *(SAL-uh-fahy), verb*
To mix with salt.
> *By his efforts to SALIFY the fish, Orson hoped to find a means of preserving it.*

salubrious *(suh-LOO-bree-us), adjective*
Favorable to one's health.
> *After father's asthma reasserted itself, the family began to spend more time at its Arizona compound due to the area's dry weather, which is SALUBRIOUS toward asthmatics.*

salutary *(SAL-you-tare-ee), adjective*
To have a soothing or healing effect; an act that helps one recover or benefit from a situation.
> *Tuberculosis patients were often sent to the mountains, where the fresh air was thought to have a SALUTARY effect on their condition.*

sanctimonious *(sank-tih-MOAN-ee-us), adjective*
Overbearingly self-righteous and smug in the (perhaps mistaken) belief that one's opinion is correct, and possessing an air of moral superiority about one's opinion.

> *"Not but I've every reason not to care / What happens to him if it only takes / Some of the SANCTIMONIOUS conceit / Out of one of those pious scalawags."*
> —Robert Frost, *American poet*

sangfroid *(san-FWAH), noun*
The attitude or state of possessing a cool head and steadfast composure in the face of danger, adversity, or stressful situations.

> *The car crash shook him, but within seconds he recovered his SANGFROID and went to check on his driver.*

sanguine *(SANG-gwihn), adjective*
Accepting of circumstances with good cheer and a positive attitude.

> *"Many marketers were SANGUINE about the Do Not Call introduction, saying that it helped better focus their telephone communications." —Eleanor Trickett,* DM News *editor*

sapient *(SAY-pee-ent), adjective*
Wise.

> *The judge made a SAPIENT ruling in splitting custody between the two parents.*

saprophagous *(sah-pro-fay-gus), adjective*
Feeding on decaying organic matter.

> *Catfish are partially SAPROPHAGOUS.*

sarcophagus *(sar-KOF-ah-gus), noun*
A tomb.

> *Superstitious people do not open a mummy's SARCOPHAGUS.*

sardonic *(sar-DON-ik), adjective*
Mean-spirited sarcasm.

> *When I asked the bank for another home equity loan, the president, who was called out of his office by the teller, approached with a SARDONIC grin.*

sartorial *(sar-TOR-ee-al), adjective*
Anything related to the way a person dresses, typically used to describe a man who wears finely tailored clothing.
Jonathan's personal tailor always makes sure that Jonathan radiates SARTO-RIAL splendor.

satiety *(suh-TIE-ih-tee), noun*
The sensation or feeling of being full or having eaten too much.
Although we knew we would be struck by SATIETY, we could not resist the gustatory delights offered at the Whittington's New Year's gala.

saturnalia *(sah-tur-NAIL-ya), noun*
A festival or party with wild, out-of-control behavior.
The SATURNALIA degenerated into an orgy.

saturnine *(SAT-ur-neen), adjective*
Moody; morose; gloomy; unhappy; having a pessimistic outlook on life.
Ever since his father told him he could not have another Lotus Esprit, Williams has acted positively SATURNINE.

satyr *(SAY-ter), noun*
A lascivious, lecherous man.
Harold's graceful manners disappear once he has had a few glasses of champagne, and he becomes a veritable SATYR.

savant *(sah-VANT), noun*
A person with a natural talent or genius in a particular field or skill.
With her family's background in finance, it was a given that Francine would be a Wall Street SAVANT.

savoir faire *(sav-wahr-FAIR), noun*
An evident sense of confidence, optimism, and proficiency in the task at hand.
Eileen hosted a charity luncheon for forty people with her usual SAVOIR FAIRE.

scarify *(SKARE-ih-fie), verb*
To wound with harsh criticism.
We deemed it necessary to SCARIFY Eileen for having the nerve to criticize our fashion sense.

scelestic *(skel-ESS-tik), adjective*
Wicked, evil.
> *Vlad the Impaler is a SCELESTIC figure personified.*

scintilla *(SIN-tih-lah), noun*
A spark; a tiny trace amount.
> *"The air twittered with bright SCINTILLAS of fading light." —Harlan Ellison, American author*

scintillating *(SIN-til-aye-ting), adjective*
Witty, brilliant, or sparkling.
> *I did enjoy our SCINTILLATING conversation.*

scion *(SIGH-uhn), noun*
A descendant or heir.
> *"SCION of chiefs and monarchs, where art thou? / Fond hope of many nations, art thou dead?" —Lord Byron, British Romantic poet*

sclaff *(SKLAFF), noun*
In golf, when your club bounces off the ground before striking the ball.
> *He got a birdie on hole three despite his tee-off SCLAFF.*

scree *(skree), noun*
A slope covered with loose stones.
> *The footing on the SCREE was tricky and challenged my balance.*

sealink *(SEE-link) noun*
In telecommunications, an error-correcting data transmission protocol for sending files between PCs.
> *SEALINK overcomes transmission delays caused by satellite relays.*

sectarian *(sek-TAYR-ee-in), adjective*
Relating to the practices, nature, or activities of a sect.
> *"In the early 1990s, as the insurgency took on a more unambiguously religious and SECTARIAN flavor, several Pandits were killed, and most of the rest fled for their lives." —William Dalrymple, Scottish historian and author*

secular *(SEK-yuh-lehr), adjective*
Separate from or devoid of religious belief or connotation.
"The liberal humanist assumption that American society, like that of Europe, would become progressively SECULAR was always something of a delusion."
—Gordon Wood, history professor at Brown University

securitization *(seh-cure-ih-tih-zay-shin), verb*
Creating a marketable security backed by assets.
SECURITIZATION with weak assets led to the mortgage scandal.

sedentary *(SEHD-n-tare-ee), adjective*
Resting a great deal and taking little exercise.
All we have to do is hire a personal trainer if our SEDENTARY habits begin to have negative effects on our well-being.

sedition *(sih-DISH-uhn), noun*
An action that promotes discontent or rebellion.
In an act of childish SEDITION, Alex quit the club after we refused to play a round of golf with him.

sedulous *(SAID-you-lus), adjective*
Working hard and diligently.
I was SEDULOUS in writing this book.

selcouth *(SELL-kooth), adjective, noun*
Unusual.
It's not SELCOUTH to be loved by anyone.

sentient *(SEN-tea-ent), adjective*
Possessing enough intelligence to be self aware.
"Many years ago, a particular creature was selected to develop into the dominant life form on this planet. It was given certain breaks and certain challenges, all of which, when utilized or overcome, marked it indelibly with particular traits as it moved along the road to a higher SENTIENCE." —Roger Zelazny, American science fiction writer

separatists *(SEP-prah-tists), noun*
Those who believe a particular region or group should be separated from a larger whole.
> *Some SEPARATIST Canadians want Quebec to be a separate nation from the rest of Canada.*

sepulchral *(suh-PUHL-kruhl), adjective*
Hollow and deep; characteristic of a tomb; often used to describe certain voices.
> *Our butler's SEPULCHRAL voice instantly impresses our social contacts when they come to visit.*

sequester *(see-KWESS-ter), verb*
To remove and isolate a portion from a larger whole.
> *"A great deal of genetic engineering must be done before we have carbon-eaters SEQUESTERING carbon in sufficient quantity to counteract the burning of fossil fuels." —Freeman Dyson, English-born American physicist and mathematician*

serendipity *(ser-en-DIP-it-ee), noun*
Attaining success, good fortune, or the object of your desire more through luck and random circumstance than deliberate effort.
> *What made him an Internet billionaire was SERENDIPITY more than brains or talent.*

serpentine *(SUR-pen-teen), adjective*
Snake-like in shape or movement.
> *"For it is not possible to join SERPENTINE wisdom with columbine innocency, except men know exactly all the conditions of the serpent." —Francis Bacon, English philosopher, author, and statesman*

sesquipedalian *(ses-kwi-pih-DAL-yin), adjective*
A writer or speaker who prefers big, complex words and arcane jargon to plain, simple English, or a piece of writing containing such prose.
> *"Recently a strange whimsy has started to creep in among the SESQUIPEDALIAN prose of scientific journals." —Stephen Hall, American architect*

sibilant *(SIH-bih-lent), noun*
The sound made when one pronounces *z*, *s*, *sh*, or *ch*.
> *"The vowels were purred, the SIBILANTS rich." —John D. MacDonald, American author*

The Big Book of Words You Should Know to Sound Smart

sidereal *(sigh-deer-ee-ul), adjective*
Determined by outside forces, particularly the positions of the stars and planets in the evening sky.

"Thoughts give birth to a creative force that is neither elemental nor SIDE-REAL." —Philippus Paracelsus, Swiss alchemist, astrologer, and physician

sinecure *(SIN-eh-kyoor), noun*
A job or office without regular duties but with regular pay; a position requiring minimal labor but conveying prestige or status to one who holds it.

Being elected as the new president of his trade association bestowed on Bill some much-needed SINECURE.

siren *(SY-ren), noun*
A destructive but seductively beautiful, beguiling woman; or, anything considered dangerously seductive.

"It is natural to indulge in the illusions of hope. We are apt to shut our eyes to that SIREN until she 'allures' us to our death." —Gertrude Stein, American author

slubberdegullion *(sluh-brrr-deh-GULL-yun), noun*
A bum; a person of low character.

It remains to be seen whether history will consider Nixon a good president or a SLUBBERDEGULLION.

socioeconomic *(so-see-oh-ek-uh-nom-ik), adjective*
Having to do with social and economic factors.

"The surest way of producing SOCIOECONOMIC mobility was through educational attainment." —Nicholas Lemann, professor, Columbia University

soi-disant *(soy-dih-SAHNT), adjective*
Self-styled.

A SOI-DISANT lady's man, Gary's focus was always on his next conquest.

sojourn *(SO-jern), noun*
A temporary visit or stay.

The Israelites' SOJOURN in the desert lasted for forty long years.

solidarity *(sol-ih-DARE-ih-tee), noun*
Bonding of people to others because of shared interests, beliefs, goals, or attitudes.
> *"It was the middle-class female SOLIDARITY, defending a nice girl from charges of calculation and viciousness." —Saul Bellow, American author*

soliloquy *(suh-LIL-ih-kwee), noun*
A dramatic or literary form of speaking in which a character reveals his innermost thoughts when he is alone or thinks he is alone.
> *The most famous SOLILOQUY in all of literature is the "To be or not to be" speech in* Hamlet.

solipsism *(SAHL-ip-sihz-uhm), noun*
The notion that one's own experiences and thoughts are the only source of true knowledge.
> *The SOLIPSISM of some members of the leisure class is distasteful to those of us who, for example, know what our servants need even more than they do.*

solstice *(SOUL-stis), noun*
A day of the year during which the sun is at its highest or lowest point in the sky, causing the shortest day of the year on December 21 (winter *solstice*) and the longest day of the year on June 21 (summer *solstice*).
> *We open our lake house for the summer season every year at the SOLSTICE.*

sonorous *(SON-er-russ), adjective*
A deep, rich, resonant sound.
> *The B-flat bass saxophone is the most SONOROUS member of the saxophone family, with the baritone saxophone coming in a close second.*

sophist *(SAHF-ist), adjective*
Sounding reasonable, yet patently false.
> *One can argue that what is learned in law school is largely the skill of making SOPHIST arguments that a jury can believe.*

soporific *(sop-uh-RIFF-ick), adjective*
Something so boring, tedious, or exhausting that it makes one start to fall asleep.
> *If Cassandra weren't such an important social contact, her SOPORIFIC speech would surely cause us to avoid her.*

spatium *(SPAY-she-um), noun*
An open space or region.
> *There is a SPATIUM between the peritoneum and the fascia transversalis.*

specious *(SPEE-shus), adjective*
Something that appears correct on the surface, but is in fact wrong.
> *The judge summarily rejected the SPECIOUS arguments put forth by the defendant, which seemed to have no evidence to back them up.*

Sphinx *(SFINKS), noun*
A mythical creature with the head of a woman, the body of a lion, the wings of an eagle, and the tail of a serpent.
> *When Oedipus correctly answered the SPHINX'S riddle, the SPHINX leaped to its death in the valley below.*

spoonerism *(SPOON-er-iz-um), noun*
A phrase in which the syllables of neighboring words are accidentally interchanged.
> *A popular SPOONERISM states: "Cook a grilled cheese sandwich in lots of butter, let it get cold, and you have a chilled grease sandwich."*

spurious *(SPYOOR-ee-us), adjective*
False; inauthentic; not well thought out.
> *The belief that the sun travels around the earth was demonstrated to be SPURIOUS by astronomical observation and is now discounted by almost everyone.*

stagnation *(stag-NAY-shin), noun*
The condition of being inactive or the slowing of forward progress or lessening of activity.
> *"Economists' statistical techniques are not refined enough to analyze unambiguously the causes of this long-term STAGNATION." —Jeff Madrick, director of policy research at the Schwartz Center for Economic Policy Analysis, The New School.*

staid *(STAYD), adjective*
Fixed and settled; not distinctive; uninteresting.
> *Even though the Sandersons are an important family, we could hardly last the requisite hour at the family's STAID winter ball.*

stalwart *(STAL-wart), noun, adjective*
A loyal, reliable member of an organization; a staunch supporter of a group or cause.
Although Wayne is no longer a working engineer, he is a STALWART member of the American Institute of Chemical Engineers.

stoicism *(STOH-ih-si-zum), noun*
Enduring pain or suffering without complaining.
"He soldiered through his duties with what looked like cheerful STOICISM."
—Thomas Pynchon, American author

stolid *(STAHL-id), adjective*
Unemotional and impassive.
Thomas's STOLID demeanor hides the heart of a jet-setting playboy.

striation *(streye-AYE-shin), noun*
A series of parallel lines.
You can track the history of our planet by studying STRIATIONS in the rock walls of deep craters.

stringent *(STRIHN-juhnt), adjective*
Rigorous; strict; severe.
"No laws, however STRINGENT, can make the idle industrious, the thriftless provident, or the drunken sober." —Samuel Smiles, Scottish author and reformer

strophe *(STROF), noun*
A stanza containing lines that do not conform to the type, style, or form of the poem in which they appear.
Those not wearing haute couture stick out at our gatherings like STROPHES stick out in short poems.

struthious *(STRUH-thee-us), adjective*
Relating to ostriches and related birds.
The expression "bury your head in the sand" derives from STRUTHIOUS behavior.

stultify *(STUHL-tuh-fie), verb*
To cause to appear foolish or ridiculous.
> *The out-of-date chapeau absolutely STULTIFIED Heather's otherwise immaculate couture.*

stygian *(STY-gee-an), adjective*
Eerily quiet; so dark as to be almost pitch black.
> *"STAND close around, ye STYGIAN set, / With Dirce in one boat convey'd! / Or Charon, seeing, may forget / That he is old and she a shade"* —Walter Savage Landor, British writer and poet

subjugation *(sub-jih-GAY-shun), noun*
The process of making someone your inferior and requiring them to take orders from you.
> *"There was a flavor of SUBJUGATION in his love for Madeleine."* —Saul Bellow, American author

sublime *(suh-BLYME), adjective*
Reaching new levels of quality and perfection unduplicated elsewhere; of such immense beauty that the viewer's breath is taken away, metaphorically speaking.
> *"The SUBLIME and the ridiculous are often so nearly related, that it is difficult to class them separately. One step above the SUBLIME makes the ridiculous, and one step above the ridiculous makes the SUBLIME again."* —Thomas Paine, English revolutionary and intellectual

subliminal *(sub-LIM-inn-uhl), adjective*
Operating below the threshold of consciousness, but still having an effect on the mind.
> *SUBLIMINAL advertising was a big fad in advertising in the 1970s.*

subrogation *(suh-bro-GAY-shin), noun*
The substitution of one person for another with respect to a lawful claim or right.
> *The SUBROGATION clause in the lease says that if the landlord cannot collect rent from the tenant, she has the right to collect from the cosigner of the leasing agreement.*

subsistence *(sub-sis-tense), noun*
The minimum—of food, water, clothing, shelter, and money—a person or family needs to survive.
All we need for SUBSISTENCE is the basics: the finest of everything.

subversive *(sub-VER-siv), adjective*
Describes an act performed to challenge or overthrow the authority of those in power.
"If sex and creativity are often seen by dictators as SUBVERSIVE activities, it's because they lead to the knowledge that you own your own body." —Erica Jong, American author and teacher

suffrage *(SUF-rij), noun*
The right to vote in political elections.
"Higginson was an early advocate of women's SUFFRAGE as he was a vociferous advocate of civil rights for Negroes." —Joyce Carol Oates, American author

sultry *(SUL-tree), adjective*
In terms of weather, hot and humid, with little or no breeze. In terms of human behavior, suggestive of passion or smoldering sexuality.
"Bare-headed in the SULTRY sun, Ahab stood on the bowsprit." —Herman Melville, American author

supercilious *(sue-per-SILL-ee-us), adjective*
Feeling superior to others, and as a result, having a low opinion of or contempt for them based on your belief that they are inferior.
Too many get-rich-quick promoters imbue their advertisements with a SUPERCILIOUS attitude toward the wealth seekers they profess to want to help.

superfluous *(soo-PER-flew-us), adjective*
Excessive and unnecessary.
Some people never seem to be aware that wearing more than a hint of fine jewelry is SUPERFLUOUS.

superlative *(sue-PURR-lah-tiv), adjective*
The quality of something's being the best in its class or quality.
Our family's show horses are SUPERLATIVE to the rest of the horses one can find in the county.

supersede *(sue-per-SEED), verb*
When one thing takes the place of another or renders the former obsolete.
  "The classical laws[of physics] were SUPERSEDED by quantum laws."
  —Stephen Hawking, British theoretical physicist

supplant *(suh-PLANT), verb*
To take the place of.
  "If we would SUPPLANT the opinions and policy of our fathers in any case, we should do so upon evidence so conclusive, and arguments so clear, that even their great authority fairly considered and weighted, cannot stand." —Abraham Lincoln, American president

surfeit *(SUR-fit), noun*
Having too much of a good thing, especially generous servings of food and drink.
  "A SURFEIT of the sweetest things / The deepest loathing to the stomach brings."
  —William Shakespeare, English playwright

surreal *(suh-REEL), adjective*
Possessing a quality that makes something seem unreal; strange; bizarre; almost otherworldly.
  "He seemed to toss them all into the mixed salads of his poetry with the same indifference to form and logic, the same domesticated SURREALISM, that characterized much of the American avant-garde of the period." —Frank O'Hara, American poet

surreptitious *(suh-rep-TISH-us), adjective*
Done in secret.
  With little more than SURREPTITIOUS glances, Alison was able to entice Quentin to her side at the spring gala.

susurration *(soo-suh-RAY-shun), noun*
A soft sound such as the murmuring from a hushed conversation in the next room or the rain gently falling on the roof.
  He bought a device to help him sleep: an electronic synthesizer that mimics the SUSURRATION of a drizzle or a rainstorm.

suzerainty *(suh-ZER-ant-tee), noun*
Paramount, unquestioned authority.
> *"The account executives are sufficiently mature to manage every phase of their accounts without challenging the ultimate SUZERAINTY of the copywriter."*
> —David Ogilvy, British advertising executive

S

sybaritic *(sih-bar-IT-ik), adjective*
Relating to self-indulgent sensuous luxury and pleasure.
> *Selena rubbed the suntan lotion over her tanned middle slowly, and the whole thing had an erotic, SYBARITIC quality that made the men's eyes pop out of their heads.*

sycophant *(SIK-uh-fuhnt), noun*
A person attempting to get on your good side by constantly sucking up and flattering you.
> *Outwardly polite, the rock star secretly viewed his fans as slobbering SYCOPHANTS.*

syllogism *(SILL-oh-jiz-em), noun*
A logical conclusion drawn from statements made.
> *"The SYLLOGISM would be: social capital leads to educational attainment, which leads to mobility."* —Nicholas Lemann, professor, Columbia University

symbiosis *(sim-bee-OH-sis), noun*
A close interdependency between two organisms from two different species.
> *The nouveau riche would like to believe they have a SYMBIOSIS with us, but, in fact, they remain wholly separate and distinct.*

synchronous *(SIN-kro-nus), adjective*
Two events or processes that take place at the same time.
> *The Smythingtons and the Lyttons caused quite a stir among their social contacts after they scheduled SYNCHRONOUS galas.*

syncopation *(sin-ko-PAY-shun), noun*
Music in which the beats are reversed: the normally loud beats are softer, and the beats normally subdued are emphasized.
> *The weird SYNCOPATION in the score made the music very difficult for the percussionists to follow.*

syncretistic *(sin-kre-TIH-stik), adjective*
A set of beliefs obtained by combining elements of multiple cultures, religions, societies, or schools of thought.
   Pauline's SYNCRETISTIC worldview comes from the fact that her family has traveled extensively across the globe.

synecdoche *(sih-NECK-duh-kee), noun*
A type of shorthand speech in which a partial description is understood by the reader or listener to represent the whole; e.g., saying "New York" in a discussion of baseball when you mean "the New York Yankees."
   Marla could not stop using a SYNECDOCHE after she returned from her trip to England at which she met the royal family, saying repeatedly that she had met and socialized with "the crown."

synoptic *(sin-OP-tik), adjective*
Forming or involving a synopsis or summary.
   The close of a presentation should be SYNOPTIC in nature.

syntax *(SIN-tacks), noun*
The arrangement of words in a sentence.
   "Beerbohm's SYNTAX derived from the study of Latin." —Phillip Lopate, editor

systemic *(sih-STEM-ik), adjective*
Relating to a system as a whole and not just its component parts.
   The discarding of couture clothing that is less than a year old has become SYSTEMIC among our group.

syzygy *(SIZE-ih-gee), noun*
In astronomy, *syzygy* takes place when the earth, sun, and moon all line up along a straight path.
   Astronomers predict an eclipse for the next SYZYGY.

"To the artist is sometimes granted a sudden, TRANSIENT insight which serves in this matter for experience. A flash, and where previously the brain held a dead fact, the soul grasps a living truth! At moments we are all artists."

———

Arnold Bennett, English novelist

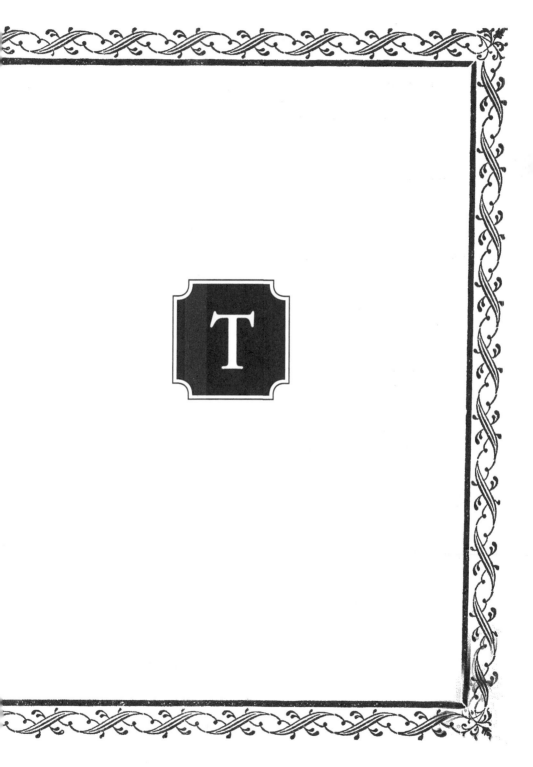

tabernacle *(TAB-err-nak-el), noun*
A portable sanctuary used by the Israelites during their time of wandering in the wilderness, often used to hold the Torah.
> *The Ark of the Covenant is probably the most widely known TABERNACLE, thanks to the movie* Raiders of the Lost Ark.

tableau *(tah-BLOW), noun*
A memorable scene created by the grouping of objects and people.
> *When Jeannette walked into the room, the TABLEAU of angry faces that greeted her revealed that we knew it was she who had gossiped to the society pages.*

tabula rasa *(TAB-yuh-luh-RAH-suh), noun*
A clean slate; lacking preconceived notions, prejudices, beliefs, and attitudes; receptive to instruction and information.
> *"Classic writer's fear of the blank page: call it TABULA-RASA-phobia." —John Jerome, American nonfiction writer*

tachistoscope *(tak-ISS-toe-skope), noun*
An instrument that projects images on a screen in rapid succession.
> *The TACHISTOSCOPE was invented to test memory recall.*

tachymetry *(ta-KEM-eh-tree), noun*
A method of surveying that determines distance and height.
> *TACHYMETRY precedes the design and construction of any major bridge or tunnel.*

tachyon *(TAK-ee-on), noun*
Theoretical particle that travels faster than light.
> *Isaac Asimov was the first to think of TACHYONS.*

taciturn *(TAH-sih-turn), adjective*
Reserved; uncommunicative; a person of few words.
> *"Nature is garrulous to the point of confusion, let the artist be truly TACI-TURN." —Paul Klee, German-born Swiss painter*

tactile *(TACK-tile), adjective*
Related to the sense of touch.
> *This year's Parisian couture is distinguished by its use of highly TACTILE fabrics.*

tangential *(tan-JEHN-shull), adjective*
Divergent or digressive; having little to do with the subject or matter at hand.
   "New York is full of people . . . with a feeling for the TANGENTIAL adventure, the risky adventure, the interlude that's not likely to end in any double-ring ceremony." —Joan Didion, American journalist

tanistry *(TAN-iss-tree), noun*
The system of determining heirship by election.
   TANISTRY determined the heir apparent to the Celtic chief.

tantamount *(TAN-tuh-mount), adjective*
Equivalent in value or effect.
   Eleanor considered our snub of her TANTAMOUNT to betrayal, and, in truth, she was correct.

tantric *(TAN-trik), adjective*
Anything related to the school of thought that views sex as a sacred and deeply spiritual act.
   "Both religions [Hinduism and Buddhism] were patronized by the same kings, ministers, and merchants, many of whom indulged in the same TANTRIC heterodoxies." —William Dalrymple, Scottish historian and author

tarradiddle *(TARE-ah-did-el), noun*
Pretentious and empty talk.
   His babbling produced a nonstop stream of TARRADIDDLE.

tatterdemalion *(tah-ter-deh-MAIL-yun), noun*
A ragamuffin.
   His ragged clothes marked him as the town TATTERDEMALION.

tautology *(taw-TAHL-uh-jee), noun*
A statement, principle, or phrase repeated many times in different ways for emphasis and resulting in redundancy.
   After his wealthy father's death, Gerald consistently referred to his mother with the TAUTOLOGY, "widow woman."

tawdry *(TAW-dree), adjective*
Gaudy, showy, and cheap, as clothes; or, base and mean, as motives.
"Far from being the basis of the good society, the family, with its narrow privacy and TAWDRY secrets, is the source of all our discontents." —Sir Edmund Leach, British author

tchotchke *(CHACH-kee), noun*
A Yiddish word meaning trinkets.
My mother loves to buy TCHOTCHKES at flea markets and swap meets.

tediferous *(ted-IF-err-us), adjective*
One who bears the light.
Carrying the only torch, our leader was TEDIFEROUS.

teem *(TEEM), verb*
To abound or swarm.
As we walked into the nightclub, the paparazzi TEEMED around us like so many manic worker bees.

telecine *(tel-eh-SEEN), noun*
The transfer of footage from movies to TV.
A TELECINE machine prepares films for television broadcast.

teleological *(tee-lee-uh-LOJ-ik-uhl), adjective*
The notion that things exist for a purpose.
The fact that we have unsurpassable wealth and taste, while others who are less important endure hardship, is surely proof that we live in a TELEOLOGICAL universe.

temerity *(teh-MER-ih-tee), noun*
Possessing of boldness and confidence perhaps unwarranted by the situation at hand.
Anne, the girl who just moved to our gated community, had the TEMERITY to ask if we would invite her to one of our galas.

temper *(TEHM-per), verb*
To moderate or lessen the impact of.
"Yet I shall TEMPER so / Justice with mercy." —John Milton, English poet

temperance *(TEM-per-ance), noun*
Abstinence from consuming alcoholic beverages.
> *Cicero said that TEMPERANCE is "the firm and moderate dominion of reason over passion and other unrighteous impulses of the mind."*

tempestuous *(tem-PESS-chew-us), adjective*
Tumultuous and turbulent, as a personality.
> *Claire's TEMPESTUOUS personality is most likely linked to the fact that her father has married and remarried an excessive amount.*

temporal *(tem-PORE-uhl), adjective*
Relating to time.
> *"Science is the language of the TEMPORAL world; love is that of the spiritual world." —Honoré de Balzac, French novelist and playwright*

temporize *(TEHM-puh-rize), verb*
To gain time by being evasive or indecisive.
> *When an officious socialite tries to get too close to us, we do not feel the need to TEMPORIZE with our response; we simply remind her of her place.*

tenacious *(tuh-NAY-shuss), adjective*
Persistent; stubborn; obstinate.
> *"Women are TENACIOUS, and all of them should be TENACIOUS of respect; without esteem they cannot exist; esteem is the first demand that they make of love." —Honoré de Balzac, French novelist and playwright*

tendentious *(ten-DEN-shus), adjective*
Statements or actions designed to promote one's beliefs or point of view.
> *Laura is TENDENTIOUS in her efforts to prove that she believes that a plentitude of fine jewelry is the key to happiness.*

tenebrous *(TEN-uh-bruss), adjective*
Dark and gloomy.
> *Eloise and Marcus spent the day exploring the TENEBROUS forest that surrounded their family's Maine compound.*

tenet *(TEN-et), noun*
A central philosophy; a core belief; a rule or principle one lives by.
"Christian writers from the third century on pointed out the deleterious effect of Platonism on Christian belief—even while adopting many of its fundamental TENETS." —Harold Attridge, dean of Yale University Divinity School

tenuous *(TEN-you-us), adjective*
Unsubstantiated and weak.
Roland's arguments to prove to us that it's better to give than to receive were TENUOUS at best.

tepid *(TEHP-id), adjective*
Characterized by a lack of enthusiasm.
We greeted the new opera, with its mawkish plot and poor acting, with TEPID applause.

terpsichorean *(terp-sih-CORE-ee-an), adjective*
Relating to dancing.
Amy and I took lessons to brush up our TERPSICHOREAN skills prior to our wedding.

tertipara *(ter-tiP-ah-rah), noun*
A woman who has had three pregnancies resulting in viable offspring.
As a TERTIPARA, she was the proud mother of three healthy boys.

tessellate *(TESS-el-layt), adjective*
Arranged in a mosaic pattern.
The TESSELLATE tile arrangement worked well in the kitchen backsplash.

tête-à-tête *(tayt-ah-tayt), noun*
A face-to-face meeting.
Some of us had begun to believe that our servants were pilfering from us, so we sat down the allegedly guilty parties and had a TÊTE-À-TÊTE.

thaumaturge *(THAW-mah-turj), noun*
A person who works miracles.
If you were ever to see Hannah early in the morning, just after she has awoken, then you would know Hannah's personal make-up artist is the epitome of a THAUMATURGE.

theocracy *(thee-AH-krah-see), noun*
A system of government in which priests rule in the name of God.
The Vatican is the ultimate THEOCRACY.

theodolite *(thee-OH-doh-lyte), noun*
A surveying instrument used to measure angles.
The surveyor used a THEODOLITE and simple geometry to calculate the height of the building.

theologian *(thee-oh-LOW-gen), noun*
A student or scholar of religious doctrines.
"The French THEOLOGIAN Alfred Loisy declared that although Jesus proclaimed the coming of the celestial kingdom, it was the church that actually arrived." —G. W. Bowersock, Institute for Advanced Study, Princeton, New Jersey

thigmotaxis *(thig-moe-TAKS-iss), noun*
The motion of an organism in response to touch.
The THIGMOTAXIS of worms is to recoil from physical contact with larger animals, including humans.

tincture *(TINK-cherr), noun*
A trace amount or slight tinge.
The tragic opera was leavened with a TINCTURE of comic relief.

tintinnabulation *(tin-tin-ab-you-LAY-shin), noun*
A ringing or chiming sound.
The bells gave off a lovely TINTINNABULATION.

titillate *(TIT-l-ate), verb*
To excite in an agreeable way.
With its stirring performance of Beethoven's Eroica symphony, the full orchestra TITILLATED us at the Van Gelder's gala.

titration *(ty-TRAY-shin), verb*
Determining how much of a substance is in a solution using a glass vessel made for that purpose.
TITRATION is a common laboratory procedure in organic chemistry.

titular *(TITCH-uh-luhr), adjective*
A person who is a leader by title only, but lacks any real power.
The Queen is the TITULAR head of the British Empire.

T

tmesis *(tim-EE-sis), noun*
The separation of the sections of a compound word using an intervening word.
Fan-freaking-tastic! is an example of TMESIS.

toadyism
Obsequious behavior or excessive flattery for self-serving reasons.
"Note the perfect pitch parody of literary TOADYISM." —Phillip Lopate, editor

tokophobia *(toke-oh-FOE-bee-uh), noun*
Fear of childbirth.
I suspect my sister, who never had kids, suffered from TOKOPHOBIA because she is a small person and also because she felt she did not want to be a mother.

tombolo *(TOM-bo-low), noun*
A split that joins an offshore island to the mainland.
Until they decide to build a bridge, the single-lane road on the TOMBOLO is the only way onto and off of the island.

tome *(TOAM), noun*
A large or scholarly book.
"She carries a book but it is not / the TOME of the ancient wisdom, / the pages, I imagine, are the blank pages / of the unwritten volume of the new." —Hilda Doolittle, American poet and memoirist

toothsome *(TOOTH-suhm), adjective*
Voluptuous and sexually alluring.
Dorienne is TOOTHSOME thanks mainly to her plastic surgeon and her family's attractive fortune.

topical *(TOP-ih-kuhl), adjective*
Having to do with issues of current or local interest.
All the debutantes at the ball wasted our time with inane attempts at TOPICAL conversation about politics and other distasteful matters.

topography *(tuh-POG-ruh-fee), noun*
The arrangement of the physical features of a place, area, or physical object; the "lay of the land."
>*After her return from Europe, Lauren spent most of her time talking about the dazzling alpine TOPOGRAPHY of Switzerland.*

torpor *(TORE-purr), noun*
Apathy; indifference.
>*"A multitude of causes unknown to former times are now acting with a combined force to blunt the discriminating powers of the mind, and unfitting it for all voluntary exertion to reduce it to a state of almost savage TORPOR." —William Wordsworth, British Romantic poet*

torrid *(TORE-ihd), adjective*
Ardent and passionate.
>*The TORRID romance between Alison and her family's stable boy lasted only a short time before the family discovered the tryst and fired the young man.*

tort *(TORT), noun*
In law, a civil misdeed requiring compensation of the victims.
>*Cutting the branches off a neighbor's tree that went over the fence into your yard is, at most, a TORT, not a felony.*

tortuous *(TORE-chew-us), adjective*
Intricate and indirect; not straightforward.
>*"[Critics] don't know that it is hard to write a good play, and twice as hard and TORTUOUS to write a bad one." —Anton Chekhov, Russian dramatist*

totem *(TOH-tuhm), noun*
Anything that serves as a venerated symbol.
>*Our various formal and informal gardens are TOTEMS to our emphasis on the importance of the natural world.*

tout *(TOWT), verb*
To publicize in a boastful, extravagant manner.
>*Eloise TOUTED the excellence of her family's new personal chef to a gauche and distasteful degree.*

tractable *(TRACK-tuh-bull), adjective*
Easygoing; easily managed.
> *The occasional kind comment seems rather enough to keep our servants TRACTABLE.*

tractate *(TRAK-tayt), noun*
A treatise.
> *Amanda's mother delivered a TRACTATE to her daughter about socializing with the right people after she learned that Amanda had been spending time with middle-class families.*

traduce *(truh-DOOSS), verb*
To speak maliciously of; slander.
> *We have snubbed Katrina permanently because she has, at one time or another, TRADUCED each one of us in the society pages.*

transcendent *(tran-SEN-dent), adjective*
Going beyond normal everyday experience; existing beyond the known physical universe and its limitations.
> *"Genius . . . means the TRANSCENDENT capacity of taking trouble."*
> *—Thomas Carlyle, Scottish satirist and historian*

transcendentalism *(tran-sen-DENT-ul-iz-um), noun*
A philosophy that seeks to discover reality through thought.
> *The problem with TRANSCENDENTALISM is that it ignores physical evidence.*

transfiguration *(trans-fig-yuh-RAY-shun), noun*
An extreme change in appearance; a metamorphosis.
> *By the time of her coming-out party, Brigitte had undergone a TRANSFIGURA-TION from gawky child to poised and beautiful adolescent.*

transgress *(trans-GRESS), verb*
To go beyond acceptable bounds.
> *"Unjust laws exist; shall we be content to obey them, or shall we endeavor to amend them, and obey them until we have succeeded, or shall we TRANSGRESS them at once?" —Henry David Thoreau, American author and transcendentalist*

The Big Book of Words You Should Know to Sound Smart

transient *(TRAN-zee-unt), adjective*
Temporary; lacking permanence.
> *"To the artist is sometimes granted a sudden, TRANSIENT insight which serves in this matter for experience. A flash, and where previously the brain held a dead fact, the soul grasps a living truth! At moments we are all artists." —Arnold Bennett, English novelist*

transmogrify *(trans-MOG-ruh-fie), verb*
To change appearance in a disturbing way.
> *We cannot abide that particular interior decorator because he always manages to TRANSMOGRIFY tasteful displays of luxury into pompous tableaus of arrogant wealth.*

transubstantiation *(tran-sub-stan-she-aye-shun), noun*
The notion of endowing something with symbolic value beyond its physical construct.
> *TRANSUBSTANTIATION is used as a technique in marketing, transforming shabby and gauche items into supposed examples of tasteful luxury.*

travail *(truh-VAIL), noun, verb*
Pain and suffering due to a mental or physical hardship; or, to endure such pain and suffering.
> *Charlotte recently had to endure the TRAVAIL of going an entire week without her family's Olympic-sized swimming pool because the pool had developed a crack.*

treacle *(TREE-kuhl), noun*
Contrived or mawkish sentimentality.
> *That writer's work is suffering in quality, as we could hardly sit through the TREACLE of her recently opened opera.*

tremulous *(TREHM-yuh-luss), adjective*
Timid and fearful.
> *With TREMULOUS mien, Anthony asked Gwendolyn if she would consent to a joining of their families.*

trenchant *(TREN-chunt), adjective*
Sarcastic; direct and to the point; intelligently analytical and accurate.
> *Michael's TRENCHANT commentary on American politics and society have made him a popular radio talk show host.*

trepan *(trih-pan), noun*
A person or thing that ensnares or traps you.
> *Addiction is a TREPAN.*

T

triptych *(TRIP-tick), noun*
A picture or carving on three panels, or a set of three associated paintings or other works of art.
> *Scott wanted to buy just the center painting, but the gallery owner refused to break up the TRIPTYCH.*

Triton *(TRY-ton), noun*
A mythical creature, similar to a mermaid, with a human torso and arms, gills under the ears, and a tail like a dolphin.
> *TRITONS served Neptune as his attendants.*

troglodyte *(TRAHG-lah-dyte), noun*
A person considered to be primitive, out of date, coarse, uncouth, ill-mannered, or brutish.
> *Sick and tired of going out with TROGLODYTES, Janet told her friends she was through with blind dates.*

tropism *(TRO-priz-um), noun*
The tendency of a plant or other organism to change direction in response to a stimulus; also used as a pejorative to describe reflexive or instinctual (i.e., mindless) human behavior.
> *The socialites demonstrate TROPISM as they flocked to the newly opened store of the newest high-fashion designer.*

truckle *(TRUHK-uhl), verb*
To submit obsequiously to a command.
> *We have trained our servants to TRUCKLE to our every whim.*

truculent *(TRUK-you-lent), adjective*
Belligerent; argumentative; always ready for a fight.
> *Short-tempered and TRUCULENT, Lucy could be set off by the slightest incident or comment.*

trumpery *(TRUHM-puh-ree), noun*
Something without value; a trifle.
> *The TRUMPERY that the Smythingtons collect and call "art" is, clearly, distasteful dreck.*

truncate *(TRUN-kate), verb*
To shorten something by cutting off the top or one of the ends.
> *Ellen looked ridiculous because she had chosen to TRUNCATE her floor-length party dress to tea-length hem.*

tryst *(TRIST), noun*
An appointment made by lovers to meet at a certain place and time.
> *Since their families are of equal station, no one worries much about the supposedly secret TRYSTS between Josephine and Brock.*

tumescent *(too-MESS-ent), adjective*
Becoming or already engorged, full, swollen, or rigid.
> *After the hurricane, our Florida compound was flooded by the TUMESCENT Intracoastal Waterway.*

tumid *(TOO-mid), adjective*
Pompous and swollen with pride.
> *We cannot stand it when Katherine wins arguments about couture and art collecting because the TUMID expression that crosses her face after a conversational victory is so loathsome.*

turgescent *(tur-JESS-ent), adjective*
Becoming or appearing swollen or distended.
> *His abs were so neglected, his stomach became TURGESCENT after a big meal.*

tyro *(TIE-roh), noun*
A beginner or novice.
> *Though a TYRO, Madeline quickly mastered cross-country skiing during her jaunt to Switzerland.*

"A gentleman doesn't pounce . . . he glides. If a woman sits on a piece of furniture which permits your sitting beside her, you are free to regard this as an invitation, though not an UNEQUIVOCAL one."

———

Quentin Crisp, British writer, actor, and model

uberty *(YOU-ber-tee), noun*
Abundance.
The law of attraction says everyone can enjoy a life of UBERTY.

ubiquitous *(you-BICK-wih-tuss), adjective*
Something that is everywhere, all around you, constantly surrounding you, and you cannot escape from it.
Wireless communication in the United States became UBIQUITOUS toward the close of the twentieth century.

ufology *(you-FAH-la-gee), noun*
The study of unidentified flying objects.
The movie Men in Black *is mostly about UFOLOGY.*

ulterior *(uhl-TEER-ee-er), adjective*
Intentionally concealed, as motives.
"When one has extensively pondered about men, as a career or as a vocation, one sometimes feels nostalgic for primates. At least they do not have ULTERIOR motives." —Albert Camus, Algerian-born French author and philosopher

ultimo *(UHL-tih-mow), adjective*
Of the last month.
We received our tenant's rent check ULTIMO.

ululation *(you-you-LAY-shin), noun*
A loud howl or cry.
"He made an unintelligible howling sound, a ULULATION of pain and rage." —John D. MacDonald, novelist

umbra *(UM-brah), noun*
A planet's shadow, especially the shadow of the earth upon the moon.
A solar eclipse is caused by the earth passing through the moon's UMBRA upon the sun.

umbrage *(UM-bridge), noun*
To take exception to and be offended by a comment or action seen as a slight or insult.
"I take UMBRAGE with people who post comments on my blog that are patently false," Bob said.

unassuming *(uhn-uh-SOOM-ing), adjective*
Modest and unpretentious.
> *The Binghamtons just bought a lovely, UNASSUMING 5,000-square-foot chalet in the Rockies.*

unbosom *(uhn-BUH-zim), verb*
To reveal feelings or what one knows.
> *On Sunday we UNBOSOM ourselves in the confessional.*

unbridled *(un-BRY-duld), adjective*
Without limitations or boundaries; uncontrolled and unrestrained.
> *The customer's UNBRIDLED fury at being denied a refund was a sight to behold.*

unceremonious *(un-sair-uh-MOAN-ee-us), adjective*
Discourteously abrupt, hasty, rude.
> *The maitre d's UNCEREMONIOUS manner only made us love the new French restaurant all the more.*

unctuous *(UNK-chew-us), adjective*
Possessing an untrustworthy or dubious nature; characterized by an insincere manner.
> *Local car dealers doing their own TV commercials often communicate in an UNCTUOUS, almost laughable manner.*

underclub *(UN-der-klub), noun*
When a shot in golf comes up short due to improper club selection.
> *His UNDERCLUB resulted in a bogey for the hole.*

undulate *(UN-jew-late), intransitive verb*
To move back and forth or from side to side in a smooth, slow motion.
> *Barbara and Bentley UNDULATED gracefully at their family's private ice rink.*

unequivocal *(uhn-ih-KWIV-uh-kull), adjective*
Possessing a clear meaning or answer.
> *"A gentleman doesn't pounce ... he glides. If a woman sits on a piece of furniture which permits your sitting beside her, you are free to regard this as an invitation, though not an UNEQUIVOCAL one." —Quentin Crisp, British writer, actor, and model*

ungainly *(un-GAIN-lee), adjective*
Awkward and clumsy.
> *One of the hallmarks of this year's fashionable shoes is that they make one seem UNGAINLY on anything other than marble flooring.*

unguent *(UN-gent), noun*
A greasy substance used as an ointment or for lubrication.
> *You can treat a minor burn by breaking off a leaf of the aloe vera plant and applying the UNGUENT inside to the injury.*

unicameral *(you-nih-CAM-ah-rul), adjective*
Having only a single compartment.
> *Large corporate jets have two luggage compartments, but midsize jets are UNICAMERAL.*

unicast *(YOU-nih-kast), noun*
The communication from one device to another device in a network.
> *UNICAST used to be called point-to-point communication.*

uniformitarianism *(you-ni-form-ih-TARE-ee-uhn-iz-um), noun*
The belief that change on earth takes place slowly, gradually, and at a uniform rate rather than through short, sudden, catastrophic events.
> *The fact that the families of our servants have been with us for many, many generations would seem to be proof of UNIFORMITARIANISM.*

unilateral *(you-nih-LAT-ur-uhl), adjective*
A decision that affects many people or states but that is made independently by a single authority, without consulting those whom it affects.
> *We made a UNILATERAL decision to exclude Edwin from our group of possible paramours due to his distasteful habit of kissing and telling.*

unimpeachable *(un-ihm-PEE-chuh-bull), adjective*
Above reproach; impossible to discredit or slander.
> *We promoted Carla to upstairs maid because her job performance has been UNIMPEACHABLE.*

unitary *(YOU-ni-tare-ee), adjective*
A thing that exists or occurs in discrete units, sections, parts, or steps.
 "Today we can see life as a UNITARY process, made up of a number of smaller processes." —Julian Huxley, English evolutionary biologist

unrenumerative *(un-re-NEW-mer-ah-tiv), adjective*
A job, investment, business venture, or other activity that pays little or no financial return.
 "We find the wealth of our cities mingled with poverty and UNRENUMERA-TIVE toil." —Grover Cleveland, American president

unsavory *(un-SAYV-err-ee), adjective*
Distasteful; unpleasant; disreputable; of dubious reputation.
 "Our future is inextricably linked to what happens in Washington DC, and we know that is a very UNSAVORY reality." —Don Libey, direct-marketing advisor

untenable *(uhn-TEN-uh-bull), adjective*
Not possible to defend, as an argument or position.
 "Are the legitimate compensation and honors that should come as the result of ability and merit to be denied on the UNTENABLE ground of sex aristocracy?" —Bertha Honore Potter Palmer, American socialite

unwieldy *(un-WEEL-dee), adjective*
Not easy to handle or to manage.
 "Now mark me how I will undo myself. / I give this heavy weight from off my head, / And this UNWIELDY sceptre from my hand, / The pride of kingly sway from out my heart." —William Shakespeare, English playwright

unzymotic *(un-ZEYE-mow-tik), adjective*
Fabulous.
 Celebrities live an UNZYMOTIC life.

upbraid *(up-BRAYD), verb*
To censure or to find fault with.
 We had to UPBRAID our butler severely when we learned he was gossiping to other members of our staff.

uptick *(UP-tik), noun*
A price of a share sold that is higher than the previous price.
> *An UPTICK in the market caused a major sell-off.*

urbane *(err-BANE), adjective*
Suave, sophisticated, refined, cosmopolitan, and well versed in the ways of high society.
> *Even in his knock-around tennis whites, Brett always manages to appear URBANE.*

urbanization *(ur-ban-ih-ZAY-shun), noun*
The growth of cities brought about by a population shift from rural areas and small communities to larger ones.
> *URBANIZATION, which began in the United States in the late 1800s, was in part triggered by the shift from an agricultural economy to an industrial one.*

urtext *(ERR-tekst), noun*
The original text of a work.
> *The Beethoven manuscript contained the URTEXT of Moonlight Sonata.*

usurper *(you-SIR-per), noun*
A person who seizes a position of power through illegal means, force, or deception.
> *"A USURPER in the guise of a benefactor is the enemy that we are now to encounter and overcome." —William Leggett, American poet and fiction writer*

usury *(USE-err-ee), noun*
To charge illegally high or excessive interest rates on a loan.
> *Loan sharks lend money at USURIOUS rates, and break your legs if you don't make back the principal with interest on time.*

utilitarian *(you-till-ih-TAYR-ee-an), adjective*
Showing preference for things and ideas that are practical and utterly pragmatic while eschewing the fanciful and useless.
> *Paul's UTILITARIAN mindset makes him an ideal trader on Wall Street.*

utopia *(you-TOE-pee-uh), noun*
A perfect or ideal society.
> *Many of us who are accustomed to wealth have learned to accept that we must make our own UTOPIAS rather than rely on the actions of outside forces or agencies.*

uxorious *(uhk-SAWR-ee-us), adjective*
Doting on one's wife to an excessive degree.
> *"The same things change their names at such a rate; / For instance—passion in a lover's glorious, / But in a husband is pronounced UXORIOUS." —Lord Byron, British Romantic poet*

vacillate *(VAH-sill-ate), verb*
To swing back and forth between two points.
> *"But modern character is inconstant, divided, VACILLATING, lacking the stone-like certitude of archaic man . . ." —Saul Bellow, American author*

vacuous *(VAK-yoo-us), adjective*
Devoid of emotion, intelligence, or any normal human thought processes; stupid; moronic.
> *The VACUOUS stare from her two eyes, looking like raisins pushed into a lump of dough, made him shiver with loathing and contempt.*

vagary *(VAY-guh-ree), noun*
A random or unexpected occurrence.
> *One needs to accept the VAGARIES of life if one is to be happy or at least content.*

vainglorious *(vayne-GLOR-ee-us), adjective*
Conceited; boastful; prone to showing off and bragging.
> *Although the scion of a well-established family, Gordon is so VAINGLORIOUS that you'd think him a parvenu!*

valuation *(val-you-AYE-shun), noun*
The calculated worth or value of an asset, based on a rigorous appraisal.
> *One of the accounting firm's services is business VALUATION, where you can pay to have an accurate appraisal of what your business would sell for if acquired.*

vanguard *(VAN-gard), noun*
That which is at the forefront or the leading edge; the most advanced group.
> *Robert is among the VANGUARD of area oenophiles.*

vapid *(VAH-pid), adjective*
Dull; void of intellectual curiosity or intelligence; lacking spirit and enthusiasm; routine; unchallenging.
> *What irked him most about his sister-in-law was her VAPID stares in response to simple questions, conversation, and jokes.*

variegated *(VAIR-ee-ih-gate-ed), adjective*
That which changes color or contains different hues of the same color.
> *A lawn covered in VARIEGATED fallen leaves is the sign that autumn is finally here.*

vehement *(VEE-heh-ment), adjective*
Insistent; unyielding in one's opinion or decision; intense inflexibility about matters.
> *Milly, a chronic worrywart, was VEHEMENT about her children calling her if they were going to be late getting home from school.*

venal *(VEE-null), adjective*
Refers to people who can be bought, bribed, or otherwise persuaded to deviate from their beliefs and purpose.
> *"Give me but the liberty of the press, and I will give to the minister a VENAL House of Commons." —Richard Brinsley Sheridan, Irish playwright and statesman*

venerable *(VEN-err-uh-bull), adjective*
An individual or institution that is respected and revered, sometimes because of achievement, intelligence, or character, but just as often as a result of being around a long time.
> *"Is the babe young? When I behold it, it seems more VENERABLE than the oldest man." —Henry David Thoreau, American author and transcendentalist*

venial *(VEE-nee-ul), adjective*
A pardonable offense; a minor misdeed for which one is easily forgiven.
> *Cassidy was initially angry that Carley lied to her about where she bought her vintage handbag, but soon deemed the deed VENIAL.*

veracity *(ver-ASS-ih-tea), noun*
The characteristic or habit of being truthful and conforming to accepted standards of behavior.

"The world is upheld by the VERACITY of good men: they make the earth wholesome." —Ralph Waldo Emerson, American poet, essayist, and transcendentalist

verbiage *(VER-bee-ij), noun*
Words; in particular, prose written to fill space and impress others rather than communicate ideas and information.

"There's some white space on the back page of the sales brochure," the marketing manager told his ad agency, "so let's fill it with some VERBIAGE about service and quality."

verbose *(ver-BOHS), adjective*
Describes a person or composition using more words than are needed to get the point across.

Long-winded and VERBOSE, Mitch made his team members groan whenever he stood up to speak at a charity event.

verdant *(VUR-dant), adjective*
Lush with trees, bushes, ferns, and other green foliage.

With its careful mix of plants, the Whittingtons' formal garden remains VERDANT year-round.

veritable *(VER-ih-tah-bull), adjective*
Genuine; the real thing; a perfect specimen or example.

"For me, the child is a VERITABLE image of becoming, of possibility, poised to reach towards what is not yet, towards a growing that cannot be predetermined or prescribed." —Maxine Greene, American philosopher and educator

vernacular *(ver-NAK-you-lar), adjective, noun*
The language of a particular region or specific group of people.

Communicating with stockbrokers is difficult for many investors because they do not speak the VERNACULAR of the financial world.

vernal *(VER-nul), adjective*
Related to spring.
> *"One impulse from a VERNAL wood / May teach you more of man, / Of moral evil and of good, / Than all the sages can." —William Wordsworth, British Romantic poet*

vers libre *(VERSS-LEE-breh), noun*
Free verse, a style of poetry requiring no rhyme or meter.
> *H.L. Mencken observed that VERS LIBRE is "a device for making poetry easier to write and harder to read."*

vertiginous *(ver-TIJ-uh-nuss), adjective*
Causing vertigo, imbalance, dizziness, or stumbling.
> *Mallory and Michael enjoyed their weekend getaway to Paris, spending many moments staring at the Parisian skyline from the VERTIGINOUS heights of the Eiffel Tower.*

vestigial *(vess-tih-jee-ul), adjective*
Describes a remaining sample or trace of something that is disappearing or has already all but disappeared.
> *Some babies are born with a VESTIGIAL tail at the base of the spine.*

vexation *(vek-SAY-shin), noun*
Frustration, annoyance, or irritation resulting from some action, occurrence, or statement.
> *"There is not much less VEXATION in the government of a private family than in the managing of an entire state." —Michel de Montaigne, Renaissance scholar*

vicariously *(vye-KARE-ee-uss-lee), adverb*
To enjoy imagined feelings and experiences largely by observing or hearing about another person's life and adventures.
> *Married for over twenty-five years, Roger often told his single friends that he lived VICARIOUSLY through them.*

vicissitudes *(vi-SIS-ih-toods), noun*
The constant change of one's situation or condition, common throughout life.
> *"VICISSITUDES of fortune, which spares neither man nor the proudest of his works, which buries empires and cities in a common grave." —Edward Gibbon, British historian*

vignette *(vin-YET), noun*
A brief story, incident, or episode, usually told to illustrate some point.
Adding a VIGNETTE or two to a speech can help make abstract ideas clearer.

vindicate *(VIN-dih-kate), verb*
To prove your opinion is correct, or your action justified, or that you are innocent of a misdeed you stand accused of, despite opinions and evidence to the contrary.
We laughed at Paulette's predictions about the imminent fall fashions, but, once the couture was unveiled, Paulette was VINDICATED.

virulence *(VEER-uh-lentz), noun*
Bitterness and loathing.
"We are sheep in a pen, injected with the VIRULENCE." —Harlan Ellison, writer

visage *(VIZ-aj), noun*
Face or overall appearance.
When the doctor entered the patient lounge, his grim VISAGE told the whole story before he could say a word.

visceral *(VIS-er-ul), adjective*
An immediate and strong gut reaction; a quickly formed opinion, based mainly on instinct and usually negative in nature.
"[Multiculturalism's] passions are political; its assumptions empirical; its conception of identities VISCERAL." —Joyce Appleby, American historian

Visigoths *(VIZ-ih-gahths), noun*
Members of the western branch of the Goths that invaded the Roman Empire.
"The time has come to speak out, to hold back the VISIGOTHS." —Harlan Ellison, writer

vitriol *(vih-tree-awl), noun*
An attitude of bitterness, hatred, or mean-spiritedness.
The school board reprimanded the coach with VITRIOL.

vituperative *(veye-TOO-pre-tiv), adjective*
A person who is bitter and angry, and readily takes that anger out on those around him.

> *VITUPERATIVE to an unreasonable degree, George smashed one of Jessica's prized dishes for every one of his old golf clubs she had given away when cleaning out the garage.*

vivacious *(vy-VAY-shuss), adjective*
Joyful; happy, spirited; possessing a positive attitude about and enthusiasm for life; a person who lives life to the fullest.

> *Even after her family maintained some steep revenue losses, Sandra retained her VIVACIOUS character.*

vociferous *(vo-SIF-er-uss), adjective*
Something said loudly so as to gain the listener's attention; a person who speaks loudly so as to gain attention.

> *"Let the singing singers / With vocal voices, most VOCIFEROUS, / In sweet vociferation out-vociferize / Even sound itself." —Henry Carey, English poet*

volitional *(voe-LISH-uhn-uhl), adjective*
Describes an action performed or thought achieved through deliberate and conscious effort.

> *Our servants' persistent and VOLITIONAL attention to detail makes them absolutely indispensable to us.*

voluptuous *(vuh-LUP-chew-us), adjective*
Anything arising from or giving extreme sensory or sensual pleasure.

> *A VOLUPTUOUS banquet was the highlight of the Masterlys' Thanksgiving gala.*

voracious *(vo-RAY-shuss), adjective*
Possessing a huge and insatiable appetite, whether for food, knowledge, amusement, or something else.

> *Her son always had a VORACIOUS desire for knowledge. He read anything he could get his hands on and was always willing to experience something new.*

The Big Book of Words You Should Know to Sound Smart

vortex *(VOR-teks), noun*
Liquid or gas swirling in a spiral that sucks everything in or near it towards its center; a problem or situation that draws in everyone around it.
   The permanent whirlpool where the river goes underground is a dark VORTEX sucking in everything in its current.

vox populi *(VOKS-pop-you-lye), noun*
Expression of the prevailing mood, concerns, and opinions in a country.
   In response to an environmentally friendly VOX POPULI, more and more corporations are "going green."

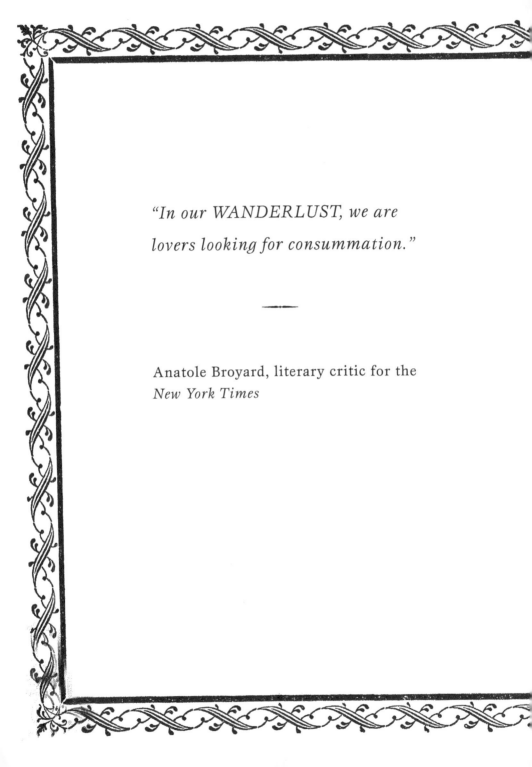

"In our WANDERLUST, we are lovers looking for consummation."

Anatole Broyard, literary critic for the *New York Times*

waft *(WAFT), verb*
To carry lightly, as if caught in a breeze.
> *"This quiet sail is as a noiseless wing / To WAFT me from distraction."* —Lord Byron, British Romantic poet

waggish *(WAG-ish), adjective*
Joking, witty, and mischievous.
> *"This species of 'fame' a WAGGISH acquaintance says can be manufactured to order, and sometimes is so manufactured."* —Herman Melville, American author

waif *(WAFE), noun*
A stray person or animal.
> *The occasional nouveau riche WAIF may float into our circle, but she rarely lasts long.*

wainscoting *(WAYNE-scott-ing), noun*
Wood paneling on the lower part of a wall only.
> *A carpenter did our WAINSCOTING for us as I am unhandy.*

wan *(WAHN), adjective*
Showing or suggesting ill health or unhappiness.
> *"So shaken as we are, so WAN with care, / Find we a time for frighted peace to pant."* —William Shakespeare

wanchancy *(wahn-CHANCE-ee), adjective*
Unlucky.
> *Being WANCHANCY, I avoid casinos and poker games, since I'd be sure to lose.*

wanderlust *(WON-dehr-lust), noun*
A strong and innate desire to travel far from home.
> *"In our WANDERLUST, we are lovers looking for consummation."* —Anatole Broyard, literary critic for the New York Times

wane *(WAYN), verb*
To gradually decrease; to fade away; to become diminished.
> *Once she finally received the Cartier watch from her father, Karen's interest in the timepiece quickly WANED.*

wangle *(WANG-guhl), verb*
To accomplish by underhanded methods.
Jennifer managed to WANGLE an invitation to the Clarksons' party, even though she is the gauchest of the area's parvenus.

wanton *(WAHN-tn), adjective*
Loose, lascivious, and lewd.
Robert is so WANTON that women stay away from him in spite of his family's connections.

waspish *(WOS-pish), adjective*
Irascible and petulant; given to resentment.
Rebecca can be WASPISH, but we forgive her because she gives the best galas.

wassail *(WAH-sull), noun*
A salute or toast given when drinking to someone's health, well-being, or success.
We lost count of the mugs of beer consumed with the numerous WASSAILS to our teacher wishing him a happy retirement.

watermark *(WAW-terr-mark), noun*
A faint design, graphic, or lettering pressed into paper while it is still in pulp form.
The CEO's classy letterhead bears a WATERMARK of the company logo.

watershed *(WAW-ter-shed), noun*
An important event that signals the beginning of a new era or phase.
We knew it was a WATERSHED event when the Smythingtons did not hold their annual New Year's Eve gala last year.

wayfaring *(WAY-fair-ing), adjective*
Traveling on foot.
We spent many WAYFARING weekends during our month-long jaunt in France last year.

weal *(WEEL), noun*
Prosperous well-being; vitality.
> *Jordan is convinced that expensive jewelry is necessary for one's WEAL and welfare.*

weanling *(WEEN-ling), noun*
A recently weaned animal.
> *The WEANLING pandas were absolutely adorable.*

weir *(WEERE), noun*
A low dam or barrier built across a river either to control water levels or catch fish.
> *When the water level in the Passaic River lowered during a drought, a stone WEIR built by Indians for catching fish became visible.*

weltschmerz *(VELT-schmayrtz), noun*
A lingering sorrow that some believe is a given in life.
> *When we snubbed Margaret for buying so many fashion knockoffs, her WELTSCHMERZ lasted until we forgave her.*

wend *(WEND), verb*
To go; to proceed.
> *"As they WEND away / A voice is heard singing / Of Kitty, or Katy, / As if the name meant once / All love, all beauty." —Philip Larkin, British poet, novelist, and jazz critic*

whelky *(WELL-key), noun*
A large carnivorous snail with a spiral shell.
> *WHELKIES are the largest of the edible snails.*

whelp *(WEHLP), noun*
A despised person or his or her offspring.
> *"'Twas Slander filled her mouth with lying words, / Slander, the foulest WHELP of Sin." —Robert Pollok, Scottish poet*

wherewithal *(WAIR-with-all), noun*
Means or resources; money.
> *We certainly have the WHEREWITHAL to visit that restaurant, but we will not because the maitre d' does not know his place.*

whicker *(WIH-kerr), verb*
To muffle your laughter.
> *When our math professor taught the class with his fly open, we WHICKERED.*

whimsical *(WIHM-zih-kuhl), adjective*
Erratic; unpredictable; capricious.
> *"How truly does this journal contain my real and undisguised thoughts—I always write it according to the humour I am in, and if a stranger was to think it worth reading, how capricious—insolent & WHIMSICAL I must appear!"*
> *—Frances Burney, British novelist, diarist, and playwright*

wily *(WHY-lee), adjective*
Crafty and cunning.
> *When it comes to parting Brock from his inheritance, the normally charming Mallory can be quite WILY.*

winnow *(WIN-oh), verb*
To find what one is looking for through a process of elimination in which many candidates are considered but only a few are chosen.
> *Selma WINNOWED through her wardrobe until she found the perfect Vera Wang gown to wear to the New Year's Eve ball.*

winsome *(WIN-suhm), adjective*
Winning and engaging; charming.
> *Lydia looked quite WINSOME throughout her coming-out party.*

wistful *(WIHST-full), adjective*
Yearning, pensive; having an unfulfilled desire.
> *"I never saw a man who looked / With such a WISTFUL eye / Upon that little tent of blue / Which prisoners call the sky." —Oscar Wilde, Irish playwright and poet*

witticism *(WIT-uh-siz-uhm), noun*
A witty or clever remark.
> *We love our servants because they are so full of WITTICISMS about people of their class.*

wizened *(WIZ-uhnd), adjective*
Withered; shriveled; dried up.
> *Moira spent so much time out in the sun during her Mediterranean trip that she came back positively WIZENED.*

wont *(WAWNT), adjective, noun*
Accustomed; or, a custom or practice.
> *"I am WONT to think that men are not so much the keepers of herds as herds are the keepers of men, the former are so much the freer." —Henry David Thoreau, American author and transcendentalist*

wontless *(WANT-less), adjective*
Unaccustomed.
> *When it came to gourmet food, he was WONTLESS, never having had the opportunity of eating well before.*

wormhole *(WERM-hole), noun*
A channel or shortcut through space-time, originating at a black hole, that connects to another part of the universe.
> *One theory is that white holes are on the opposite end of the WORMHOLE from the black hole.*

wormwood *(WERM-wood), noun*
Strong-smelling plants with white or yellow flowers.
> *One sniff told us the WORMWOODS were in full bloom.*

wrest *(REST), verb*
To pull away; to take something by force or threat.
> *"WREST once the law to your authority: / To do a great right, do a little wrong." —William Shakespeare*

writedown *(RIGHT-down), noun*
A reduction in the recorded value of an asset.
> *Big WRITEDOWNS caused the value of his real-estate portfolio to plummet.*

wunderkind *(WUHN-der-kind), noun*
One who succeeds in business, or a similar endeavor, at a comparatively young age.

Alex would be a WUNDERKIND in the firm even without his father's connections.

wuthering *(WHUH-there-ing), adjective*
Moving with force or impetus.

Heathcliffe and Cathy met on the moor, where the wind came WUTHERING across the heather.

Such epithets, like pepper, / Give
ZEST to what you write; / And, if
you strew them sparely, / They whet
the appetite: / But if you lay them
on too thick, / You spoil the matter
quite!"

———

Lewis Carroll, English author and
logician

X, Y, & Z

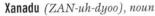

Xanadu *(ZAN-uh-dyoo), noun*
A place of perfect, idyllic beauty.
> *"In XANADU did Kubla Khan / A stately pleasure-dome decree: / Where Alph, the sacred river, ran / Through caverns measureless to man / Down to a sunless sea." —Samuel Taylor Coleridge, English poet*

xanthic *(ZAN-thick), adjective*
Of a yellowish tint or color.
> *After Laura wore a XANTHIC dress to the spring ball, the area's nouveau riche followed her example at subsequent galas.*

Xanthippe *(zan-TIP-ee), noun*
An ill-tempered, shrewish woman.
> *Felicia is far from a XANTHIPPE simply because she interacts only with certain members of the household staff.*

xanthospermous *(ZAN-tho-sperm-us), adjective*
Having yellow seeds.
> *Some members of the squash family are XANTHOSPERMOUS.*

xebec *(ZEE-beck), noun*
A small, three-masted ship used in the Mediterranean for commerce that once was a favorite vessel of the leisure class.
> *All of the amassed XEBECS ruined the otherwise spectacular views from our villa during the month we spent on the Greek Isles.*

xenocurrency *(zen-uh-KURR-uhn-see), noun*
Money that is circulated or traded in money markets outside its country of issue.
> *The Wallaces stopped speculating in XENOCURRENCY once rumors of a worldwide recession began circulating.*

xenogamy *(zih-NAHG-uh-me), noun*
Cross-pollination among plant species.
> *The secret of our award-winning formal gardens is the careful use of XENOGAMY.*

xenophile *(ZEN-uh-file), noun*
Someone who is attracted to foreign styles, customs, manners, etc.
> *All of us are XENOPHILES because American customs and cultural products are so gauche.*

xenophobic *(zen-ah-FOE-bik), adjective*
Having an irrational fear of foreigners and immigrants.
> *We are not XENOPHOBIC; we dislike all strangers, regardless of their backgrounds, unless they are brought to us by other social contacts.*

xenoplastic *(zen-uh-plass-tick), adjective*
Of, or occurring between, distantly related individuals.
> *We always have the senders of cards and letters carefully screened because some of us have been involved in XENOPLASTIC schemes by which total strangers suggested they belong to our family.*

xerochilia *(zeer-uh-kile-ee-uh), noun*
Dryness of the lips.
> *Kyle may be cute, but the way he treats his chronic XEROCHILIA with common lip balm is nothing short of distasteful.*

xerophyte *(ZER-oh-fight), noun*
A cactus, succulent, or other plant that has adapted to living in a desert with limited rainfall or irritation.
> *We make use of a XEROPHYTE garden at our Southwest desert estate.*

xerosis *(zih-ROH-sis), noun*
The typical hardening of aging skin and tissue.
> *Ophelia constantly visits European spas to slow the onset of XEROSIS.*

xerotic *(zer-AH-tik), adjective*
Dryness of the skin.
> *My XEROTIC skin caused white, scaly growth on my elbows.*

xiphoid *(ZIE-foid), adjective*
Shaped like a sword.
> *We can always spot Carlson's private plane because it is covered with the same XIPHOID shapes that adorn his family's crest.*

xylography *(zie-LAHG-ruh-fee), noun*
The art of engraving wood.
> *Even though it is not particularly valuable, we keep great-grandfather's XYLOGRAPHY collection because it meant something to him.*

yahoo *(YAH-hoo), noun*
A boorish, uncultivated, common person.
> *"Factory windows are always broken. / Somebody's always throwing bricks, / Somebody's always heaving cinders, / Playing ugly YAHOO tricks." —Vachel Lindsay, American poet*

yammer *(YAM-uhr), verb*
To whine or complain loudly and at length.
> *The way Roland YAMMERS about being thrown out of Yale, you'd think he hadn't begged his father to make the expulsion happen!*

yantra *(YAHN-truh), noun*
A geometric diagram used to help one meditate.
> *During Eloise's foray into Buddhism, she kept forgetting her mantra, so her teacher gave her a YANTRA that she could affix to the wall in front of her meditation cushion.*

yarborough *(YAR-berr-oh), noun*
In whist and bridge, a hand with no card above nine.
> *I usually bet against a YARBOROUGH hand.*

yardarm *(YAHRD-arm), noun*
Either of the outer portions of a square sail.
> *During the regatta, the yachts sailed YARDARM to YARDARM, appearing as though they may collide at any moment.*

yare *(YARE), adjective*
Quick and agile; lively.
> *Thanks to the gymnastics she performed at finishing school, Amanda has a YARE and limber body.*

yaw *(YAW), verb*
An erratic, side-to-side motion; or, to swerve.
> *A fast-moving cold front caused Sasha's Learjet 60 to YAW dangerously for several minutes.*

yawnful *(YAWN-full), adjective*
Arousing tedium or boredom.
> *Eleanor's YAWNFUL story about her month doing volunteer work made many of us bolt for the doors.*

yawp *(YAWP), noun, verb*

A raucous, clamorous noise; or, to make such a noise.

"I sound my barbaric YAWP over the roofs of the world." —Walt Whitman, American poet and humanist

yearling *(YEER-ling), adjective or noun*

Of a year's duration; or, an animal in its second year.

Many of our family's racehorses are YEARLINGS, which we put to pasture after their retirement.

yen *(YEN), noun*

A strong desire or urge.

"Perhaps one subtext of the health care debate is a YEN to be treated like a whole person, not just an eye, an ear, a nose or a throat." —Anna Quindlen, American author and opinion columnist

yenta *(YEN-tuh), noun*

A woman considered a busybody or gossip.

Spreading rumors amongst ourselves is one thing, but Rebecca has gained a repu-tation as a YENTA because she also blabs to the help.

yeoman *(YOH-muhn), adjective, noun*

Pertaining to or one who performs arduous tasks in a loyal and workmanlike manner.

We promoted Helga to upstairs maid because of her YEOMAN work ethic.

yob *(YAHB), noun*

A cruel and loutish young man; a bully.

"Mick Jagger, alternately slurring YOB and lisping lordling, is classlessness apo-theosised." —Phillip Norman, British author

yokel *(YOH-kuhl), noun*

A gullible inhabitant of a rural area.

"[A human being] is the YOKEL par excellence, the booby unmatchable, the king dupe of the cosmos." —H.L. Mencken, American magazine editor, essayist, and critic

younker *(YAHN-kuhr), noun*

A young man or child.

Alex has been a fine horseman since he was a mere YOUNKER, playing with his family's thoroughbreds.

The Big Book of Words You Should Know to Sound Smart

zabaglione *(zah-buhl-YOH-knee), noun*
An Italian dessert delicacy featuring a foamy, custard-like mix of egg yolks, sugar, and wine.
> *Even though the café has been discovered by the general public, we still go to the café for its delectable ZABAGLIONE.*

zarf *(ZARF), noun*
A small metal holder used to carry a cup of hot coffee.
> *She served the coffee with ZARFS so her guests wouldn't burn their hands.*

zazen *(ZAH-ZEN), noun*
Meditation in a cross-legged posture.
> *Christopher has taken to practicing ZAZEN, but at heart, we know his goal is still acquisition of wealth and power, not personal enlightenment.*

zeal *(ZEEL), noun*
Great enthusiasm and energy for a cause or activity.
> *"The living, vital truth of social and economic well-being will become a reality only through the ZEAL, courage, the non-compromising determination of intelligent minorities, and not through the mass." —Emma Goldman, Bolshevik anarchist*

zealot *(ZEL-it), noun*
A rabid follower; a true believer; a fanatical advocate.
> *"What a noble aim is that of the ZEALOT who tortures himself like a madman in order to desire nothing, love nothing, feel nothing, and who, if he succeeded, would end up a complete monster!" —Denis Diderot, French philosopher*

zegedine *(ZEG-eh-dyne), noun*
A silver drinking cup.
> *Drinking wine from a ZEGEDINE, he looked like a king.*

zeitgeist *(ZITE-gahyst), noun*
The prevailing viewpoints, attitudes, and beliefs of a given generation or period in history.
> *In the twenty-first century, "going green" is very much at the forefront of the nation's ZEITGEIST, as people have been made aware of the importance of being good stewards of our planet's natural resources.*

zelig *(ZEH-lig), noun*

A chameleon-like person who seems omnipresent.

The parvenus try so hard to be ZELIGS, blending in seamlessly at our functions, but we can always spot them for the intruders they are.

zen *(ZEHN), verb*

Generally speaking, to figure out the answer to a difficult problem with a flash of sudden insight.

After days of indecision regarding which gala to attend on a particular night, Danielle managed to ZEN the answer and make her choice.

zenith *(ZEE-nith), noun*

The highest point attained; the peak.

"This dead of midnight is the noon of thought, / And Wisdom mounts her ZENITH with the stars." —Anna Letitia Barbauld, English poet and children's author

zenzizenzizenzic *(zen-zih-zen-zih-zen-zik), noun*

An obscure mathematical term for the eighth power of a number.

I have never encountered a math problem involving a ZENZIZENZIZENZIC.

zephyr *(ZEFF-uhr), noun*

A gentle breeze.

"Soft is the strain when ZEPHYR gently blows, / And the smooth stream in smoother numbers flows." —Alexander Pope, British poet

zest *(ZEHST), noun*

Extreme enjoyment; a lust for life.

"Such epithets, like pepper, / Give ZEST to what you write; / And, if you strew them sparely, / They whet the appetite: / But if you lay them on too thick, / You spoil the matter quite!" —Lewis Carroll, English author and logician

Zionism *(ZYE-on-iz-um), noun*

The modern political movement to establish a Jewish homeland in Palestine.

The Wasserstein's give charitably, not only to the community, but also in support of ZIONISM because the family has many relatives living in Palestine.

zoetrope *(ZOH-ee-trohp), noun*
A mechanical toy consisting of a spinning cylinder with figures inside.
> *When you look through slits in the side of the ZOETROPE as it spins, the figures inside appear to be moving.*

zonifugal *(zoh-niff-YOU-gull), adjective*
Passing out of, or away from, a region.
> *Our multinational European jaunt contained many ZONIFUGAL changes that often caused us to feel disoriented.*

zonk *(ZAWNK), verb*
To stun or stupefy.
> *We were positively ZONKED by Marie's choice of couture for the very important Sanderson gala.*

zoomorphic *(zoh-uh-MORE-fihk), adjective*
Having the form of an animal.
> *The Rossington's formal garden is peppered with delightfully ZOOMORPHIC topiaries that seem to mix flora and fauna in equal measure.*

zooscopy *(ZOO-scope-ee), noun.*
Seeing animals when you hallucinate.
> *Drunks are said to undergo ZOOSCOPY and see pink elephants.*

z-snap *(ZEE-snap), noun*
Snapping one's fingers while moving one's arm and hand in a Z pattern.
> *The Z-SNAP is a way of emphasizing that you are sure about what you are saying.*

zwieback *(ZWIE-back), noun*
A type of biscuit.
> *After baking, ZWIEBACKS are sliced and toasted.*

zygote *(ZEYE-goat), noun*
A cell formed by the joining of an egg and a sperm.
> *All humans start life as a ZYGOTE.*

ABOUT THE AUTHOR

Bob Bly is a freelance copywriter whose clients include IBM, Brooklyn Union Gas, Praxair, AT&T, Intuit, and dozens of other companies. He has written more than 100 articles appearing in numerous publications including *Writer's Digest*, *Cosmopolitan*, *New Jersey Monthly*, *City Paper*, and *Successful Meetings*. Bob is the author of more than eighty books including *The Ultimate Unauthorized Star Trek Quiz Book* (HarperCollins), *How to Sell Your House, Condo, or Co-op* (Consumer Reports Books), and *The Copywriter's Handbook* (Henry Holt). Mr. Bly can be found on the web at *www.bly.com*. He once interviewed for a job as a reporter for the Associated Press but lost out when he failed the spelling test.